BONUS TIME

Brian Pennie

Gill Books

Gill Books
Hume Avenue
Park West
Dublin 12
www.gillbooks.ie

Gill Books is an imprint of M.H. Gill and Co.

978 07171 8635 8

Print origination by O'K Graphic Design, Dublin
Copy-edited by Jane Rogers
Proofread by Emma Dunne
Printed by CPI Group (UK) Ltd, Croydon, CR0 4YY

This book is typeset in 11.5/17.5 pt Sabon.

The paper used in this book comes from the wood pulp of managed forests. For every tree felled, at least one tree is planted, thereby renewing natural resources.

A CIP catalogue record for this book is available from the British Library.

5 4 3 2 1

About the Author

On 8 October 2013, Brian Pennie experienced his first day clean after fifteen years of chronic heroin addiction. Instead of perceiving his addiction as a failure, he embraced a second chance at life and went to university to study the source of his suffering.

In 2017 he graduated with a degree in psychology, winning several awards, including a fully funded PhD scholarship from Trinity College Institute of Neuroscience. Since then, he has become an author, keynote speaker, university lecturer in both Trinity College Dublin and University College Dublin, and a life-change strategist.

With a relentless belief that we are what we think, Brian's mission is to show people that change is possible, demonstrating actionable steps through a lived experience.

To write this book, I relied upon diaries, called upon my memories, researched facts where possible, and consulted with those who appear in the book. Many of the names in this book, along with other identifying details, have been changed to protect the privacy of those involved.

CONTENTS

Prologue VII

1 The body remembers 1

2 The lure of chaos 17

3 Falling in love 27

4 The darning needle 35

5 The secret 45

6 Panic attack 55

7 Planting my flag 65

8 Not a 'real addict' 73

9 When worlds collide 91

10 Not a 'real drug dealer' 105

11 Vodka bread 121

12 I don't care 137

13 The drugs don't work 151

14 Cockroach 171

15 The end of the race 189

16 The life of Brian 209

17 Relapse 227

18 A programme for life 245

19 Wonderfully weird 263

20 Magic and miracles 279

Appendix: My programme 290

Acknowledgements 291

PROLOGUE

I was lying on the ground, face down and motionless. I couldn't feel my body, but I was strangely aware of my right cheek, pasted to the wooden floor by my warm sticky blood. Frightened and confused, I tried to peel myself off the ground, but my arms gave way and I slumped back onto the floor. As I lay there, pain pulsating through my body, especially my tongue, I attempted to make sense of what had just happened.

I soon realised I was in my sitting room, the familiar stink of overflowing ashtrays hanging in the hot, humid air. It was getting dark outside, the curtains were half drawn, and the lamp in the corner was spitting out an eerie orange hue. The TV was playing loudly, and there was someone in the room, but as I scanned around me, everything was a blur – a slow-motion blur. That's when my bodily senses began turning back on, sluggish and sequential, like a damaged computer struggling with a reboot. I was in serious trouble, and I knew it.

My limbs felt heavy and itchy, like how your jaw feels in the aftermath of a dental numbing, and sweat was streaming off my pale, freckly skin. My heart, which was pounding out of my chest, ached as if clamped by the sharp edges of my ribcage. But none of this compared to the throbbing in my mouth. My tongue, or 'thhuunggg' if I could have said it out loud, felt huge. I tried to gently massage it against the inside of my mouth, but that was a mistake. The pulsing sensations turned to a steady piercing stab. It felt like something was growing inside my mouth. I was struggling to breathe, thick lumps of blood congealing at the back of my throat. I thought I was going to suffocate, and I began to panic.

I didn't know it then, but I had just experienced my first ever convulsive seizure, a violent one at that. The convulsions had driven my teeth through my tongue; that's where the blood was coming from, and it was dribbling from my mouth onto the floor.

I don't know what I looked like, but when I woke up on a hospital trolley several hours later, I remember how I felt. I was physically, emotionally and mentally broken. I tried to get up off the trolley, but I didn't have the strength. Disturbed by odd bodily sensations, I pulled myself into a sitting position in small sluggish bursts. With my body slumped over, and my legs dangling off the side of the trolley, my focus landed on a red fire extinguisher. I could barely keep myself upright, and my head was swaying from side to side, but this random object sucked me into the moment. As I sat there, hypnotised by the fire extinguisher, something wasn't quite right. I knew the colour red, and I knew it was a fire extinguisher, but it wasn't a 'red fire extinguisher', not to me – not this night. I could not link the two together. It was just 'red' and 'fire extinguisher', like floating links of a chain, completely detached. I looked around the room and tried to focus on other objects, but nothing made sense.

Time slowed down, and I remember thinking, 'Holy shit, that's fucking brain damage. Game over, man.'

I awaited the dreaded panic, but it didn't come. I just sat there, unmoved by what had just occurred. Something like that would have sent the old me into a panic, but it didn't, not this time. I had nothing left, no more fight. I was utterly defeated, and for the first time in my life, I surrendered. I had just experienced the most painful night of my life, but it was also the most important. I didn't know it then, but I had just entered bonus time.

THE BODY REMEMBERS

'*Congratulations. You have survived the war. Now live with the trauma.*'

LORI JENESSA NELSON

'm the happiest person I know. I shouldn't be. Not by society's standards anyway. I'm not rich. I didn't win the genetic lottery. And I lost most of my life to addiction. So why the hell am I so happy?

I was given a gift, the gift of not caring. I'm not talking about people. I care deeply about people. My mission in life, and the reason for writing this book, is to help others. What I'm talking about is the silly things in life, the things that once tormented me, like comparing myself to others, worrying about situations I couldn't control, agonising over what people thought of me and pointlessly wishing I had done things differently.

This gift, which gave me a second chance at life, is what I call bonus time. It forced me into the present moment, and helped me to overcome my fears. Instead of letting anxiety consume me, which is how I lived for most of my life, I now dream big and act boldly. By doing so, amazing things have come into my life, and for that, I'm eternally grateful. To receive this gift, however, I had to jump a few hurdles along the way, which started from the moment I was born.

* * *

I was only five weeks old, but that didn't stop me yanking the needle out of my arm. So what did they do? They pulled down the sleeves of my babygrow, pinned my arms together and inserted the needle in my head. It sounds like torture, but it wasn't. It was a drip. It was also keeping me alive. My mother was desperate to help me, but the nurses held her back. Forced to watch me from a distance, she was powerless as I frantically grasped the needle, trying to tear it from my scalp.

Two weeks earlier, my mam had been becoming increasingly worried about my health. I couldn't keep a bottle down, and I wouldn't stop crying. As the days progressed, the problem got worse, gifting me with an ability to projectile vomit several feet; pretty impressive for a newborn. Instead of happy memories with her infant son, my mam describes those experiences as something akin to *The Exorcist*, as I sprayed the walls with milky white vomit.

My mam brought me to the doctor in a panic, but he said it was only colic, seemingly a little sceptical about the projectile vomiting story. Feeling a little silly, she went home thinking there was nothing to worry about, but things soon took a turn for the worse. I continued to vomit, and the crying intensified.

She brought me to the Rotunda Hospital the following day – that's where I was born – but they weren't much help either. After three more visits to the hospital, they were getting a little annoyed with this 'overly concerned' young mother, and insisted it was only colic.

That's when things got serious. I would drink my bottle, but then I would vomit and my body would go floppy and limp. I was getting sicker by the day. Even my cries sounded sick, turning to frail, feeble whimpers as the hours passed. My mother didn't know what to do, but the neighbours insisted that she go back to the hospital. I'm sure the nurses were thinking, 'Here she comes again,' but when my mother told them my nappies had been bone dry for several days, the alarm bells went off. They snatched me from my mother's arms and weighed me immediately. I was less than four pounds – half my birth weight – and the soft spot on my head had sunk deep into my skull.

The hospital staff knew they had made a huge mistake, and now we got the royal treatment. Two nurses scooped me up, drip in tow, and rushed me to Harcourt Street Hospital for emergency surgery. There was no ambulance available, so we were bundled into a taxi and given a police escort. I must have had some fighting spirit about me, because even in the taxi I was trying to snatch the needle from my head.

The sirens of the police motorbikes cleared the path ahead, as the taxi dashed through the narrow Dublin streets. When we arrived at the hospital, the nurse took me in her arms and ran straight to the operating theatre. My fight for survival had truly begun.

The operation lasted several hours. I had a condition known as intestinal malrotation. In layman's terms, my gut was twisted. That's why I could not digest any food. It was also blocking the blood flow throughout my digestive system. I spent the next week in an incubator, my family waiting in the hospital and praying for me to pull through.

My dad was in work when my mam went to the hospital, so only hours after the nurses scooped me from her grasp, she got a bus to her mother's house to tell her what had happened. Still in shock, with my vomit-laden blankets in her arms, one of the neighbours asked, 'Oh, congratulations, Jenny; can I see your beautiful baby?' That's when it hit her, all at once, and she broke down in tears in the middle of the street. When chatting to my mam about these difficult times, what pulls at my heartstrings most is an image of my brother Kelvin. He was only three years old at the time, but over the next year, my mam had her hands full with me. Starved of much-needed attention, he would walk behind her holding on to the belt of her coat.

The hospital released me after a few weeks, but my recovery would not be easy. Due to several complications, the doctors told my mam I would be crying for the best part of the next year. I didn't let them down. When I asked my aunt Tess about those times, the answer was always the same: 'You *never* stopped crying, *ever*.' Anyone who came into my orbit was affected, no one more than my mother.

The medical practice at the time was also a problem. As crazy as it sounds, it was only in the mid-80s that doctors recognised that newborns could experience pain. Based on weak neurological evidence from the 1940s, the research suggested that infants had not yet developed the capacity for pain because they didn't react to pinprick tests. Even as life-saving surgeries became more invasive, most newborns, including myself, went under the knife without an anaesthetic. They received a muscle relaxant to stop them squirming during the operation, but that was about it. Based on the latest evidence, the researchers were shockingly wrong.

The hospital treated me like an organism, but I was only a baby, and I learned to view the world as a terrifying and painful place. I am convinced that these early experiences primed me for a life of anxiety. That's how I spent my first thirty-five years in the world: tormented by my mind and consumed by anxiety. These claims are backed up by the nature of my symptoms, all based on my heartbeat, pulse and the scar from the operation. I don't suffer from anxiety as I used to, but simply talking about these experiences makes me feel uneasy.

I did not receive an anaesthetic for my operation; nor was I given any medication to ease the pain. This, I believe, was a defining moment of my life, one I was blind to until recent times. I needed that anaesthetic, and I finally found it, but not until I was in my teens.

* * *

When I was five, I passed another traumatic milestone. It was 1983, and Ireland was in the midst of a prolonged recession. Unemployment was high, living standards were low and my parents decided to move to Canada. All the arrangements were made, but a few days before we set off, the airline told my mother that she couldn't travel. She was pregnant with my younger brother James, and they had strict guidelines on allowing pregnant women to fly. My parents decided that my dad, my brother Kelvin and I should travel without her, a decision they later regretted.

I remember the day we left. All the extended family came to Dublin airport to see us off. 'Your mam won't be going with you today,' I was told, 'but she'll be following you over soon.' I heard it, but I didn't get it. It was so confusing. Everyone was celebrating, as if something good was happening, but they all felt sorry for me at the same time. It was like a wedding and a funeral all at once. Despite the attention, and the celebrations, I knew something terrible was looming; there was just something in the air. I was right. It would be four months before I saw my mother again.

We lived in Calgary, Alberta during those first four months, in an apartment block with my uncle Frank and his family. My memory is sketchy, but I remember spending lots of time in bars. The adults drank a lot, something that wasn't on my radar at the time, not consciously anyway. Alcoholism, which runs in both sides of my family, was beginning to play a significant role in my life. This was the first time I felt its sinister grip, and it had my dad firmly in its sights. I don't specifically recall missing my mam during those four months, but emptiness, darkness and anxiety dominate the few memories I do have.

I must have been excited when my mam arrived in Canada, but I have no memory of the day, not a second of it. Maybe I was in shock, because when she did land on our doorstep, I wasn't the baby any more. She arrived with my infant brother James. I'm not sure what kind of an impact this had, but it couldn't have been a good one. I craved my mother's attention, but despite us being a whole family again, things were about to get worse, and she simply wouldn't have the time.

When my mam arrived, we all moved into a big wooden house in the Calgary suburbs, including my uncle, aunt and two cousins. My cousins were the same age as me and my brother Kelvin, and I have some fond memories of those days. I loved ice skating, and we'd often go to the nearby ice rink. It was the home of the Calgary Flames, and I was mesmerised by the sight, sound and sheer size of the arena. During winter, we would play in the snow at the back of the house. When it was too cold, we would play games in the basement or use the huge ventilation system to talk to each other from different rooms in the house. We had some fun times, but I never felt happy, not in Canada.

We were finally a whole family again. Life should have been great. But it wasn't. I don't remember anything specific, but I do remember how I felt. Fear was my primary emotion. It wasn't a normal fear, however; it felt hollow. I was afraid, but of what I didn't know. Maybe I have my parents to thank for that, because things were going downhill fast, and they did well to hide it from us.

My parents had sold their house to start a new life in Canada. But emigration was an epic failure. By the time my mam arrived, all the money was gone. She was horrified. Her dreams ruined in the blink of an eye. That must have been the hollow fear I was picking up, as my parents tried to keep the peace. Things quickly took a turn for the worse. In less than a year, with three young kids in tow, and nothing but the clothes on our backs, the authorities kicked us out of the country. I don't know the exact details, but on the day of my sixth birthday, we were deported.

I have vivid memories of the journey home. The police came with us to make sure we didn't come back, which was obviously upsetting for my parents. Despite that, mam and dad threw me a birthday party on the plane. I remember being happy on the way home, probably because we were coming back to Ireland, but mostly because I had policemen at my party.

Within a year of dreaming about a great life in Canada, we were back in recession-stricken Dublin. With no money and very little hope, we found ourselves living in Ballymun – in a sixth-floor flat on Balcurris Road, to be precise. I question my memory often, but from what I remember, I quite liked Ballymun, despite its bad reputation.

There was a great community spirit and the neighbours were very good to my mam. I loved going to school there, too. It was right beside the flats and I remember making lots of friends. I also loved playing in the lifts. They were filthy and smelled like urine, but we didn't care. A gang of us would get in, including my brother Kelvin, and we'd press the emergency button to jam the lift between floors. We'd then force the doors open with a bar and climb out. One time it jammed right in the middle of two floors. I was the youngest and the smallest, so it was too high for me to climb up and too scary to drop down. I cried until an adult came along and pulled me out. It was quite dangerous, on reflection, but I didn't know any better at the time.

Several other memories from Ballymun remain vivid. One is when I robbed for the first time. My brother Kelvin brought me over to the shops, and I remember putting a packet of Polo Mints in my pocket. I was only six, and some part of me knew it was wrong, but the thrill of this experience lives with me to this day.

I also remember the excitement I used to feel when the older boys threw shopping trolleys off the seventh-floor balconies. They would smash onto the ground, metal pieces flying everywhere, and we'd collect the oily ball bearings that broke away from the wheels. I thought they were silver marbles, and I'd be delighted with myself.

While I was out getting stuck in lifts, things weren't going too well at home. My parents weren't on great terms after Canada, and I don't remember seeing much of my dad, but there were happy times too. My fondest memory involves lying on the sitting room floor with my mam and brothers. We had no money, not even for furniture, but we had plenty of heat. The old Ballymun flats had heated floors, something my mam still raves about because we didn't have to pay for it. We would sit on the ground playing board-games for hours, mostly Monopoly and Buckaroo. I specifically remember putting my cheek to the warm tiled floor. They were cheap plastic tiles, but it felt strangely comforting, maybe because I was back home in Ireland.

It wasn't long – about four months – before we were moving again. I was distraught when my parents told me. Every time I settled, it was the same thing: a new house, a new school and trying to make new friends. I was an experienced nomad at only six years old. But I enjoyed living in the next place we called home, in the early days anyway.

Ladyswell was a brand new estate in the Blanchardstown area of west Dublin. It was a troubled area from the outset. Two hundred families, plucked from various disadvantaged areas around Dublin, mostly Ballymun, were simply thrown into the mix together. There were no amenities, no transport system, and it was in the middle of nowhere. We didn't even have a church or school, never mind a sports centre or playground. Despite these difficulties, there was a great community spirit, at first anyway. But over time, with tragedy after tragedy, that sense of community slowly disappeared.

I could write a whole book about the troubles in Ladyswell. Crime, violence and drug use were everyday occurrences. I personally knew over twenty people, many of them kids, who died in violent and tragic circumstances; a crazy number for such a small estate. We lived there for the next twenty-two years, but not without a fight: on several occasions, my parents told me we were moving, but I was so upset that they called it off. In hindsight, it might have been better if we had moved.

**

From the moment we arrived in Ladyswell, I was obsessed with football. I was even quite talented until a knee injury forced me to stop playing in my early teens. When I wasn't playing football, my friends and I would spend our days roaming around the surrounding fields, forests and rivers. We had some fantastic adventures. We'd climb trees, make camps, catch tadpoles and do what young kids do. I had no issues in school either, and fared quite well when it came to academic activities. On the outside, life looked good.

My sister Anne was born two years after we moved to Ladyswell, the last of my siblings. Little did I know that she'd spend most of her adult life trying to save me. Before that, however, there were some great family memories, including holidays with my parents, siblings and extended family. My aunts Tess and Gert were ever-present during this part of my life, as we'd travel all around Ireland together, especially Donegal and Achill Island in County Mayo.

Like everyone in life, my parents had their faults, but I consider myself very lucky with the ones I had. My mam is a real-life superwoman. How she handled four kids in such difficult circumstances, I'll never know. As for my dad, he wasn't around as much as he should have been, and yes, alcohol played a role, but he was an incredible worker and always provided for the family. Even during the recession, he found work and always put food on the table. He's also one of the most helpful men you could ever meet, a real-life teddy bear, and would do anything for anyone.

We were a close-knit family, but besides my dad, and only when he was drunk, my parents never openly showed us affection. I was jealous of other kids who got hugs from their parents, but at the same time, I knew they loved me deeply. Hugging just wasn't a thing in our family, expect for my aunt Tess, who'd shower us with hugs and kisses any time we met. She was incredible.

Between the ages of six and twelve, I was relatively happy, on the outside anyway, but anxiety was never far away. It hung over me like a dark cloud, whispering in my ear. I was always worrying about what might happen, overly sensitive to the most trivial things. I remember watching a war film with my dad when I was about eight – I think it was about the Vietnam War. The soldiers were chatting away in their tents when a siren went off. It was warning them of an impending attack. It didn't faze me at the time, but a few days later, when I was playing in my bedroom, I heard a siren-like noise from out on the street. I froze mid-play, action figure in hand. My heart began beating so loudly I could hear it pulsing in my ears. My chest tightened, and disturbing thoughts flashed through my head. I ran down the stairs as fast as I could to warn my family about what was going on, but I caught myself on the way. Yes, for a moment I had thought it was World War III starting right outside my house. This wasn't normal, and I knew it, so I kept it to myself.

This experience became a core feature of my childhood. The sirens in my head never switched off. I was always thinking, forever worrying and constantly on the lookout for an impending attack. But it wasn't all in my head. There were some very real concerns that would make any normal kid anxious.

Our family home was dysfunctional and not always a happy place. There were many rows between my parents, always drink related. Alcohol played a substantial role in every aspect of my life. All family events ended up in the pub, and often started there.

My dad was particularly fond of the drink, and he regularly drove under the influence. Christmas Day was the worst. We'd go over to my nanny's and meet up with the relatives. It would be fun for a few hours, but then the sing-songs would start. I'm not sure if the singing made people drink quicker, or it was just the long day, but everyone would be legless when it was time to go home. It was usually after midnight, and that's when the mood changed. Someone always passed a smart remark, often my mam or dad. I hated how it made me feel, and then, as if it was the most normal thing in the world, my dad, who was struggling to walk straight, would drive us all home.

* * *

A persistent experience from my childhood scarred me more than others. I was seven years old when it started, and it continued for many years. My parents would go to the pub every weekend. I knew they would be driving home drunk, and I would wait by my bedroom window, desperately hoping that they would get home safely. They always arrived home in the early hours, usually after two in the morning, but as a hopeless optimist, I'd start my window-watch early.

There was a big field in front of my house, so I could see all the cars as they came into the estate. As I watched from my bedroom window, peeking from behind the net curtains, my hopes would build with every passing car. 'This could be them now,' I'd think. As my hopes built up, so did the pressure in my chest. But as I learned over the years, hundreds of cars passed each night, and my hopes would be blown away in an instant. As each car passed, I would lie down in my bed, cursing my parents for putting me through this. I'd convince myself that I didn't care and try to go to sleep. But it was hopeless. The sirens were incessant. The same tune kept replaying in my head: '*Your parents are going to die.*' Then, as soon as I heard another car engine, I'd jump back up to the window.

My two brothers were in a bunk bed in the corner, but it didn't seem to bother them. They'd fall asleep as soon as their heads hit the pillow. I was glad they could sleep – I didn't want them to suffer as I was – but I wished I could sleep too. Instead, I was being tormented by anxious whispers in my head: '*Your parents are lying dead in a ditch. You're going to be all alone.*'

I often tried to distract myself and pretend everything was fine. I'd watch TV, play video games or make something to eat. But no matter what I did, even if I was laughing at something on TV, I'd feel an overwhelming sense of dread, as if my world was about to end.

When they eventually got home, a huge sense of relief would wash over me. It felt like a lead weight had been lifted off my chest. But it wasn't over. Sometimes I'd make a noise to let them know I was awake, but it never stopped their drunken rows. It was never violent, not physically, but it was traumatic all the same, and I always feared it would escalate into something worse. It usually settled down after an hour or so, when one of them went to bed. That's when I could relax and finally go to sleep.

* * *

Some of my best childhood memories are of playing football in Ladyswell Park. But even those good days could turn in the blink of an eye. When I was thirteen, a few friends and I were kicking a ball around in the park. There are hills everywhere, and a gang of older lads were flying around on a motorbike. The park was full of kids – it was a tragedy waiting to happen. All of a sudden, we heard a terrifying shriek from a woman on the pitch above us. Something awful had happened – it was obvious from the screams. We ran up the hill to see what was going on. The woman was still screaming and there was a small kid lying on the ground. The motorbike was about thirty yards away, also on the ground. It was obvious what had happened. That's when my friend shouted something I'll never forget: 'Pennier, that's your ma!' I froze on the inside, but my body kept running. The words, 'Please no, please no, please no,' flashed through my mind. But he was right. It was my little brother James lying on the ground. He was only six years old.

My mam was hysterical. A motorbike had killed her father, and all those memories came flooding back. When she saw me, she cried, 'Run down and get your da.' My house was minutes away and I ran as fast as I could. Thankfully, my dad was home. I don't know what I blurted out but he got the message. As we ran back up to the park, I pleaded with the universe, 'Please don't let him die, please don't let him die ...' As we got closer, I could see that James was still lying on the ground. My heart sank. It felt like the whole world was closing in around me. I immediately thought the worst and began to cry, but as we got closer still, I noticed that my mam was talking to him. He was conscious. A surge of relief flooded my head and chest, which only seconds earlier had felt like they were about to explode. I was still crying, but now they were tears of joy. My little brother was still alive.

With my brother out of immediate danger, my dad's attention quickly turned to the guy who was riding the bike. My dad uses anger to cope with his fear, so that only meant one thing. He dragged him off the ground, grabbed him by the throat and began to choke him. I thought he was going to kill him, but the guy started crying, 'Please, mister, I'm sorry, I didn't mean it … please, mister.' The motorbike driver was drunk – I could smell the cider from miles away – and had hurt his leg, but my dad didn't care. He kept choking him and the guy kept crying. After a few minutes, my dad released his grip, gave him a few slaps and dropped him on the ground.

James was conscious, but my mam still feared the worst. Her father, my grandad, had died of internal bleeding, so that was firmly on her mind. She screamed at my dad to bring James to the hospital. He picked him up and carried him down to the house. My dad was actually drunk too, but this was not the time for a row about drink driving.

Miraculously, after getting flipped into the air like a rag doll, James only injured his legs, but the scars from that day live in our memories.

2

THE LURE OF CHAOS

'Living in continual chaos is exhausting, frightening. The catch is that it's also very addictive.'

LORNA LUFT

was fourteen years old when my life began veering off course. Football was my world, but I was having trouble with a knee injury. My parents didn't have the money to pay for physiotherapy, so I faked my age to get a part-time job at a local supermarket to pay for it. It turned out to be a muscular problem related to my running style, and they gave me exercises to correct it. I had every intention of following through with the treatment, but my motivations were changing. I didn't realise it then, but this was a critical juncture in my life.

All of my friends smoked, but not me. No way. That would interfere with my football. I thought they were crazy, sucking dirty smoke into their lungs. But now, for the first time in years, I wasn't playing football every day, and I was bored. I was never one to conform to peer pressure, and I certainly didn't think it was cool, but that's when I took my first puff of a cigarette – on the roof of the football dressing rooms, of all places. I remember my friend Alan saying, 'I love the head-buzz ye get from smoking,' and that's what tempted me. It was a big dirty Samson roll-up, and nobody could roll properly, so it looked like a used nappy. I took one big inhale and nearly coughed my lungs up. It tasted terrible, but it made me feel wonderfully lightheaded. I liked that feeling. I liked it a lot. Looking back now, this was the start of my love affair with chasing highs, and it wasn't long before I was chasing bigger game.

My motivation to recover from the knee injury was soon replaced with a desire to get high. Within weeks of my first cigarette, I was smoking hash. My brother Kelvin had been smoking it for a few years, and now we'd smoke it together. It didn't take much to get stoned back then. One joint would KO the both of us. I remember watching TV with our parents in the sitting room, waiting for them to go to bed. As soon as they did, I'd switch off the lights and excitedly watch Kelvin prepare for the rolling ritual. He'd start by sticking three cigarette papers together. He'd then break open a cigarette and pour the tobacco into a U-shaped groove he made with the papers. It was new to me back then, and I'd be bouncing with anticipation as he burned the hash into the joint – the smell of it was hypnotising. Once he'd finished, we'd lie down on the carpet near the fire and spark up the joint. We'd take a puff each, hold it in for as long as we could and then blow the smoke up the chimney.

Over the next two years, I began experimenting with lots of drugs. Drinking became a weekend thing; drug-taking was my new day job. When I was fifteen, I began abusing petrol. A gang of us would go down to the local garage after school and buy a pound's worth of it. We'd head into the fields and spend the next few hours inhaling the fumes. Petrol is a powerful drug, and we'd be completely out of our heads. I don't exactly know what it does to your brain, but it produces a very distinctive sound in your head, like a siren, so we called it the 'wah-wahs'. The noise always came from the same direction in the sky, which still intrigues me. After a while, the petrol would turn milky white and we'd be like zombies trying to suck on the bottle, pulling it out of each other's hands.

The zombie fest would only stop when someone sober came on the scene. Freaked out by what they'd see – I've been there – they would burn the petrol and only then would we snap out of our trance. There were some seriously disturbing scenes, and many scary experiences, but it didn't seem to faze us. On one occasion, I'm not sure if I was conscious or not, I slipped into a weird dark void. It felt like I was in it for hours, or days even, a spinning vortex from which I couldn't escape. I was terrified, and in this nightmare-like state, I remember thinking, 'Am I dead? Is this what death is like?'

It felt like another world, and as I lingered there, the memory of doing petrol in a field, or anything from my real life, began fading further into the distance. I tried to grab onto something familiar – not physically, it was more of sensory thing – but I was losing touch with reality, falling deeper into the void. Then, unexpectedly, a sense of acceptance came over me, 'This is it. This is what eternity feels like.'

The next thing I knew, I was lying on the ground, filthy dirty and miles away from everyone. How long was I lying there? I don't know, maybe an hour. But I knew one thing: it freaked me out. How could a bit of fun in the fields turn into something sinister so quickly? I jumped up, grabbed the bottle of petrol and set it alight. That was one of the last times I did petrol. But no matter, I had other ways of getting high.

* * *

By the time I was sixteen, I was taking all kinds of drugs: LSD, Valium, antipsychotics, ecstasy, sleeping tablets. I didn't even know what half of them were, especially the tablets and capsules; they just made me feel good. Hash was still a daily ritual, so I started selling it to fund my habit. I always fancied myself as an entrepreneur, and because our gang were smoking so much of it, it seemed like a natural thing to do. Little did I know then that selling drugs would play such a big role in my life.

Despite the damage I was doing to myself, and the fact that my life revolved around drugs, I had some fun times during my teens. I had a close-knit group of friends, and we all had the same interests: football by day, drugs by night. Although the balance of these interests became skewed over time. There were about twelve lads in our group, but my four closest friends were John, Gar, Barry and Dano. Gar, my best mate, had a steady girlfriend and didn't go too crazy. As for the rest of us, we'd spend the summer months getting off our faces in the fields and the winter months chilling in our rooms getting drunk and stoned.

I'd always been good in school, and prided myself on getting good results. It was the same with sport. I was a competitor, always have been, and I wanted to be the best. This made me very driven, but with the help of drugs, this advantage was slipping away. I was slowly losing my drive, and I was quickly losing my spirit.

At the start of fifth year, I had high hopes for a good Leaving Cert, but then I started skipping school. It was also around this time that I stopped playing football. I made a few comebacks over the years, but my knee injury always came back to haunt me. Dano was expelled at this stage, so we'd sit in his ma's house smoking hash all day. But that got boring, so we started doing heavier drugs – acid, Valium, E's – to pass the time. Things were getting out of hand, but we just didn't think it was a problem.

* * *

We weren't what you'd call troublemakers, not at that stage anyway, but as our drug use increased, our morals took a nosedive. I'm probably using drugs as an excuse here, because I'm not proud of what I'm about to say. Even now, as I write this paragraph, I've caught myself thinking, 'Sure that's what lads do at that age. You didn't know any better.' But the fact is, I did know better. I just chose to ignore it. A few incidents come to mind, and all of them involved bullying. One family, where we completely abused the hospitality of the mother of one of our friends, got the brunt of it. We were always welcomed into their home, but we paid them back by acting like scumbags. One time we put their left-over dinner into their DVD boxes, just for kicks. Another time, one of the lads pissed on their toothbrushes. I didn't do it personally, but I laughed about it afterwards. These incidents are only the tip of the iceberg.

Like every gang of young lads, there was a hierarchy. The abuse dished out to the people at the lower end of the spectrum was disgraceful. One lad, who often tagged along because his brother was in the group, wanted to come with us one day. I'm not sure why, but we didn't want him coming. He insisted, so one of the lads whipped him with a stick until he went home. It was vicious. Another time, when we were doing acid in the forest, one of the lads had his jeans ripped from ankle to thigh because someone thought it would be funny. The sad thing is, we all laughed.

Most of these incidents happened in the moment, but we planned the most shocking one for weeks. I've thought long and hard about it since, and I'm reluctant to talk about it because of how people might react. I'm still deeply ashamed of it, but it happened, and I cannot change that fact.

It was 1993, and we suspected that one of our friends was gay. Although I've several gay friends today, I don't know much about the gay scene, and I certainly didn't know anything about it back then. What I did know, however, was that in places like Ladyswell it was safer to act as if you hated gay people in case someone thought you were one. Anyway, we got it in our heads that our friend Tessy was gay. I have no idea why we gave him that nickname, but it's ironic considering the story. Tessy was quiet and softly spoken, but there was no reason for us to think he was gay, and it's quite possible that the name we gave him drove the actions we were about to take.

We hatched a plan. One of our more easily persuaded friends, Charlie, was told to bring Tessy into a camp we had made. I'm not sure what fourteen-year-olds do now, but we made camps.

We gave Charlie a script that went something like this: 'Tessy, I know you're gay. I'm gay too. It's hard to admit it around these guys, but you can tell me.' We were all hiding in the bushes about thirty yards away. When he said he was gay, which we convinced ourselves he would, we were going to run in and give him a serious hiding. I am forever grateful that Tessy said, 'What the fuck are you talking about? I'm not gay,' as I have no idea what would have happened.

Writing about this incident has made me reflect on my own actions. I was never one to conform, and I wasn't afraid of anyone in our crew, so why the hell did I go along with it? The fact is, I was just weak, and my belief about nonconformity is obviously bullshit. I remember inwardly hoping that Tessy wasn't gay. Even if he was, I knew what we were doing was disgraceful. But I wasn't willing to speak up. I was terrified of the consequences. They might think I was gay, and that was something I wasn't willing to risk. I was simply too afraid.

***

Whether it was worrying about my parents dying, avoiding the sound of my heartbeat while I slept or threatening friends for being gay against my better judgement, anxiety was never far away. What's strange is that I didn't realise it; or, more precisely, I didn't know it was an issue. It was all I had ever known, so I had nothing to compare it with. I honestly believed that's how everyone felt. It was consuming my entire life, but that all changed when I was sixteen. I wish I could say that I found therapy or spirituality, but I didn't. I found opiates.

Without realising it was a substitute for heroin, I advanced straight on to methadone, called Physeptone at the time. Methadone is a liquid opiate, prescribed by doctors to help wean people off heroin. It works by reducing the high people get from taking heroin, but if you don't have an opiate habit, it mimics the effects of heroin. In other words, it gets you really fucking stoned.

I have no idea why I wanted to do methadone without knowing exactly what it was, but I do remember the first time I heard about it. Liam, a friend of John's sister Debbie, was a slick dude. He was much older than we were, and we both looked up to him. We were telling him about our tablet-popping exploits one day and he asked us if we ever tried methadone, which he called 'phy'. We said no, and he told us he could get us some if we wanted to try it. 'It's like Valium,' he said, 'but much better. Yiz will love it.'

I'll never forget the day we bought methadone for the first time. It was a beautiful day, warm and breezy, with the sun splitting the clouds. We agreed to meet Liam in John's parents' front garden, which was just around the corner from my house. John and I arrived early. We were both giddy and nervous as we waited for Liam to show up. Trying new drugs was fun, but it was also dangerous. The latter we usually ignored, but the reality was not lost on us.

When Liam arrived, we had a casual chat about the everyday goings-on in Ladyswell – robbed cars, drugs, violence – and then he handed John a paper bag. We paid him £15 each and said our goodbyes. He had a smirk on his face that made me feel uneasy, but that was just his way. John and I walked around to my house and went up to my room. We had a peek in the bag on the way and realised that there was a plastic bottle in it, like the ones you get from a pharmacy. We were expecting tablets, so that surprised us. There was a gloopy orange liquid in the bottle. It was unexpected, but I didn't really care. I looked at John, shrugged and put the bottle under my bed for later that night. I wasn't too worried about my parents finding out either – they always respected my privacy – but I shoved it towards the wall just in case.

It was Friday. I had a new drug. And I was bursting with excitement. John and I had planned to do it together, but he had to meet someone later that evening, and he needed to be sober. We decided to split it up and meet later that night. The plan was to chill out with the rest of the lads while they drank and smoked hash at the shop, a corner house eleven rows down from mine.

We went to my house at around 7 p.m. and took the bottle out from under the bed. John had brought a big empty two-litre bottle of TK lemonade so he could take his half with him. It looked stupid when we poured the 30 millilitres into it, but it did the job.

Today's methadone is green and much easier to drink, but Physeptone is an entirely different animal. It is sickly sweet and more like a syrup than a liquid. I sipped it at first and nearly threw up. It was disgusting. John laughed and told me to hold my nose. The taste wasn't going to stop me, so I pinched my nose and poured it down the hatch in one go. Big mistake. Its gloopy consistency coated the inside of my throat. I couldn't stop gagging. The last thing I wanted was to throw up – it wasn't easy to get and I didn't want to waste it. I managed to keep it down with a few glasses of water, and despite a few shudders from the aftertaste, I was ready to rock.

John left to go about his business, and I went down to the shop where my friends were hanging out. They were drinking and smoking hash, and probably doing tablets. That's what we did every Friday night. I sat there smoking joints with them waiting for the methadone to kick in. It didn't take long, about twenty minutes or so, but immediately, I knew this was something I was going to love. As the night passed by, I slipped through the gears of several amazing feelings. At first, I felt warm and tingly, as if my bones were being heated from the inside. Then I felt soft, but also invincible, as if nothing could hurt me. I even felt comfortable in my own skin; that was a first. I also felt quiet. It was loud on the outside, with the lads acting the dick as usual, but I was quiet on the inside, as if nothing could penetrate my new invisible shield, my methadone shield. I didn't drink that night, I felt way too queasy, but mixing hash with methadone was a match made in heaven. This was the first time my brain tasted opiates. I was soft, warm and free. The sirens went quiet. My mind said 'thank you'.

3

FALLING IN LOVE

'It's such a perfect day. I'm glad I spent it with you.'

LOU REED

Upstairs, sitting down the back of the bus, I'm both excited and afraid. Am I going to die from a heroin overdose? Or am I going to have the best night of my life? I was the one who insisted we should try heroin, so I can't back out now.

It had only taken me two years to advance from hash to methadone, with many other drugs in between. Now I had just gone seventeen, and I was about to graduate to heroin. It was supposed to be a one-time thing. 'You should try everything once,' Jim Morrison said. I was a huge fan, and that's why I insisted we should do it – once.

As we joked around on the bus, five skinny kids – four guys and John's girlfriend, Katie – we tried to hide the fact that we were all scared shitless. We talked about everything except what we were about to do, but every now and then it crept into conversation, and the mood shifted from jovial to a dark silence.

We were on our way to meet John's cousin, Cian. He had done it many times before, so all we had to do was go with the flow. We arrived at a nice, if somewhat old, house in north County Dublin. Cian invited us in and we all sat in the sitting room. The furniture reminded me of my nan's house – good quality, but it had seen its fair share of visitors. I felt the need to do something – anything – to get my mind off the anxiety I was experiencing from my new surroundings. So I took Anto's lead and began rolling a joint. Back then, I would never admit it, but I always felt uneasy whenever I ventured outside my comfort zone, beyond my Ladyswell bubble. And rolling a joint made me feel in control.

There was a nervous, giddy atmosphere in the room. Cian didn't waste any time. He walked into the kitchen and came back with a roll of aluminium foil, a pair of scissors and some kitchen roll. Then he took five bags of heroin from his pocket and placed them on the glass table. They were tiny – less than an eighth of a gram each. That's about the size of the letter 'O' on a normal-sized keyboard. He unrolled the foil, tore off a piece about ten inches wide and shaped it into a neat square. He then scorched every inch of the foil with a lighter. It went black, but he quickly wiped off the residue to leave a beautiful silver sheen. He tore off another piece of foil and rolled it into the shape of a straw. He called this a tooter, and the square piece of foil he called a tray.

I was like a sponge, sucking in the experience as if my life depended on it.

Using the scissors, he snipped the knot off one of the bags and sprinkled the powder, light brown in colour, into a long groove he had crafted on the foil. It looked like a little valley. Using a lighter, he heated the underside of the foil, directly beneath the heroin, and that's when the magic happened. The mousy brown powder transformed into a majestic brown puddle. It wasn't a dirty brown; it was golden brown, just like the song by The Stranglers.

I was hypnotised by this flawless gold puddle glistening in the light. When heated, heroin turns into a thick liquid, but when you take the heat away, it quickly transforms into a glass-like substance, like a crystal. You can pick it up. You can play with it. You can caress its smooth belly and feel the beauty of its curves. You can rub your fingers along the edges, but be careful not to break it. It's brittle. You don't want to waste it. You can even see yourself in its crystal reflection. Heroin stole fifteen years of my life, and nearly killed me, yet for some perverse reason I still revere it like a god from the heavens.

Cian placed the tray at an angle and, with a flick of his lighter, dissolved the brittle brown shard into a golden liquid puddle. Like lava rolling down a mountainside, it oozed down the valley of the foil, leaving white smoky fumes in its wake. Cian went first, using the tooter to hoover up the fumes, some of which clung to the foil. With barely a breath left, he took a pull on a cigarette, and held it in for as long as he could – a process often called chasing the dragon. I was mesmerised by the ritual. I hadn't even tasted heroin, but I was already hooked by its charms.

Heroin has a pungent odour, a cross between smelly fish and old forest foliage. It wafted through the air, making everyone feel nauseous. I hated feeling sick, but this time it didn't bother me. I was captivated by the strange smell and by everything about this sun-kissed puddle.

It was my turn. I could barely contain myself as I bobbed on the edge of my seat. Cian tilted the tray and began caressing the lighter on the underside of the foil, right behind the glossy shard. It liquefied immediately, rolling down the valley like molten rock. I inhaled deeply, chasing the fumes that followed in its trail. With my last breath, I sucked on the cigarette, the filter collapsing with the intensity of my grip. One, two, three, four, five, six, seven ... I held it in for as long as I could, then gasped with a breathless exhalation.

I was lightheaded at first, from a lack of oxygen I think, but within a minute or so, maybe less, it hit me: a warm, gentle tingling. A lull in the voices. A softening of the muscles. A faint tilting of the head. I plunged into the armchair as everyone else took their turn. Thoughts left the room. Anxiety left the room. Fear left the room. Agitation and those damned bodily sensations – they all left the room. As I lay there, sinking into stillness, a thought crossed my mind: *'That was only one line.'* It wasn't an impulsive thought, I was still effortlessly calm. Then the words *'Do another line'* echoed from beneath the stillness. Suddenly I was eager for more. Again I heard a voice, but this time it felt different, as if someone was whispering in my ear: *'Do another line. It will protect you.'* The voice sounded caring, so I listened.

I've always been a quick learner, and my sponge-like focus paid off. I made my own tooter, fashioned another tray and snipped the knot off a second bag of heroin. It was sloppy, but within minutes I had my own golden puddle. I chased the first line down the foil, but angled the tray too far. The molten blob shot down the groove and attached itself to my index finger. It was painful, hardening instantly around the contours of my skin. I peeled it off, leaving a bubble on the tip of my index finger and my fingerprint on the inside of the shard. It was a nasty little blister, especially when I bit into it with my teeth, but the powerful effects of heroin were already evident, and I forgot about it in an instant.

I was soon chasing lines up and down the foil. One line. Two lines. Three lines. Four lines. Five lines. I was falling deeper into stillness with every inhalation, as my fears, my attempts to escape my own mind, to get away from myself, began to dissolve. I was drifting between two worlds – my inner world of bliss, where I floated weightlessly, and the outer world, where I could get another hit. With every line, the external world faded further away, until finally it was gone. In my new world, my inner heroin world, I felt safe. I felt sheltered. Everything went quiet. Then, through the veil of stillness, I heard another whisper: *'I told you.'* The voice was right. I felt like there was a soft warm blanket wrapped around my soul, protecting me from my demons. In the words of Pink Floyd, I was 'Comfortably Numb'.

I woke at 3.30 a.m., still immersed in a sea of calm. Through squinted eyes, I lazily scanned the room. Everyone was gone, except for Anto, who was comatose in the armchair to my left. I looked at the glass table, eyeballing the remnants of the night before. I smiled and dissolved back into my chair. As I lay there, a beautiful itch tingled across my body, mostly on my face. I lifted my fingers up to my left cheek and then, slowly and deliberately, as if in slow motion, scrawled my fingernails across my skin. Dipping in and out of consciousness, I scratched at my face and thighs for the next hour. It was one of the most gratifying experiences of my life, despite the rawness of my skin the following day.

It was getting bright outside. I could see a flicker of light creeping around the edge of the curtains. Normally, when I was at a house party, the morning light used to shock me into a mini-depression. I waited for the gloom, but it didn't come. Draped in my new protective blanket, I was unmoved by my former foe. Again, I smiled.

As I sat in the sitting room, cheerfully watching the sun sneak around the drapes, I began to feel nauseous. 'Fuck, no.' Ever since having a horrible choking experience as a child, I hated throwing up. It terrified me. But I didn't have time to think. I was going to vomit, whether I liked it or not. I jumped up and ran into the kitchen. I could feel a mass of vomit moving up my throat, and just as I got to the sink, it spewed from my mouth, landing with a clatter. Not a splash, a clatter, because it was so thick. It was like my mam's stew after sitting in the pot for three days: dense, stodgy and full of lumps. I had never seen anything like it, and I couldn't stop throwing up. When I thought I was finished, I would throw up some more. It was an endless mass of vomit, more forceful than I'd ever experienced, filling my mouth and oesophagus and pushing out through my nose.

When I finally finished throwing up, and spat out the remaining vomit, it was two inches deep in the sink. I turned on the tap, but the vomit was so dense it wouldn't mix with the water. I swished it around with my hand, trying to force it to mix, but it didn't work. As the watery vomit drained down the sink, the heavier, lumpier bits remained. I clawed most of it out with my hand and threw it in the bin. Then, using my fingers, I forced the remaining undigested lumps of food through the bars of the plughole. Finally, the sink was empty, and I walked back into the sitting room.

This should have been one of the most disgusting moments of my life, but it wasn't. With heroin coursing through my body, it was one of my most cherished. As soon as I threw up, a wave of euphoria washed over me, just as powerful as my initial hit. Even as I threw up, with vomit forcing its way out of my nose, I felt a sense of ease, as if I hadn't a care in the world. That night heroin felt like my guardian angel, but I didn't realise it was bringing me to hell.

As I plunged back into my seat, itchy, warm and comfortably numb, heroin whispered in my ear: '*Don't worry. No matter what happens, no matter what pain you're going through, I'll look after you. Everything will be okay. All you have to do is keep me close.*' Heroin spoke. I listened.

4

THE DARNING NEEDLE

'Drugs are a bet with your mind.'

JIM MORRISON

JUNE 1993

Have you ever seen the game where somebody puts the palms of their hands together, like in a prayer position, then points them towards the person they're playing with, who then tries to slap their hands before they can pull them away? I used to like that game until the darning needle incident.

When I was fifteen, before heroin had entered my life, we had a ritual in Barry's house every Friday night. It was a homage to our favourite musicians. We worshipped The Doors, Jim Morrison in particular, and a gang of us would spend the night sitting around the table in Barry's kitchen doing drugs. We'd knock off the lights, light a few candles, play some Doors music and smoke a load of hash.

There could be fifteen of us in the room at any one time, rolling joint after joint. We'd close all the doors and windows to heighten the heavy vibes, and just sit there, stoned out of our heads, as the room filled with smoke. With the jazzy, rocky music playing in the background, and with the candles flickering through the dense fog, it made for a peculiar atmosphere.

One night, we were going through a phase of the hand-slapping game. One of the lads, Jay, was having a laugh with Dano. He put an eight-inch darning needle between his fingers and said, 'Imagine being a cruel fucker and doing that to someone.' Unfortunately for me, that's when I turned around. I was half-baked from god knows how many joints, and I saw Jay with his hands placed together. I've always been super-competitive, so I pounced, as quick and as hard as I could, clattering both of his hands. First, I noticed the shock on Jay's face, then I felt a searing pain in my left hand. I let out a shout, 'Aaaagh,' and one of the lads turned on the lights. The darning needle had impaled itself right through the centre of my hand, with four inches of needle sticking out on either side.

Jay looked like he had seen a ghost, as I stood in the centre of the room with the needle sticking through my hand. John, who nearly fainted, gave Jay a box in the head for his trouble; more for making him feel faint as it turns out. Sweat was streaming down my face as I screamed at someone to pull it out. Barry stepped up and began pulling the needle, yanking it from side to side, but his fingers kept sliding down the edges. It wasn't budging. 'Will someone pull the fucking thing out?' I shouted. No one moved. They just stood there looking at me, so I shouted at Jay, 'It's your fucking fault. Pull it out!' He reluctantly grabbed the head of the needle and began tugging at it. I could feel the needle jerking and pulling at the inside of my hand, as if it was glued to my sinews, but no matter how hard he pulled, his fingers kept slipping, and it wasn't coming out.

Things were getting freaky at this stage. Someone suggested using pliers, but they couldn't find one. I began feeling weak, so I walked into the sitting room to calm myself down. I sat down on the sofa and took a few deep breaths. Out of options, I rubbed the sweat off my good hand, gripped the needle between my thumb and the side of my index finger, and pulled as hard as I could. It was still tugging the inside of my hand, but I just kept pulling it. Eventually, the needle began to move. My fingers kept slipping down the edges, but after several attempts, it slowly slid out of my hand.

I collapsed in a heap on the sofa. One of the girls wanted to ring an ambulance, but when I looked at my hand, the holes had closed over. The inside of my palm looked like a large ear piercing hole, and the other side had a flap of skin sticking out. How on earth it had missed the bone I have no idea, but I just thanked my lucky stars that it had. It was a painful and trippy experience, and my hand was throbbing, but otherwise I was fine. My next thought was a joint, and within twenty minutes, I was back in the kitchen listening to Jim in the smoky candlelight.

* * *

My teens were full of weird and wacky experiences like the darning needle story. Thankfully, they didn't always involve pain. If I wasn't gloriously spitting chunks of vomit into a sink, or floating in my inner world of bliss, I was wobbling around a field doing petrol, listening to the 'wah-wahs' soar through the sky.

However, some of my craziest memories involve LSD. On one occasion, when I was nineteen, a gang of us were doing acid beside an electricity box at the top of the estate. They were potent acid tabs called Black Stars, and we were on the cusp of a bad trip. Things can go very wrong very quickly on a bad trip. It was around midnight and one of the local piss-heads came wobbling up from the pub. Paddy was about forty, and he stopped to have a chat with us. He was talking all kinds of shit, thinking he was hilarious. It was sort of funny, but you'd laugh at anything when you're on acid. We were having fun, when out of nowhere he began taking the piss, pretty much slagging us to our faces. The mood changed quickly. That was bad enough on a normal night, but when someone is on a bad trip, paranoia can kick in fast.

Paddy said something nasty to one of the lads in our group. It was seriously out of order, and this fella takes no shit. Then, before we even knew what was happening, Mikey caught him with one of the cleanest uppercuts I've ever seen. The noise of his fist on Paddy's jaw was terrifying. Paddy's head smashed off the concrete before his legs even touched the ground. That was bad enough, but then Mikey jumped in the air and landed on Paddy's head with both feet. That was the first so-called 'head-stomping' I ever witnessed and it frightened the life out of me.

'Fuck me, what the fuck did ye do that for?' I shouted.

'Fuck him, prick deserved it,' said Mikey, dismissively.

'Yeah, but ye didn't have to jump on his fuckin' head … he's fucked, seriously, he's not fuckin' moving.' Blood was beginning to pool around Paddy's head.

'Let's get fuckin' out of here,' said one of the lads.

We were all starting to panic, but hid it as best we could. We were hurrying towards the park, which was on a slight hill above the electricity box, when one of the girls started freaking out: 'He's fuckin' dead! We have to call someone ... call an ambulance!'

With acid surging through our bodies, we weren't in control – paranoia was pulling the strings – and something was about to go off. As we stood at the edge of the park, watching Paddy's limp body for what felt like an eternity, he finally began to move. A huge relief washed over me. He stumbled to his feet and wobbled on down the road.

That was one of many experiences of normalised violence in Ladyswell. We simply walked back down to our spot by the electricity box and continued as if nothing had happened, all in the space of a few minutes. We were literally standing in his blood, laughing about the whole incident. Looking back, I think we were all scared shitless, but we couldn't show it, not the lads anyway. That would be a sign of weakness.

Paddy was so drunk I doubt he even remembered what had happened. He'd feel it the next day, though, that's for sure. We never did find out how he was after that – I honestly didn't give it much thought – but I saw him a few weeks later and he looked okay. That was good enough for me.

That wasn't the first or the last of my encounters with acid. It played a big role in my life during my teens. During the summers, a gang of us would take acid and go down to a cool forest in the Tolka River valley. A steep hill, about fifty feet high, led to a big opening where a large tree had blown down. We'd all sit around the tree waiting for the acid to kick in. Taking acid can be a bizarre experience at the best of times, but in the pitch black of the forest, the shadows, the silence and the tracers from our lighters, it was mesmerising.

Trying to emulate Jim Morrison, I'd run off through the trees on my own, pondering the essence of life. Well, that's what I thought I was doing. Either way, I felt indestructible. LSD is fickle, however. With acid coursing through my veins, it didn't take much for my mind to do a U-turn. I'd soon hear a noise in the bushes, shit myself and scurry back to the gang in a panic.

An acid trip can last anything from ten to eighteen hours, and it's a roller-coaster of a ride. Sometimes I couldn't stop laughing. Other times I'd be afraid of the grass. But most of the time I felt invincible, as if my lungs and veins were bursting with energy. Then there were the hallucinations. I never saw giant bunny rabbits or anything like that: for me, the world seemed to have a rubbery or bendy texture to it, as if it was twisting, melting or swaying from side to side. I loved the way acid altered my mind.

But acid wasn't always fun, particularly for some of the lads in our group. When people are on acid, they are often on edge, especially in the latter stages of the trip. We loved to wind each other up, like making weird noises and pretending we hadn't heard anything. This often ended in extreme paranoia – and even the people doing the winding up got paranoid. For some reason, anytime this happened, we always chose a victim, and anyone was fair game.

On one such occasion, we walked up from the forest and sat on a railing at the side of the estate. There were at least ten of us, and we had taken a lot of acid. Ladyswell was an unpredictable place, particularly at night, so it was smart to be on your guard, even when you were sober, never mind when you were off your face on acid. With people walking up and down the lane, usually drunks, addicts and drug dealers, this set the tone for our edginess that night.

Someone began tapping a coin off the railing. The idea was, when someone asked them to stop, we pretended they were imagining things. That's when Marlo, who was doing his first ever acid, made a fatal mistake. 'Ah, lads, this is my first trip. Can yiz stop messing?' Like vultures, we were on it in seconds. 'What are you talking about, you mad thing? Stop what?' It didn't take long before we were all tapping the railing, perfectly co-ordinated, and we'd keep tapping until Marlo would ask us to stop. 'Ah fuck off, lads, I'm freaking out here,' he pleaded. He was scared shitless, I could see it in his eyes, but that only egged us on. Then it got semi-aggressive, just to make it more real. 'No one is doing fucking anything. Now shut the fuck up or we'll all be freaking out.' This persisted for over an hour and it got more malicious by the minute.

Finally, Marlo had enough and decided to walk away. But like proper little vultures, we followed him up the lane. I don't know what possessed us to do it, but we began making hissing noises and jumping in his face. He began to cry, 'Will yiz fucking leave me alone?', but that only made things worse. He started running, but we all kept pace, hissing as we chased him up the lane. He tried to get away by running into the field, but there were too many of us. The field was pitch black, and like the raptors out of *Jurassic Park*, we began circling him, taking turns as we leapt into his face from the darkness.

We all had a laugh about it the following day, including Marlo, but I think he was just happy it was over. Not surprisingly, he never took acid again. I didn't admit it out loud, but I felt terrible. It was by far the cruellest incident I was ever involved in, but I got my comeuppance a few weeks later.

I've had many bad trips, but the night with the chicken was one I'll never forget. Jay, Dano and myself took four Black Stars each. There was something odd about that night – we all had a bad trip, nervously laughing at each other, and scared shitless of our own shadows. We spent the whole night lurking out of sight, afraid that someone would start playing with our heads.

It was around 1 a.m., and there was no sign of us coming down, so we decided to make our way over to a friend's house, hoping we could stay the night. Jonesy lived in Wellview, and it was a long walk across the fields. When we were halfway there, we heard a weird noise in the distance. It sounded like the cries of an animal, but it was hard to tell. It was coming from the direction we were going and I was freaking out.

'Fuck this, I'm not walking up there, lads.'

Dano couldn't go back to his house that night, so he was pushing us to keep going.

'Nah, lads, I'm too fucked-up. I'm gonna go home and look at the ceiling for the night.' Lying in bed, staring at the ceiling, is one of the worst experiences you can have on acid. You could be lying there for hours, until the following morning even, with no chance of sleeping, but it seemed like the lesser of two evils that night. So that was that. The lads went one way, and I went the other.

Now I was walking through the fields on my own, having one of the worst trips of my life, and my mind went into overdrive. 'What the fuck was that noise? Should I run after the lads? Why do I feel so detached from my body? What's that weird taste in my mouth? Am I going to die?' Acid can play with your mind, and then I got it into my head that my mam and dad were waiting up to catch me.

With my head in a spin, someone screamed from the darkness: 'Pennierrrrr, what's the fucking craic?' I absolutely shat myself.

'Jaysis, Sammy, ye fucking scared the crap out of me. I'm off me tits on acid.'

Sammy was a mad bastard, but I liked him, and was relieved it was someone I knew.

'What's in the bag?' I asked.

'What's in the bag?' he said, breaking his heart laughing. With that, he swung the bag towards my face. What came next is an image I'll never forget. 'It's a fighting chicken,' he roared. As he held the legs of the chicken, swinging its head towards mine, it felt like the whole world stood still. I locked eyes with the chicken, as it stared me right in the face. Then it began screeching, the same noise that made me go home in the first place. It was frantic, flapping its wings to escape. It was obviously scared, being carried around Ladyswell by the legs, but not half as scared as me. I can only imagine what I looked like, and Sammy couldn't stop laughing.

With that, I was gone, running down to my house to put an end to this messed-up night. With my pupils like saucers, the last thing I wanted to do was bump into my mam or dad. As I got close to my house, I noticed that my brother Kelvin was in his

43

car with his friends, or at least that's what I thought. My head was still spinning from the bloody chicken, and I was dying to tell someone about it. As I walked up the drive, I knocked on the car window. With that, my mam spun her head around to look at me. My parents had taken Kelvin's car to go to the pub and were having a drunken row inside. It was too much. I ran straight into the house and up to my bed. My mam and dad were drunk, so I got away with it, but I spent the next six hours staring at the ceiling, promising that I would never do acid again.

I never kept my promises when it came to giving up drugs, and this time was no different. But that didn't matter when it came to acid, because at nineteen years old, I was only interested in one drug, and that was heroin.

5

THE SECRET

'If you want to keep a secret, you must also hide it from yourself.'

GEORGE ORWELL

SEPTEMBER 1995

By the time I finished my Leaving Certificate, heroin had me firmly in its sights. Like a teenage crush, I couldn't get it out of my head: *'I'll protect you. I'll take away your pain.'* It was all-consuming – I thought about it night and day. Despite my obsession, however, using it regularly wasn't an option. 'Sure then I'd be a drug addict, and I'm way too clever for that.' This was the story I told myself. But heroin is cunning. Heroin is shrewd. Heroin is patient. I had big dreams, lots of ambition and a burning drive to succeed, so it wasn't going to take me head on. Instead, it tried to convince me, ever so gently, ever so slowly, that I could have the best of both worlds.

If I'm honest with myself, heroin already had me. It's like a wily child snatcher. First it entices you with sweets. *'You'll like these sweets.'* Then it tells you there are more in the car. *'The more you eat, the better you'll feel.'* And before you know it, you're looking in the rear view mirror as your house gets smaller and more distant. *'Sorry, I forgot to mention that.'* Was it possible to escape? I'm not sure. Did I want to escape? I honestly don't know. What I am certain of is this: on my first night chasing the dragon, heroin helped me to forget myself. Anxiety left me. My busy mind went quiet. And all my insecurities dissolved in an instant. But now I was back in the real world, and I was struggling to cope. How could I live with my mental poverty, having tasted riches that were still within reach?

That's when I came up with a new story: 'Maybe you could do heroin once a month, like a treat.' I liked my new story and quickly decided that the first month started now. Heroin agreed: *'Yes, that makes complete sense.'* John was keen to do it too, and so was Barry, who couldn't make it the first time. There was just one problem. Apart from a few close friends, I didn't want anyone to know I used heroin. More specifically, I didn't want anyone calling me a junkie. Such a horrible word. Even in Ladyswell, where drug use was rife, it was a terrible slur. 'Sure he's only a fucking junkie,' you'd often hear. That meant you were a nobody, the lowest of the low. And if someone did find out, they wouldn't understand that it was only a treat, that I wasn't a 'real' addict.

This turned out to be a blessing in disguise, for a short while anyway. It was easy to get heroin, but nearly impossible to score a bag without people knowing about it. The first time was supposed to be a one-off, so I couldn't ask Cian. Then there was the problem that most people wouldn't expect, especially if you believe what you see on TV – most heroin addicts, in my experience anyway, don't want to get other people strung out, especially young people. Obviously there are exceptions, but that's what they are, exceptions.

I knew many addicts, and when I asked them to sort me out on the QT, what I generally found was a decent human being. 'Look, ye don't want to be getting involved with that,' said one. 'Best off sticking to the hash, Pennier,' said another. Both of these addicts became my friends over the years. One of them died from addiction. The other is one of the most courageous people I've ever known.

I struggled to score gear off anyone I trusted, so, over time, I stopped caring about who might find out. Or more accurately, I told myself that people would keep their mouths shut. That was a lie, a lie to myself. I became very skilled at believing my own lies, especially as my addiction took hold. I often wonder how I became so self-deluded, and I keep coming up with the same answer: I didn't like the person I was becoming, and twisting my mind to make it feel okay was the only way I could live with myself. I began to tell myself all kinds of stories – I'm not a real addict. I'm not a real drug dealer. I'm not hurting anyone but myself – and I swallowed every one of them.

I soon found someone who would sell me heroin, one of the exceptions. He didn't tell anyone either. Not because he was kind or caring. He just didn't give a shit. It turns out most addicts are worried about their own problems, like getting drugs and trying not to die. They don't spend their days gossiping about some newbie scoring the odd bag of gear. Who knew!

I smoked heroin once a month at first, although that didn't last long, and soon became more frequent. I always did it with one of my two best mates, John and Barry. John was in a serious relationship, so it wasn't his main priority. But Barry and I became obsessed. We would buy two or three bags a few days before the big day, and I'd be bouncing out of my skin with anticipation. For the next week, that's all we could talk about, and for the next month, all I could think about was my next hit. We kept it from the rest of the gang. Maybe we knew something we weren't admitting to ourselves. But over time, we began talking about it openly, as if it was the most normal thing in the world.

* * *

When I was eighteen, I thought I had life licked. I had a good job, a good social life, great friends, and I had stumbled across a secret that no one else knew about: *'If you're not a real addict, you can do heroin once a week, feel fucking amazing and have a normal life.'* So that's what I did. Clever boy! I genuinely thought people were crazy not to do it. *'Those eejits haven't a clue,'* I'd often think.

Was I trying to convince myself that my secret was true? Probably. Either way, I didn't think about how it might affect others, and I tried to convince anyone who'd listen that they should try heroin too.

I started my first proper job around this time and, after only a few weeks in the place, I was trying to convince a colleague about the benefits of doing heroin. Darren was very cool and looked like a young high-flyer in the company. We shared an office and hit it off straightaway. I began telling him all about my secret, and how only 'real addicts' get strung out. He was fascinated by what I had to say and curious as to what heroin looked like. The following Monday, I showed him the remnants of Friday night's binge. The golden puddle is a thing to behold, but the blackened foil in the aftermath is not a pretty sight, and the smell is toxic. He was not impressed, but that didn't put me off.

By the time I was twenty, I was doing heroin once a week, always on Fridays. That was my rule, so I wouldn't get strung out. I caught myself reflecting one day, 'How did this creep into a weekly thing?', but I justified my actions with a new story. *'As long as you don't get physically addicted, you're okay.'* I was careful to keep a full week between using, and I would never do it during the week. *'Sure only real addicts do that.'* I had no idea that heroin already had me.

Barry and I now needed more heroin to get the same hit, so we were buying twice as many bags, usually two or three each. We didn't need as much as that to get high, so we'd wake up in the early hours of Saturday morning, stoned out of our heads, and still have some to spare. This made me smile. When we woke up, we'd smoke the rest of the gear, which meant we were using on Saturday. Yeah, I was breaking my rule, but not on purpose. That's what I told myself. Still, this did not sit well with me, so I had to change my story. Saturday was now fair game, but I would never do it during the week. Only 'real addicts' do that.

Despite the drift, I was completely unaware of the danger I was putting myself in. I believed my own lies and every little tweak I added to my story. So what did I do? I pushed my secret on anyone who might be interested or whose life I wanted to improve.

I became tight with several work colleagues over the years, but since they weren't swallowing my 'once a week' solution to life, I changed tack. 'Look, you at least have to try it once. It's one of life's greatest treasures. It's a bloody sin to deny yourself this experience.' I remember how they looked at me. I thought they were confused, as they grappled with one of life's big secrets. They *were* confused; not about the secret, but by my irrational beliefs, and the look on their faces was pity. They tried to warn me, many times, but I simply refused to hear them.

* * *

I met Lena on a skiing holiday in Austria. She was stunning. I couldn't believe my luck. She was from Vienna, so I thought it was just going to be a holiday fling. But we really clicked, and stayed in touch afterwards. We'd spend hours on the phone to each other, and she decided to come over to Dublin for a holiday. It was one of the best weeks of my life, and I convinced myself that she might be the one. I missed her terribly when she went home, and swore I'd make it work.

Within a few weeks, we made plans to meet in Vienna. I was desperate to see Lena again. All I had to do was save up the money. I'd spend my days dreaming about our perfect week together. I even watched *The Sound of Music*, only realising afterwards that it was set in a different city. Either way, it was going to be a magical trip. But as the weeks rolled by, I didn't save a penny. Instead, I spent everything I had on drink and drugs.

Looking back, I could have made it work. I always found money when push came to shove. Maybe the problem was that what I really wanted was my true love – heroin – I just didn't know it yet. I came up with all kinds of excuses why I couldn't make it to Vienna, mostly lies. I suggested it would be better if we went skiing together instead. It was only three months away after all. In reality, this was an invitation to join me on a drug-induced ski trip with the lads. I would have loved her to be there, but she couldn't make it because of college and financial commitments.

Despite my growing drug use, I was still crazy about Lena. I'd send her roses on her birthday, and we were constantly on the phone to each other, planning all kinds of adventures for our future together. She was dying to see me too and was soon on her way back to Dublin, this time with two of her friends, which worked out great for my mates Dano and Barry.

I didn't tell Lena about the secret when she first came to Dublin, or any drugs for that matter, which leads me to believe that I knew on some level I was playing with fire. But when she came to Dublin for a second time, things were different. Heroin had dug its claws in, and it decided to come to the party.

On the second night of the trip, she told me she wanted to study in Ireland for a year so we could be together. I was ecstatic. We chatted all night about moving in together, what college she might attend and what our days would look like. I was falling for this girl big time. I remember saying to myself, 'Wow, you're a lucky shite. Don't fuck this one up,' which makes the following night all the more bizarre.

We went to the Buddha Bar. It was the place to be in Blanchardstown back in the day. It should have been a night to remember. I was going out with a beautiful girl who was crazy about me, and me about her. She was moving to a different country just to be with me. I thought I was falling in love.

Turns out, it was a night to remember, but for all the wrong reasons. There was only one thing on my mind that night, and it wasn't Lena. Instead, all I could think about was: 'It's Friday.'

There were six of us in the bar. Dano, Barry, myself, Lena and her two friends from Vienna. Barry had scored four bags of gear earlier in the day. They were physically in his pocket, but they were mentally boring a hole into my head. Lena was chatting to me about moving to Dublin, I think, but I was completely ignoring her. Not on purpose. I was lost in my own thoughts, scheming and planning, trying to figure out how we could get back to Ladyswell to smoke the gear without fucking up the night.

Barry and I had developed a telepathic connection when it came to heroin. We only had to look at each other. With a furrowed brow, I gave him a glance and he suggested we go back to his parents' house. 'Here, we should all go back to my gaff for a few drinks. Me ma and da are out.' Let's just say we came from modest households, so compared to the Buddha Bar, this was a terrible idea if we were really going back for a drink. Dano, the little fucker, knew what we were up to and painted a terrible picture of how the night would unfold, pretty much slating Ladyswell in the process. 'What, sit in that kip when we could be chilling here? Fuck that.' Quickly picking up on the bad idea, Lena told me she would rather stay in the bar.

I conceded defeat and decided to enjoy the night, or that was my plan. As the evening wore on, I became increasingly agitated. Everything was grating on me. The loud music. The purple lights. The conversations. Dano's cheeky laugh. And Lena. Her chirpy chit-chat about moving to Dublin felt like a chisel grinding into my brain. Even her Austrian accent, and the way she said 'Doblin', which I previously thought was cute, began pissing me off. I became extremely restless and started honing in on the negatives – or making them up. Lena had elfin features, which is what made her so attractive. But when she wouldn't stop talking about 'Doblin', I turned to Barry and said: 'That fucking elf is doing my head in. Let's get out of here.' And that was that.

This was the first time Lena had seen me acting like a complete dickhead. I didn't even bother to make an excuse. I just said, 'Here, I have to go somewhere. I'll be back in a few hours.' I don't know what she thought, or how she felt. I was too self-centred and pathetic to ever ask her about it.

'They'd do your nut in, wouldn't they?' I said to Barry as we left the bar. I genuinely believed that's why we left. It was far easier to blame others, and tweak my internal story, than it was to face the harsh truth. We skipped down the road, delighted with ourselves, smiles stretched across our faces, completely unaware that we were already strung out.

Dano was smart. He never touched heroin, so he stayed in the Buddha Bar with Lena and her friends. After Barry and I got our fix, I was dying to meet up with Lena. I knew I had acted like a dick, but my little blanket of numbness made it feel okay. It was 2 a.m. and we knew they'd be up in Dano's house. He didn't like heroin, but he loved to party and never knew when to call it a night. We knocked at his door, and they were there, but Lena was mad as hell. That was the first time she was ever angry with me, in a passive, Viennese kind of way. Blanket or no blanket, I knew I had to act. Then it hit me, a moment of inspiration, and I told her all about the secret.

To this day, I have no idea if she knew what I was talking about. We'd smoked all the gear, so I couldn't show her. Either way, telling her about the secret was pointless. Sure she wouldn't be able to reap the rewards back in Vienna anyway, unless she started scoring gear herself. And even I knew better than that.

Thankfully, there was no heroin to share that night, but with my drug-taking out in the open, I asked Dano to grab my stash. I sold a lot of cannabis at this stage, so we burned joints off nine-ounce bars to show off. Lena was not impressed. She smoked hash for the first time that night, but she didn't like it. She didn't like anything about that night. Not that she said so, she didn't have to. She thought I was an idiot. Yeah, Lena was smart.

I never made it to Vienna, but we continued our long-distance relationship for a few years. Lena came to Dublin a few more times, and we met up on skiing holidays twice, but I had already found my true love in Dublin. Her name was heroin.

6

PANIC ATTACK

'*Never a frown with golden brown.*'

HUGH CORNWELL

Despite being stoned for half my exams, I got a decent Leaving Cert. I wanted to go to the National College of Art and Design, and all I needed was two honours in honours subjects and an overall pass. Even though I messed up some of my exams, I got an A1 in honours art and a B1 in honours geography, so I was delighted with my results.

Now all I needed was an art portfolio. I signed up for a one-year course at an art college in Ballyfermot. My first day felt like something out of the *Twilight Zone*. I was a very young seventeen-year-old, and everyone was so grown up. Half the students were mature students in their thirties, but even the ones who were my age seemed so mature. But it wasn't just that. Everything about the place felt unusual, in a zany, and unsurprisingly arty, kind of way. I was a long way from my Ladyswell bubble, and this was completely different from anything I'd experienced before.

In my first class, a strange-looking lecturer strolled into the room. He had these odd tufts of hair growing high up on his cheekbones, like an older Wolverine gone tragically wrong. I was already way out of my comfort zone, so his opening statement left me baffled. 'You see ... I'm an atheist. It's important that you all know that,' he proclaimed. I didn't even know what an atheist was, but I had a feeling it had nothing to do with art. I can't recall another second of that lecture, and although I stuck it out for a few months, I believe that was the moment when I decided art college wasn't for me.

In the months that followed, I slowly lost my love for art. I blamed the weirdness of the college, but in reality I was falling deeper into addiction, and maybe I was the one who was weird. The 76A was the only bus that would bring me to Ballyfermot, and it would take nearly two hours. Every morning, I got on at the first stop and sat upstairs, right down the back of the bus. Then I'd roll a five skinner (a very long joint) and smoke my brains out until I got to Ballyfermot. The bus would be full of smoke, especially on cold mornings, when the windows were closed, but no one ever said anything. I could see it in the passengers' eyes, though – they hated me on that bus.

Despite my growing addiction, I was determined to succeed in life. I had tremendous belief in my abilities. It may have been somewhat delusional at times, but it drove me forward. This made it difficult to quit college, so I made new plans. 'I'll do my portfolio at home on my own, and in the meantime, make as much money as I can.' As luck would have it, my dad was giving up his coal run, so John and I took it off him and did it ourselves. I also continued to sell hash. We'd collect the money on Friday nights, and, funnily enough, some of my customers had a bill for hash and coal. That was Ladyswell in a nutshell.

That's when opportunity came knocking. A printing company called Kenilworth Products rang the college looking for students interested in graphic design. The college gave them my details and they called me up for an interview. I didn't have much knowledge in graphics – I'd only done four months of my course – but I landed the job, and in the process skipped four years of college. I was ecstatic, and I would end up spending the next seventeen years in the company.

We were a close-knit gang in the graphics department, and we had a great little upstairs office that was separate from the rest of the factory. We had our own mini kitchen and huge bay windows that swung open in the summer. I have many fond memories from that time of my life, especially the early days. We'd take extended lunch breaks and have the best of laughs playing cards. However, when I was twenty-one, this office was also the scene of my first panic attack, an event that would change the course of my life.

It was a normal Monday, and we were chatting away as usual. Due to my excessive use of drugs – uppers and downers – I was feeling much more agitated than normal. I'd never even heard of anxiety at this stage, not on a conscious level, and I was completely unaware of how restless I was. I've since come to realise I was using heroin to suppress my anxiety, but I just didn't see it at the time. On that morning, however, my anxiety levels hit new heights, and I was about to become very aware of its power.

There were five of us in the office, and we were having a laugh about something or other. I was standing in the middle of the room, and in the blink of an eye, I began feeling detached from my body. My vision went blurry, and I felt as if I had lost control of my limbs. I ignored the sensation at first, thinking it would pass, but it grew stronger by the second. Suddenly, my chest began to tighten and I found it difficult to breathe. 'I feel fucking weird,' I said, nervously. Two of the lads start laughing, thinking I was taking the piss. I could see and hear them laughing, but it was as if there was a barrier between my sensory experiences and the real world. Everything seemed fuzzy, and their laughs sounded terrifying. 'Seriously, something is very fucking wrong here,' I said, with greater urgency.

Everyone still thought I was messing, except my boss, Kim. She knew that something was wrong, something serious. We were quite close and I think she saw the fear in my eyes. She asked me if I was okay. I wasn't. I was petrified, the most terrified I've ever been in my entire life. I thought I was having a heart attack, or a stroke, but the macho side of me, the side that wouldn't object to the trap we set for Tessy, decided to play it down: 'Ah, ye know what, I'll be grand. I just need a bit of fresh air.'

I ran down the stairs and out to the back of the building. There was a little boiler room outside, where we used to hide when we were having a smoke. I didn't want anyone to see me like this, so I climbed in. It was a horrible room, dark and damp, with a big rusty boiler and cobwebs everywhere. Not an ideal place to have a panic attack, but that's where I went.

I leaned against the boiler and tried to steady myself, to get my bearings, but my attack was only starting. It was like an opera song gradually reaching its climax, or a roller-coaster steadily climbing to the top of the hill, before frantically hurtling to the bottom. I didn't know what was happening, but I knew it wasn't over. Something was coming, something bad. And then it happened.

'Oh my god. What the fuck is going on? I can't breathe. What's happening? Am I having a heart attack? Am I having a stroke? My head is about to explode. It must be a stroke. It feels like something is about to pop. Oh my god. Fuck me, my heart. It can't keep beating that fast, can it? Jesus, I can't breathe. What the fuck is happening to me? I'm dying, I must be fucking dying.'

My mind was in overdrive, intense bodily sensations driving every thought. With my heart pounding against my chest, it felt like my ribcage was being squeezed in a vice, with the lever pulling tighter anytime I tried to breathe. Chills were surging up and down my torso, and my face, back and hands were dripping with sweat. Again, I tried to get my bearings, to take a few deep breaths, but my vision was scrambled and I couldn't focus. It felt like I was looking at the world through an old VHS recorder, with someone tapping rewind to keep me trapped in my new world. I was sure I was going to pass out, but finally, after what seemed like an eternity, it began to subside.

I sat in the boiler room for about twenty minutes. I was over the worst of it, but my nightmare wasn't over. Throughout the whole ordeal, I felt a terrifying pressure in my head – that's why I thought I was having a stroke. But the worst thing was the overwhelming sense of dread, of impending doom, as if my existence was about to end. I'd never felt anything like it, and both of these experiences stayed with me after the attack, along with a level of agitation that was now fully in my awareness.

Today, as a researcher and lecturer in neuroscience, I have a unique insight as to what was going on in my body and mind. Our brains are malleable, like playdough, and our experiences determine its shape. Just like physical exercise, thirty reps in a gym won't make your muscles bigger, but thirty reps every day for a year will. The same is true for your brain, and over time, its shape will change. As a perennial worrier, I always felt tense, uneasy and anxious. If my mind wasn't scanning the world for potential threats, it was looking for ways to relieve my unrelenting anxiety. Over time, I literally transformed my brain into a finely tuned anxiety machine. In times of stress, the fear centre of my brain would light up like a Christmas tree, sending stress signals throughout my body, and once that happened, I'd do anything to relieve my pain. Including heroin.

When I woke the following morning, I thought I felt normal, but within seconds, the whole experience spilled back into my body. I couldn't sit easy, as I tried to shake the nervous tension out of my hands. My biggest concern, however, was the tightness in my head and chest, caused, no doubt, by my stroke or heart attack. There was only one thing to do – go to the doctor to figure out which it was.

It never occurred to me that this could be a psychological issue, or that my once-a-week heroin habit might provide a solution, albeit a temporary one. But as I sat in the doctor's office, telling him about my ordeal, he was in no doubt about what had occurred. 'You had an anxiety attack,' he declared confidently. He didn't mean to belittle the most terrifying event of my life, but that's how I took it. I didn't even know what anxiety was, but a psychological issue? No way. I wasn't having it. I was too strong for that. Either way, I thought he was wrong. 'How could something so powerful, so physical, be simply in my head?' I thought to myself. He prescribed me medication and gave me a book to read, but in my mind, his diagnosis was way off.

When I looked at the prescription, it said Valium. I had taken variations of Valium before, such as duck eggs and Zopiclone. I liked them a lot, so I went straight to the chemist, regardless of whether it could help with heart disease or a stroke. I was still feeling highly agitated when I went home. My chest was still tight and the tension in my head was getting worse, not better. I took two of the Valium tablets – five milligram yellow pills, if I remember correctly – and I was astonished. Within thirty minutes, my symptoms had all but disappeared. I wasn't dying, which came as a huge relief, but I also had the perfect cure for my distress. It was better than perfect. It made me feel amazing.

This was a dangerous time for me. I was in the middle of my once-a-week heroin habit, and to my amazement, when I mixed it with Valium, it lifted my high to another level. What the hell was going on? From thinking I was dying only a few days before, I was now getting free drugs off my doctor – drugs that made heroin even better. It seemed too good to be true. It was.

The doctor suggested that I pop in to see him the following week. I was eager to get more Valium, so I duly obliged. He must have seen the excitement in my eyes, or the addict within me waiting to explode, because there was no way he was giving me another prescription. I was devastated. He went on to tell me that Valium was just a short-term fix, not a solution. Then he told me to read the book he had given me. 'Fuck you and your book,' I thought, 'I want a fucking prescription.' This was worrying. Despite the success of the Valium, I could feel the anxiety bubbling under the surface, especially as the week wore on. In that very moment, right there in his office, I stepped onto the anxiety treadmill. I became anxious about becoming anxious.

I have a vague memory of reading the book, but in my mind, there was only one solution. I quickly realised that heroin was even better than Valium for targeting anxiety. It was my guardian angel, after all. It would swat anxiety aside. There was only one problem, the same problem that kept coming back to haunt me. Only drug addicts take heroin every day, and I was way too clever for that. I thought.

I suffered terribly the week after the doctor's appointment, especially in work. Sitting at my desk felt like torture. I was so agitated. I kept clenching my fists and squirming in my chair, trying to escape my own body. I tried to get Valium everywhere, but it was harder than I thought. I don't know how I got through that week without drugs. I knew one thing, however – I wasn't going to make a habit of it.

Around this time, Barry and I had begun using heroin on Mondays and Tuesdays. We were still keeping a five-day gap in between using, but decided we were missing out on normal Friday and Saturday nights, which involved getting off our heads on drink and E's. So in a moment of insight, I suggested, 'Let's do smack on Mondays and Tuesdays and keep weekends for parties.'

We swore to each other that we'd stick to the new plan. It made sense at the time, but this was addiction at its conniving best.

Barry was a barber, and I was a budding graphic designer, but we were now doing heroin on work nights. I knew we were playing with fire, but I never said it out loud. Besides, I still thought I was too clever to get strung out. The signs were there though. We began hiding it from all our friends, even John, who had decided to take a step back. We were on a slippery slope, and before long I was buying bags and doing it on my own.

A few weeks after my panic attack was a defining moment in my life, and I must have known it; I remember it like it was yesterday. It was Friday night, and we were all partying in Dublin city centre. Sticking to our pact, heroin was off the table, so I was drinking hard to smother the anxiety. That worked initially, but alcohol always came back with a vengeance. Hangovers are different for everyone, but for me they were a concentrated dose of anxiety, and when mixed with uppers like cocaine or E's, they were my worst nightmare.

From what I remember, we were having a great night, but there was only one thing on my mind, and Barry's. Just like the time I bailed on my girlfriend Lena, we didn't need to say anything. We just looked at each other, smiled and walked out of the bar.

7

PLANTING MY FLAG

'Hard choices, easy life. Easy choices, hard life.'

JERZY GREGOREK

31 DECEMBER 2000

The moon shone brightly in the night sky. It was cold but fresh. The laneway was long and narrow, and the light breeze softly stroked my face as I strolled at a leisurely pace. It was a beautiful night, or at least it should have been. For me, however, things were about to change.

An hour before my midnight stroll, I had left a party. But not just any party. It was New Year's Eve, a night I used to live for. Tonight was different, however. For several months, addiction had been tightening its grip, and as I sat in the Greyhound Inn with my friends, all of them in high spirits, I felt completely disconnected – from everyone and everything.

All evening, instead of having a good time, I was fighting with my own mind, toying with a very appealing idea: *'Forget about ringing in the New Year with friends and get a few bags of gear.'* Barry, my partner in crime, had moved to America for a few months, and the thoughts of going home to smoke heroin on my own was alluring. It would obliterate my anxiety, that's for sure, but it would also fill that ever-growing void, the one which was making me feel so lonely and disconnected.

This was not an easy choice, however, as I would have to ask myself a big question, one that scared the life out of me. *'Am I a drug addict?'* I was a smart twenty-two-year-old with a good job, great friends and a cool social life, even if it was a bit hectic. On the outside, life looked great. Surely I couldn't be a drug addict. Until this night, I didn't think I was, but the tide was turning, and tonight I was going to plant my flag.

I'm not sure how I convinced myself to leave – what story I spun so I wouldn't feel like a real addict – but I'm certain it was a good one. I was becoming very skilled at that. Now that I had made my decision, I ran outside to make a phone call. I had one mission on my mind: to score a few bags of gear. It was 11.15 p.m., and I was kicking myself for leaving it so late. I had been fighting the idea all day, and in retrospect, it was just a matter of time.

My main concern was that the dealers had taken the night off. But as I've learned over the years, the heroin trade doesn't do holidays. It's always on. I frantically rang my dealers and got through after several attempts. 'Anything doing?' That was the code, and Franner, who I knew well, said, 'Yeah, where you at?'

If you've never been addicted to anything, it's difficult to understand how you feel when you realise you're getting your fix, especially heroin, and particularly when it had been looking unlikely. It's one of the most thrilling feelings in the world. I still get excited just thinking about it.

I told Franner I'd be back in Ladyswell in thirty minutes, and hung up. That's when the agitation kicked in. I didn't have my drugs yet, and that thrilling feeling could turn to despair in an instant. Dealers won't hold your drugs just to be nice. If they sell out before you get there, tough.

Far too restless to wait for a taxi, I decided to walk and flag one on the way. It was only twenty-five minutes on foot, so I'd make it on time either way. With no taxi in sight, I decided to pick up the pace and take a shortcut through the fields. I'd spent my youth in these fields, the same ones where I did acid and petrol, but it's not an ideal place to walk in winter.

My shoes were filthy and my feet got soaked, but none of that mattered as long as I got my fix. Now five minutes away, I took out my old Nokia and made the call. Absolute dread … his phone was off. I was fuming. I began looking for other numbers, but within minutes, Franner called back. That only meant one thing – he wouldn't have called otherwise – and that thrilling feeling surged through my body again.

There was a laneway that stretched along the side of the estate, and that's where we arranged to meet. As I walked along the gravelly path, now a little calmer, the beauty of the crisp evening pulled me into the moment. The moon glistened in the misty night sky, and the trees, which lined either side of the laneway, fluttered in the light wispy breeze. It was enchanting, and then it began to snow.

That's when I heard Franner's voice, and just like that, he knocked me out of the moment. I didn't realise it then, but it would be thirteen years before I appreciated the beauty of nature again.

'Alright, Pennier?'

'Alright, Franner? What's the craic? Good stuff?'

'Yeah, it's a lovely bit of brown,' he said, proudly.

'Nice. That's what I wanted to hear, man.'

He handed me two £20 bags of heroin, and at that exact second, the New Year bells began to ring. It sent shudders down my spine. I was ringing in the New Year in a laneway scoring gear. I couldn't believe it. 'Am I a fucking junkie?' How could I deny it? I deserted my friends on New Year's Eve to smoke heroin on my own. I was in trouble. I had planted my flag.

As I spun around in the direction of home, I'm not sure what I was supposed to be feeling. Misery, fear, loneliness, worry? But I felt none of those things. I was a little confused, sure, but that's as far as it went. I looked down at the two bags of heroin, and a caring voice whispered in my ear, *'No need to worry, I'll always have your back.'* Within minutes, I was strolling back to my house, bags in hand, happy as could be. Heroin was my saviour, my liberator, my one true love, and nothing else mattered.

* * *

When I woke up the following morning, I kept replaying the previous night's events in my head. New year, fresh start, they say. It felt like the universe was mocking me. The timing of the handover is what troubled me most. The very second the bells went off. 'Are you having a fucking laugh?' I grunted to myself. I couldn't shake the feeling. Was it a sign? Was this my future?

To make matters worse, anxiety was getting the better of me. It was several months since my diagnosis, but without heroin, I couldn't see a way out. I was restricting my heroin use with the help of street Valium, sleeping tablets and alcohol, but it was still getting out of control. I was now using smack four days on, three days off. 'That's over half a week,' I thought. 'How the fuck did that happen?' I'd promised myself I'd never cross that line, but now I couldn't even remember stepping over it. Who the hell was calling the shots? This was worrying.

I was due to go back to work in a few days, and I was dreading it. I had loved my job before anxiety reared its ugly head, but tediously clicking away on a mouse all day was now my worst nightmare. The repetitive nature of it made me feel so restless. I'd wake up every morning with tightness in my chest and head; that was a given. But when I was in work, the agitation in my body was beyond belief, mostly because I couldn't go to work stoned to ease the anxiety, but also because the chemical addiction of opiates was kicking in.

My brain was craving more and more dopamine – the neurotransmitters that are released when we feel pleasure. I was giving myself a lot of pleasure by taking heroin to avoid anxiety. Through these repeated bursts of dopamine, my brain needed more of the drug to get the same hit. This is the essence of craving, tolerance and withdrawal, which makes you feel like crap if you don't get your dopamine hit. For me, that meant extreme agitation while I sat in work.

It would start in my hands, mainly from the repetitive clicking, and then travel around my whole body. I'd flick my fingers, clench my fists, take strolls around the factory, anything to relieve the tension, but nothing worked. I'd then spend the day squirming in my seat, wishing the hours away until I could sedate myself for the evening.

I couldn't go on like this, not in the long term, so I began to look at my options. I was over £20,000 in debt from credit cards and bank loans at the time. That was a problem, and my job paid well, so quitting was non-negotiable. Along with selling hash, my job also paid for my growing drug habit, which was now costing me a small fortune. If I stayed in work, however, I also had to perform. But I couldn't do my job properly any more, certainly not without medication.

My other option was self-medication. Valium worked, but it was difficult to get. Heroin worked, but I couldn't go to work stoned out of my head on smack. Either way, I couldn't use it every day without officially becoming a drug addict, and despite the overwhelming evidence, I still thought I was a million miles away from that. I played with the idea of using heroin in small doses, a few lines here and there, but even in my delusion state, I knew I couldn't pull that off.

I decided to go back to the doctor, convinced he could offer me an alternative. To this day, I have no idea why he never prescribed me some kind of anti-anxiety medication, not that I have much faith in them anyway. What does surprise me is that we never discussed therapy. I didn't even know it was an option, or what was involved, for that matter. Any knowledge I did have I learned from TV. I now know that several therapies are highly successful in treating anxiety disorders, but he never mentioned them. He kept directing me towards the book he gave me. I couldn't believe it, back to the bloody book.

I'm sure it was a great book, and if I had practised the techniques, it might have made a difference. But the fact was, I needed a lot more than a book. I needed therapy. To be fair to the doctor, he didn't know about my heroin problem, or the extent of my anxiety, and even if he had offered me a therapeutic route, I wouldn't have taken it. I was terrified of facing anxiety without drugs. 'Sit with your pain,' they would have said. 'Fuck you,' would have been my reply. I was far too cocky, fearful and unaware to have even considered it.

I stormed out of the doctor's office, mad as hell, but in hindsight, I got exactly what I wanted. There was only one thing in my head as I drove home: *'I have no choice, then. I have to do heroin if I want to keep my job.'* I had the permission I needed, and it wouldn't be my fault.

Looking back, I had two choices. I could face my demons and work through my suffering. That was the hard choice, which would have made for a much easier life. Or I could take drugs, numb the pain and face the consequences later. That was the easy choice, which made for a much harder life. Was I too weak? Was the pain too much? I don't know the answer to either of those questions. What I do know is this: there was only ever one winner.

8

NOT A 'REAL ADDICT'

'Who are we but the stories we tell ourselves, about ourselves, and believe?'

SCOTT TUROW

JUNE 2001

f you use heroin to suppress your emotions, then withdrawal is the rebound. Just like a spring pushed beyond its limits, emotions are unleashed in one ferocious burst. Heroin obliterated my anxiety, so the rebound was going to sting. That's why, on the days I wasn't using, I was feeling more on edge, more agitated and more panicky than ever before. I didn't know how withdrawal worked back then, so I was using more and more heroin to overcome anxiety.

What most people don't realise is that heroin addicts, especially long-term addicts, spend most of their time in withdrawal. When they use, they're high, but once the drug wears off, they go into withdrawal. On the streets, it's called 'dying sick'.

I was avoiding daily use so I wouldn't become physically addicted, but it didn't work, and I was now beginning to experience the physical symptoms of withdrawal. The first time, I immediately went into denial, blaming the weather for my sniffles, even though it was the summer. Deep down, however, I knew I was in trouble. Cold sweats, chills, a runny nose, all of which I'd experienced before, but something about it was different, hauntingly different.

I should have been terrified, one of my greatest fears being realised, but I wasn't. I remember thinking, 'Right, you've brought this as far as you can. Time to stop.' On one level, I genuinely believed I could stop, just like that. I've always had an unwavering belief in my own abilities, sometimes to my own detriment. This was one of those times. I was telling myself another little story, another little lie, one that would help me to accept the person I was becoming.

I needed to make sure that it wasn't just a cold, so I bought a bag of smack to find out. Still enchanted by the ritual, I crafted a tooter and poured the powder on to a foil tray. With a flick of the lighter, boom, a beautiful golden-brown puddle lay before my eyes. I smoked a few lines, following the blob up and down the foil, and I knew straight away. Heroin helps with every ache and pain, including flu, but you'd still feel the symptoms in the background. However, when I smoked a couple of lines, my symptoms dissolved in an instant. I was physically addicted to heroin. There was no denying it.

I was more shocked by my reaction than I was by my impending doom. No emotion, as if I didn't care. Heroin obviously numbed the impact, but if I'm being honest, I knew it was coming. I never allowed myself to think about it, but heroin had dug its claws in ever since my first line. I had been captivated by its charms at the tender age of seventeen. It wrapped me in a blanket, making me feel safe, connected and whole. It quietened my busy mind, soothed my childhood trauma and slapped anxiety aside as if it didn't exist. It was the solution to all my problems. I have never been able to resist heroin, and deep down, I knew I was in trouble from that very first day.

***

We in Ireland like our drug addicts to look a certain way, and despite my physical addiction to heroin, I still refused to believe I was one. I wasn't blind, or stupid, so this was a problem. How could I deny the facts?

Simple. I'd spin myself a little story, believe it and carry on as if life was great. I was becoming a master of the craft, a black belt in denial and self-deception. Completely unbeknownst to myself, I was working my *Kung Fu* magic, fabricating a whole new plotline that would keep my addiction alive.

'What do real addicts look like?' was a question I began to ask myself. The answers spewed out of me. 'They don't have jobs. They don't have cars. They don't go on holidays. They inject heroin. They sell heroin. They don't play sport. They're homeless. They rob. They mug defenceless grannies. I doubt they even wash themselves.'

'I'm none of those things,' I thought. How could I be a real addict? And just like that, I made up my mind. I could use heroin every day, crush my anxiety, and as long as I kept my job, and didn't start mugging grannies, I wasn't a real drug addict. That fleeting suspicion I had on New Year's Eve about the reality of my situation was nonsense. Heroin was my soulmate, not my enemy, and she was always there when I needed her most, whispering to me: *'I would never take advantage of you like that. We need each other, and we need to stick together. As long as we do that, everything will be OK.'*

What a relief. My GP had given me permission, and this justified my decision. I could use heroin every day and still live a normal life, and for the next year I took full advantage. I didn't get too greedy at first. After all, I wasn't a real drug addict, so why would I act like one? I also didn't want anyone to find out about my escalating problems. They wouldn't understand. Only a handful of people knew about my habit, and I wanted to keep it that way. That meant I couldn't walk around stoned out of my head, especially in work. Outside work hours, however, and especially at weekends, things were different.

I still lived with my parents at the time, but I was a master at hiding my drug use. They knew I drank and smoked hash, so if they ever saw me out of it, I'd just blame that. They wouldn't be happy, of course, but it made it easy to hide my heroin use. Adding to that, my parents didn't grow up around drugs, so they were very naive. When you use heroin, the pupils of your eyes are tiny, like pins. That's the big giveaway, but my parents had no idea, so I didn't have to worry about it.

I was also a compulsive liar, always crafting stories about how well my life was going. Without fail, my mam would have my dinner ready after work, and I'd fill her head with all kinds of lies. Getting praise and promotions in work were my two favourites. I've always been a good talker, and I'd often believe my own lies, so I was very convincing – convincing enough to even get away with smoking heroin in the house.

I fondly remember one time when Barry and I decided to smoke heroin for the whole weekend. We called it the Smackathon, thinking we were hilarious. My mam and dad were away on holidays, so we parked ourselves in my house with thirty bags of smack – that's £600 in a single weekend – and told everyone we were going to Galway. I won't lie – it was one of the best weekends of my life. With the curtains closed, days merged into night, as I floated weightlessly in my soft protective blanket. I drifted in and out of consciousness for the entire weekend, moving only to scratch, eat, smoke heroin and go to the toilet.

This event became a pivotal moment in my life. I lied to my family, friends and colleagues that I went to Galway, even though I never set foot in the place. To keep up the façade, I looked up the names of a few pubs and invented a whole story about our weekend away. I was becoming an accomplished liar at this stage, so that was easy. Several years later, however, while still deep in addiction, someone once asked me if I had ever been to Galway. Without hesitating, I dived straight in, telling them all about my experiences in the West. I immersed myself in the story, full of emotion, believing every second of it, as I relived the weekend that never occurred. In a rare moment of insight, I caught myself thinking, 'You were never even in Galway, ye mad bastard.' I sniggered to myself, not fully grasping how fucked-up this was. It wasn't until years later, when I was in recovery, that I fully realised how destructive this behaviour could be. The Galway lie was harmless, but as my addiction progressed, my ability to lie to myself took on a life of its own. As a black belt in self-deception, I could make myself do anything, cross any boundary, by making up stories and believing my own lies.

In the year following the Smackathon, I needed more and more heroin to get the same hit. I didn't want my habit getting out of control, so I began using smack with military precision. When I was in work, I'd smoke six lines in the morning, just enough to soothe my anxiety and keep withdrawal at bay, but not so much that I looked fucked-up. If I felt anxious during the day, I smoked another three or four lines in the toilets.

There was also a ready-made smack-smoking room at my company. Convenient, right? Our department used photographic negatives to make printing plates, which required a dark room to process the film. Any sort of light ruined the negatives, so you had to lock the door when you were processing film. It was also a no-go area for anyone outside of the department, so it was perfect if you wanted to hide, or, in my case, do smack in peace. I was always keen to process the film, which I'm sure seemed odd, but the guys in the plate room were always happy to oblige. They'd often complain about the strange smell, but I used to blame the electrics. I doubt they believed a word of it, but it helped me to get by at the time.

You could get anything from twelve to twenty lines out of a bag of smack, so at this stage, I was smoking a bag a day in work and, money permitting, I'd keep one or two for the way home where I'd allow myself to get proper stoned.

I was starting to pull a lot of sickies around this time, and the cracks were starting to show, but it would be many years until I lost my job. People often ask me how I didn't get sacked. There are many reasons. For one, I was very good at my job, even when I was stoned – in the early years anyway. I also had incredible support from my work colleagues, who tried to help me every step of the way, even though they didn't know the extent of my addiction. Some people call this enabling, and maybe it was, but it was done out of friendship, and it was always to their own detriment. What saved me most, however, was my reputation as a drinker, which was also true. Alcohol misuse is rampant in Ireland, accepted even, so people just thought I was hungover, and just like I was able to hide it from my parents, this helped me to cover my tracks.

There was another reason why I kept my job for as long as I did. Despite being naturally anxious, I was also a natural chameleon, gifted with an ability to fit into different environments at the drop of a hat. Back in the early days, the managing director and founder of the company asked me to join him on a plush golf outing in Malahide golf club. It was organised by one of our suppliers, BASF, who spared no expense. I don't specifically recall, but I'm sure heroin was whispering to me, *'I bet real addicts don't do this.'*

I didn't want to look stoned, especially not in front of the corporate heavy hitters – they can be sharp – so I only smoked a couple of lines that morning. The managing director and I played with a CEO from another large company, and we all enjoyed a great round of golf. I'm quite handy at the sport, which helped; and despite being a million miles away from the world I grew up in, I seamlessly fitted into my new environment, cracking jokes and talking shop as we strolled around the golf course.

I was starting to feel a little shivery as we got to the final few holes. 'The sickness' was kicking in, but it was manageable. When we finished up, I told them I'd meet them in the lobby in ten minutes, but I only had one thing on my mind. I grabbed my stash from my car, went into the fancy toilets and smoked half a bag, about ten lines. I must have stunk the place out, but I didn't care. Twenty minutes later, I met the guys in the lobby. I was a little paranoid, but they didn't suspect a thing. Who would in that context? BASF had arranged a post-golf dinner ceremony, so we took our seats in the swanky dining area and ordered a bottle of wine. There were many other leading executives in the room, but I felt completely at home, chatting away and making connections, as if I was climbing high on the corporate ladder. The contrast between my two worlds struck me that day, but it didn't bother me. If I'm perfectly honest, I was even proud. It vindicated my ever-growing conviction that I wasn't a real addict.

* * *

Despite trying to curb my habit, I was now smoking heroin several times a day. My military discipline reduced how much I used, but it was making me more obsessive. Heroin was my first thought in the morning, and my last thought at night. On work days, I was all about precision, but in the evening, I'd go nuts. At weekends, I still went out partying – it was part of my 'not a real addict' story – but I always had a good smoke before I went out. Then, when I was out drinking, like an echo in the wind, heroin called me back home for more. I always listened. It was just a matter of when.

My first big reality check came in October 2001. I had sold hash since the age of fifteen to help fund my various drug habits, and I'd seen many droughts – meaning the supply of hash ran out. I never dreamed that this could happen with heroin, but it did. It crept up from nowhere, so I had no time to stock up. I frantically rang every dealer I knew – no luck. Then I drove around Dublin to all the well-known drug spots, but no one had anything, or they were keeping it for themselves – a smart move, as I later found out. I had no idea what to do. I was stepping on new ground and it was terrifying.

Ever since I found out what methadone really was, I swore I'd never use it, but now it seemed like my only option – just while the drought lasted, of course. I knew a few people who sold it, but the law of supply and demand meant that every addict in Dublin was on the hunt, so I couldn't get it anywhere. It was the same for Valium and sleeping tablets. Nothing. Anywhere. I was willing to pay five times the price, but with a drought in full effect, it didn't matter what I was willing to pay. You can't smoke or inject money, and most addicts only care about short-term solutions, so I was running out of options – fast.

I'd felt the breath of withdrawal before, but I'd never experienced its full onslaught. 'How bad could it be?' I wondered. I'd seen the film *Trainspotting* a few years earlier, 'but that was only a film, and they were serious addicts. My situation is completely different,' I told myself. My biggest concern was coping with anxiety, especially at work. I'd be jumping out of my skin without heroin inside me. I was already getting a bad reputation for pulling sickies, so this could be a big problem.

On my first morning without drugs, I woke up feeling feverish, but physically speaking, it was manageable. My mental state, however, was an entirely different animal. I was restless and agitated – the usual suspects – but I was also afraid, very afraid. I'd never experienced anything like it. It was a lonely and helpless kind of fear, like how a lost child must feel. This was uncharted territory for me, and I had no idea what the day was going to bring – physically, mentally or emotionally. Unable to think straight, I went on autopilot, got dressed and drove into work.

It was a twenty-minute drive, and by the time I got there, I had gripped the steering wheel so tightly that I left grooves in the leather. Sweat was streaming off my forehead, and I was freezing. I folded my arms across my chest and squeezed as tightly as I could, trying to relieve the agitation, but it didn't work. When I glanced in the mirror, I got a shock. I was as white as a ghost. I looked like absolute shit. I walked into the office, turned on the computer and slumped in my seat. One of the lads, Dave, who is a good friend, took one look at me and said, 'Holy shit, you look like crap.'

'I know,' I replied. 'I think I have a dose.'

Usually I had to fight for a sick day, because no one ever believed me, so I was shocked when he said: 'You need to go home mate.'

'Really?' I mumbled disbelievingly.

'Yeah, I'll tell Kim. You need to go to bed. Plus, I don't want to catch whatever the fuck that is.'

I didn't need to think twice – I was gone.

There would be no relief at home, and I didn't want my mam to see me like this, so hoping beyond hope, I started making phone calls to see if I could score some smack. 'I'm getting sorted in a few hours, pal,' seemed to be the trend, but they'd been saying that for days now, so I didn't hold out much hope. Then finally, one of my dealers rang me to say he knew someone in Ballymun who had something. Like most drug addicts, Carl was a user and a dealer. It's on a spectrum really. Some sell more than they take; some buy a few bags in bulk and sell one or two. This particular day, like me, Carl was just an addict who needed a lift. There are no words to describe the rush I got from hearing this news. I felt like Charlie when he won the golden ticket for the chocolate factory. I sped out to Fortlawn to collect Carl, who was a crazy motherfucker and dangerous to be around, but I had bigger concerns, and off we headed to Ballymun.

We were charged triple the price, £60 per bag, but I didn't give a shit. I bought four, heating the sides to make sure it wasn't a rip-off. The side of the bag hardened, just as it should, and we drove off down the road. We pulled in on a back road beside the airport and took out the foil. I was so fucking excited. I poured the powder on the foil and cranked it up. That's when I sensed something was wrong. There was certainly a puddle, but it wasn't golden brown. It had more of an orange, rusty tint to it. It didn't smell right either. I must have gotten sixty lines from each bag, three times the usual, but it only took the edge off my sickness.

'I've seen this shite before,' Carl said. 'It always comes out of hiding during droughts. They mix it with some fucking chemical so it rolls on the foil forever.'

'Are you for fucking real?' I said. I couldn't believe it. I was raging because of the bad heroin, but I was more concerned with Carl's reaction. He was volatile at the best of times, so I knew this could set him off.

'Who the fuck does he think he is giving me that shite? I'm gonna cut that fucker up.' Carl had gone into the flats on his own so I didn't know who he was talking about.

'Who is he?' I asked, more out of concern, as I didn't want to bring Carl back out to Ballymun to cut some dealer up.

'It doesn't matter who he fucking is. No one gives me that shite.'

I'd heard stories about Carl's violence – his whole family had a serious reputation – but I sensed he was all talk this time. He never once asked me to bring him back out to cut the guy up, and despite his anger, and my whingeing, we smoked every one of the bags.

'Chasing the hungry ghosts' is a metaphor used by addiction expert Gabor Maté. It suggests that addicts use drugs to fill a hollowness that cannot be filled. It's similar to an explanation of chasing the dragon I once heard. It involves a delusional state of mind, where you think that the next line, or the next bag, will be your salvation – even when it makes no sense. You are chasing something that is make-believe. It might be a dragon or a ghost – either way, it doesn't exist. It is the only reason why what came next doesn't surprise me. We didn't just smoke all the bags that day, we went back to Ballymun and bought more, without Carl cutting the dealer up. I was still hoping the next bags would feed my hungry ghost, even though we were buying the same shite, but they didn't – they barely fed the tolerance I had built up, so my withdrawal continued as the drought persisted.

My addiction was young – only a few months of daily use – so luckily for me, the physical withdrawal was nothing compared to *Trainspotting*. I could handle the fever and the aches, but I had no defence for anxiety, especially in work. I rang my boss, Kim, and told her I'd be out sick until the following Monday, hoping that the drought would be over by then.

I'm sure I looked like a 'real' addict that week, but I was too sick to notice, begging anyone who'd listen to give me a few tablets or a few millilitres of methadone. It worked, and pity from other addicts was the only thing that got me through my sickness. I came out of that drought with one thing in mind: I would never allow myself to feel so vulnerable, weak or helpless ever again.

The drought didn't end suddenly. There was no massive rainstorm flooding the earth. Heroin dribbled back onto the streets, and it was a few months before the supply was back to normal. I struggled during this time, some days having to ration my supply, barely holding off the sickness, other days smoking everything I had just to feel normal. I couldn't continue living like this.

Despite my disdain for methadone, I began buying as much as I could in case there was ever another drought. It was still hard to get, however, especially in large amounts, and if there was another drought, it wouldn't last long. This did not sit well with me. I was not willing to let addicts and drug dealers become the masters of my fate. I had a decision to make.

I refused to be helpless in the face of another drought, so I found myself back in my GP's office, looking for a prescription for methadone. I didn't hang around with other addicts, mostly because I didn't think I was one, so I had no idea how the system worked. That's why I went to my GP.

I had been going to the same GP since I was a baby, and because there was no history of drug abuse in my family, he was surprised to hear what I had to say. He wasn't able to prescribe me methadone himself, so he told me to go to Pearse Street methadone clinic, the lion's den for naive drug users like myself.

I didn't like the sound of Pearse Street, so I began talking to a couple of addicts I trusted about my situation. Fred, an addict who later became a friend, was surprised I was in so deep, but he gave me great advice. He told me to forget about Pearse Street – 'not your cup of tea,' he said. What he really meant, and I knew it, was that I was too soft for the place – they'd eat me alive. He told me to go to a local clinic instead. I had no idea that they even existed. I didn't want to use one too close to home, so I picked a clinic in Clonsilla, ten minutes from where I lived. It was an evening clinic, which was great, because I was on day shifts at the time, so it wouldn't interfere with work.

Fred told me that the clinic was at the back of a tyre factory in Coolmine Industrial Estate. 'It's at the top of metal steps that used to be a fire escape,' he said. I went up the following day, not knowing what to expect. It was a horrible winter's day – damp, dark and cold – but I found the building handy enough. I remember looking up from the bottom of the steps, wondering how on earth it had come to this. I gripped the metal bars so I wouldn't slip on the steps. They felt cold and wet, but mostly gritty from the chipped paint. They were originally painted black, I think, but years of Irish weathering now exposed a dark grey metal, which eerily matched the colour of the sky. I held on tightly, and gingerly walked up to the door. I'm not sure if I had planned what I was going to say, but these were my very first words: 'How's it going? I'm Brian. I'm from Ladyswell. I don't know if I'm in the right place. I'm looking for a methadone clinic for a non-addict.'

The key workers were kind and caring, accepting me with open arms, despite my crazy 'non-addict' talk. They assured me I was in the right place, and it was a relief to finally talk to someone about my issues. The procedure was simple. I had to provide a couple of urine samples, and as long as they came back positive for opiates, they would put me on the programme. I would then have to attend the clinic once a week: I would provide weekly urine samples, discuss my progress with a designated key worker and meet with the doctor. The problem was, I had no intention of quitting heroin, or regularly using methadone, for that matter. It was just a backup as far as I was concerned. I thought it best to keep my mouth shut, gave my first ever urine sample right there, and within four weeks, I was on the programme. I didn't realise it then, but I had just officially registered myself as an active heroin addict.

I'm not sure how I was supposed to feel during my first few of weeks on the detox programme, but surprisingly, I felt quite comfortable. I was finally able to talk to someone about my problems – that might have been part of it – but it was a nice environment too. The metal steps on the outside were daunting, but the inside of the clinic was cosy. There were a couple of rooms in the back for private conversations between the addicts, the doctor and the key workers. Those rooms were quite clinical, but the waiting room was great. It had an orange vibe to it and reminded me of my mam's sitting room. There were armchairs, a sofa, lava lamps, lots of plants and a nice little kitchenette in the corner where we'd make tea. There was also a toilet attached to the waiting area where we all had to provide our urine samples. That wasn't ideal, but besides urinating into a bottle with a key worker standing behind me, I felt very much at home.

At the same time, I was always trying to keep my non-addict story alive. The key workers and the addicts would sit in the waiting room together, and if I wasn't talking about golf or my job, I was talking about the holidays I had planned, anything to separate myself from the 'real addicts' who attended the programme. The clinic staff had seen it all before, an addict in denial, so they just let me get on with it until I accepted my new reality. The problem was, I never accepted it.

I was now attending a drug clinic, providing urine samples and meeting key workers and doctors to discuss my problems every single week, but I still refused to admit I was a real addict. In my mind, I was only there so my fate wasn't in the hands of the drug trade. I didn't even want to take methadone. I just wanted to hoard it for future droughts. That's when I realised I could sell the extra methadone, a handy bonus. I also heard that methadone curbs the potency of heroin, something I was not willing to live with, especially as my tolerance was hitting new heights on its own.

I could work around these issues, but the urine sample was my biggest problem. The doctor prescribed me 60ml of methadone per day, but if I didn't take it, it would show up as negative on my urine test. That issue was easily avoided by taking a small amount methadone once a week, the day before my test, but there were bigger concerns. I was required to stay off all other drugs, something I was not willing to do. The urine test picked up everything except Zopiclone, a sleeping tablet which is difficult to detect, but I tested positive for heroin and Valium, and usually cocaine, every single week. When I first joined the programme, I could collect my week's supply of methadone on a Saturday, but with repeated dirty urines, I had to go to the chemist and drink it in front of the pharmacist every day. It was a nightmare.

This wasn't going to work for me, so it was time to get creative. That's when I began buying clean urine, which usually came from an addict's partner or baby. I'd heat it before I went into the clinic, and niftily fill the bottle while being watched by a key worker from behind. In later years, they put mirrors in the toilets, so I began putting urine in balloons and squeezing it from inside my trousers. It never worked, and I only ever ended up covered in someone else's urine.

How the hell did it come to this? I was buying people's piss, spilling it all over myself, just so I could get assurances for my drug use. I thought about quitting the programme, but I was afraid I'd lose my job without methadone as a back-up. What I still struggle to understand is my level of denial. Despite the evidence, and the madness of it all, it would be many more years before I admitted I was a real addict.

9

WHEN WORLDS COLLIDE

'Tricks and treachery are the practice of fools, that don't have brains enough to be honest.'

BENJAMIN FRANKLIN

Throughout most of my twenties, I was what many people call a functioning addict. For the most part, I turned up for work. I paid my bills. I wore nice clothes. I drove nice cars. And I kept myself clean and tidy. I even had what looked like a good social life.

I had many amazing experiences throughout these years, including numerous ski holidays in Europe, weekend breaks in Amsterdam, football matches in Liverpool and some fabulous work trips to Belgium. Not to mention hundreds of great nights out with family and friends. I had no interest in long-term relationships, but Barry, Dano and myself loved going to town on the pull, and every once in a while we even had a bit of luck. I did many of the things that normal lads my age did, albeit full of drink and drugs.

Underneath it all, however, I was living a lie. More accurately, I was leading two separate lives. In one life, the one I showed to the outer world, everything looked normal; in the other life, the real me, I lived in a constant state of anxiety.

My outer life had one purpose: *'Protect your addiction at all costs.'* I did this by pretending I was fine, that my life was going to plan. As long as I kept up the lie, I could continue to use drugs. My other life, the one only I knew about, was a grim and lonely place. I was constantly agitated, tortured by my mind and consumed by anxiety. It was relentless, all-consuming. To cope, I directed every thought and every action to soothing my inner restlessness and quietening the voices in my head. In reality, I wasn't soothing anything. I was running, trying to escape from my own body and mind. To do that, I gorged myself on drugs, as much as I could, especially heroin, the only thing that eased my ever-worsening anxiety.

I no longer worried about my parents lying dead in a ditch, or World War III outside my front door, but my anxiety was getting worse. Different forces were driving it now. I was anxious about losing my job if anyone found out about my drug habit. I was anxious about not getting my fix. I was anxious about getting anxious. Alcohol and uppers played a massive role, but trying to restrain my heroin use, which is a form of withdrawal, was the real villain. I was taking more and more heroin to ease my anxiety, but with increased use, withdrawal got worse, and I was actually feeding my anxiety instead of helping it. Like a snake trying to eat its own tail, I was caught in a loop, but I couldn't see it.

Despite outward appearances, as I reached my mid-twenties my heroin habit was out of control: €200 in a bad week, €600 in a good one. On top of that, I finally succumbed to taking 80 millilitres of methadone every day. But I was also drinking alcohol every day and swallowing sedatives every day. At weekends, I'd treat myself to more of everything.

I was still selling hash, but to make matters worse, I was selling cocaine too. It was far more profitable and I needed extra money to fund my growing heroin habit. Cocaine, or Bronson as we used to call it, after Charles Bronson, also began filling a new void in my life – a void which, I believe, was caused by methadone.

They call methadone a maintenance drug for opiate addiction, but it's far more insidious than that. It kills your spirit and robs you of the motivation you need to get clean. Most people who go on methadone stay on methadone, and I believe this is why. My friend Barry says, 'Methadone doesn't maintain you, it contains you.' That's why I loved cocaine. Methadone was clawing away at my soul, stealing my life energy, and I was beginning to feel empty inside, so shovelling piles of cocaine up my nose made me feel whole again – for a few hours anyway.

Something had to give. My double life could not continue, and sure enough, my two separate worlds began to collide. It started slowly, but quickly picked up speed, as glimpses of my future began rearing their ugly head.

* * *

Even in the early days, when I was only taking heroin every few weeks, it was easy to see the direction my life was going. On my first ski trip, the one where I met Lena, I arranged for the lads and myself to stay in a fancy hotel in Austria. The AlpenSchlössl, which translates as Alpine Castle, was located on the outskirts of a beautiful little Tyrolean resort called Soll. I've always pined for nice things – who doesn't? – but the madness of substance abuse always got in the way. For the staff of the AlpenSchlössl, this was unfortunate, as we caused havoc for everyone on our week at the slopes.

Four of us went to Soll: Dano, Barry, my brother Kelvin and myself. We started drinking in the airport at 6 a.m., but because of difficult weather conditions, we didn't arrive at the hotel until nine that night. Kelvin was a little more sensible and stayed in the hotel, but the lads and I went down to the town. None of us could remember checking in, never mind our room numbers. Separated in the town, where who knows what we got up to, we individually arrived back at the hotel, causing mayhem in the early hours of the morning. We randomly knocked on doors, climbed on balconies (via a milk truck), raided the bar and screamed each other's names in an attempt to find our rooms. Kelvin heard us, but he couldn't find us. I woke up the following morning lying in a corridor, and the two lads woke up on sun loungers by the pool.

When we went down for breakfast, the staff had separated our table from all the other guests. They didn't think it through, however. They put us out of sight in a little alcove near the bar. It was perfect. We pulled our own pints for the rest of the week, and even had a few for breakfast. I've no idea why they didn't kick us out, especially after the bar raid. Instead, they put us in the bold corner, and we ended up having the holiday of our lives.

That was my first foreign holiday while I was obsessed with heroin, although I wasn't physically addicted at the time. We thought about bringing some with us, but we were too nervous about getting caught. Instead, we doubled up on alcohol and went crazy for the week. Barry barely skied because he was too hungover, but the rest of us skied every day. I fell in love with skiing on that holiday, but despite being drug free for the week, the cracks were beginning to show.

* * *

My mid-twenties was a fight to look normal while my world was falling apart. Everything I did was an attempt to show people I was in control, especially my family. They knew I had problems, but they had no idea that they went so deep. I only let people see the good parts of me, and took huge steps to keep it that way.

I was still living with my parents, and to this day, my mam feels silly, and annoyed, that she didn't realise what was going on. She is also angry that I made her look like a fool. The neighbours often told her I had drug problems, but to her mind, it didn't add up, especially when I was so good at hiding my lies. She suspected I was on drugs, and often said it to my dad, but he assured her it was only hash. They weren't clued in when it came to drugs. She confronted me on several occasions, but the fact that I didn't believe I was an addict made me a very convincing liar. I'd come out with a spiel about how much I earned and how good I was at my job – most of it true. By the end of my speech,

I'd be angry, and having believed my own lies, I'd then question my mam about her faith in her own son.

I once heard that addiction is a family sport, and eventually, everyone gets to play. This line was beginning to ring true, as my drug use was starting to impact everyone in my family. At first, I mostly smoked heroin in my car, but over time, it became so normal that I just smoked it in my bedroom. Neither my mam nor my dad ever came into my room, which made it easier, but it didn't work out so well for my younger brother and sister. They used to come in and watch TV with me, but now I kicked them out, giving them no reason why. They caught me smoking heroin on several occasions, but I told myself they wouldn't know what it was. They did.

This had a huge impact on my younger sister Anne. She had no one to turn to, knowing I'd go mad if she told my mam. She looked up to me as her big brother, so she didn't see this as an option. She thought about telling her friends, but she went to school in a more privileged area outside Ladyswell, so she didn't know how they would react. Out of options, she told them anyway, but they accused her of being an attention-seeker. She was only a kid, and I forced her to face this dilemma alone.

My younger brother James had it just as bad. Before I started messing around with drugs, we spent lots of time together. I taught him how to play football, how to swing a golf club and how to play video games. We played football games non-stop. But now that I had my new friend, heroin, I just kicked him out of the room. James wasn't one to argue, especially with me, and it didn't help that he had a stammer, so he just did what I asked, even though it was also his room. Just like my sister, I left him to deal with this issue on his own. If he told anyone, he knew I'd go nuts, and I'd most likely accuse him of being a rat.

Until my mid-twenties, only my brother Kelvin and a handful of friends knew about my daily heroin use, and only Barry knew how deep it really went. Both of our lives revolved around heroin, and we did everything together. Over the next few years, our tolerance for smack hit an all-time high. It was getting more and more difficult to get the same hit, even when we mixed it with other drugs. That's when we started playing with the idea of injecting. We told ourselves it would be a one-time thing, but deep down I knew that was a lie. We got the syringes and asked an addict friend to show us what to do. We were ready to rock, but, thankfully, my morbid fear of needles kicked in, and we decided to bail out. It would be several years before I finally stuck a needle in my arm, but Barry had already made up his mind. He refused to go on a methadone programme, and within a few months he was injecting heroin regularly. Barry was one of my best childhood friends. We had so many shared experiences, practically living in each other's pockets for years. Although we spent time together after he started injecting, that was the beginning of the end. Heroin tore our friendship apart.

Barry had no interest in keeping up appearances, but I put every ounce of energy into it. If I didn't, I would have to admit that I was a real addict, and that scared the life out of me. As time went by, incident after incident, it was getting far more difficult to keep up the façade.

My dad was a taxi driver at this stage, and he would often come home in the early hours of the morning. On several occasions, he found me goofing off in the sitting room with a tray of heroin on my lap. I told him it was hash oil, and he seemed to believe me, but I don't think the apple fell too far from the tree. Just like myself, it was easier for him to believe a lie than face the reality that his son might be deep in addiction.

It still pains me today when I think about how my mother found out. She was changing the curtains in my room one day, and the rail slipped. Several of the little hooks fell behind my bed. When she pulled back the mattress, over twenty empty bottles of methadone stared her straight in the face. My name was on the sticker of every single one of them. How could I deny it? She felt sick to her stomach, her worst fears confirmed. She mentioned it to me, but uncomfortable conversations were not common practice in our family, and although it was out in the open, it was something we never properly discussed.

My heroin addiction was now becoming common knowledge among my family, friends and close work colleagues. This was going to create pressure, so I needed a new story. I decided to tell everyone I only took heroin to cope with anxiety, which was mostly true, and that I didn't take it any more. I also told them I was on a methadone programme to get off heroin, and now that I was 'clean', I was weaning myself off methadone. 'Back to normal within six months,' I said. Whatever the hell normal was. Ironically, this little story also had a positive impact on my life. For the first time ever, I believed a lie that might benefit me. I was far from getting clean, or even trying, but the thought of being normal planted a seed, a seed of possibility.

* * *

The collision between my two worlds was most evident in work. I was still doing a good job, but my standards were starting to slide. It was obvious I had issues, but I don't exactly remember how my work colleagues found out about how deep my addiction ran. I must have told them on a drunken night out.

My boss Kim did her very best to help me. Anytime I looked sick, Kim would ask me if I had taken my methadone – 'your green stuff', as she used to call it. I'm not even sure if she knew what it was at first. She soon began reading up about addiction and learned that our environment plays a big role, especially in recovery. In the hope of helping me get clean, she offered me a room in her house if I ever wanted to do a detox. I'm eternally grateful for the offer, but I knew what kind of madness that could turn into, because I knew in my heart I wasn't even close to quitting.

I made this perfectly clear while travelling with my job. We were in the graphics industry, and our computer systems required frequent upgrades. This meant that we had to go to either England or Belgium and learn about the new updates. I loved these trips, except for one thing – they were heroin free. Apparently, airport security weren't keen on opiate addiction.

Apart from droughts, the only time I spent any extended amount of time away from heroin was when I was travelling outside Ireland. I could still bring my legally prescribed methadone – I wouldn't be able to go otherwise – but I was always terrified about losing it. More to the point, it would barely contain my sickness, so I'd drink like a lunatic and bring sedatives to numb the pain.

On one particular trip, I went to England to learn about a minor systems upgrade. It was only a two-day course, and the training wasn't going to be difficult, so my mind quickly turned to how wasted I could get. The course was in a town called Redditch, about fifteen miles from Birmingham, and I stayed at a nice hotel on a golf course. I still liked golf. It worked in tandem with my non-addict story. The training course was easier than I thought, and on the first day I finished up at noon. It was too early to go on the lash, so I decided to play a round of golf. But I felt like crap – shivers and cold sweats. Methadone was never enough on its own, and I couldn't get any tablets for the trip, so I decided that a six-pack of blue WKD alcopops might take my mind off it. I packed the bottles in the bag, and played my round of golf.

As I finished the round, a familiar voice popped into my head. *'Birmingham is only up the road. I bet you could get some heroin there.'* I dismissed it immediately, knowing where that could lead. But I knew, and the voice knew, it was only a matter of when. I went out for dinner, had a few more drinks, and the next thing I remember is chatting to a few lads from Birmingham. They were a little rough around the edges – my kind of people – so I asked them if they knew where I could score some smack.

I don't recall much of that night, but I do remember sitting in the back of a car, driving up to Birmingham and sitting around a kitchen table smoking weed. The lads were originally from Pakistan, and they must have thought I was nuts, some pale Irish lad over for a work course, floating around Birmingham looking for smack. I never got any heroin, as far as I remember, and I don't know how I found the hotel, but I managed to get back safely – I always had a knack for finding my way home, like I was being guided by an inner satnav. I woke up in my hotel bed the following morning, but it was late, and I missed half of the course. But I didn't care. I was due to fly home that day, back home to heroin, and that made everything feel okay.

With my two worlds colliding, the contrast between them was becoming more and more obvious. One day after work sticks out more than most. It was urine day at the clinic, and for the previous few weeks, I had given them dirty samples. This meant that I had to go the chemist daily and drink my methadone in front of the pharmacist. Before I went to the clinic, I had to stop at the chemist. It was in Corduff, and as I walked in, an addict I knew was lingering outside. This guy, let's call him Joey, was a little crazy and seriously violent. I didn't take much notice at first, but when I walked into the chemist, there was another addict inside, called Billy, and he was crying. He said that Joey told him if he didn't give him his methadone he was going to cut him up. Joey had previous convictions for serious violence, including stabbing someone with a machete, so there was reason to be scared. Like myself, Billy had to drink his methadone in the chemist. When he said this to Joey, Joey told him to keep it in his mouth and spit it into a bottle when he came out. The pharmacist felt bad, but what could he do. If he gave Billy a second dose, every addict in Blanchardstown would be spinning the same trick. Billy had a choice: go sick or risk getting stabbed. I never found out what happened. I drank my methadone and went up to the clinic. I told them what I saw, and apparently it was a trend. It could easily have been me, and maybe next time it would.

***

The closest I ever came to killing someone occurred several weeks after the Birmingham trip. It was our summer party at work, and one of the lads asked me and another colleague to join him on a hunting trip – the following morning, as it happens. Let's call them Chris and Liam. Chris and I were in our late twenties, and Liam was only nineteen, so we should have been the responsible ones, but it didn't work out that way. Liam owned two shotguns and had recently got his licence. It wasn't really a hunting trip – the plan was to drive to Cavan and shoot a few crows. I have no idea what I was thinking. I love animals, always did, especially crows – they're my favourite. Some people find that odd, but I love their bold personalities and how their heads bob up and down when they walk. I don't even kill insects today, so it disturbs me greatly to think I was willing to murder a few crows for kicks.

I picked Liam up at 8 a.m., but I was still drunk after getting home late from the party. We drove out to Chris's house and he was just as bad. We sat in his kitchen drinking coffee, joking about the night before. Chris asked me if I wanted a beer to help with the hangover. I snatched it out of his hand in a flash. Liam was a little disturbed by this turn of events – he was in charge of the guns, after all – but we didn't give a shit. I'm not sure whose idea it was, but on the way out, Chris grabbed a crate of beer – about sixteen bottles – and off we went to Cavan.

I drank nine bottles of beer that day. Not only was I driving, we had two bloody shotguns in the car. We spent the whole day driving around Cavan, searching for fields to go shooting in.

We didn't even have permission. We fired at hundreds of crows, and several other birds, but we were too drunk to hit anything. At one stage, I told Chris to take a pop out of the car window. I was joking, I think, but Chris let off a shot. The noise was deafening, and the smell of gunpowder lasted for days. That was bad enough, but it got worse. One memory in particular will stay with me until I die.

The heron incident happened late in the day. I'm not sure what drugs I had in my system – a combination of heroin, methadone and Valium, I imagine – but I was somewhere between hungover and half-wasted. My head was bobbing with every step, just like the crows we had been sneaking up on.

There was a disturbance in the grass about twenty yards to my right. Chris, who was standing between the rustling and me, shouted, 'It's a fucking heron! Get it!' The heron took flight, and without thinking, I heaved myself around, letting off a shot in the same movement. I remember the whole incident as if in slow motion. Chris ducked and fell on the ground. I don't know how I didn't hit him. I was sure I pulled the trigger while he was in my line of sight. With adrenaline pumping through my veins, I let off the remaining shots as the bird flew away, but I missed with every one. When I turned back around, Chris, still on the ground, looked like he had seen a ghost.

'Holy shit, that was close,' I laughed nervously.

'Fuck me, Brian. You could have killed me.'

'Sorry, man, I just reacted.'

Suddenly sober, we knew we had both fucked up, from that very first beer. Liam, who was ten years our junior, jokingly said, 'I'm not bringing you two out again.' It helped break the tension, but he really meant it. We walked back to the car, joking about the day, but at the same time intensely aware of how serious it could have been. A few inches to the left or right and Chris could have been dead.

How did I get myself into so many of these situations? The answer was simple. People had no idea who I truly was. They only saw the lie, the life that I portrayed. If they knew the truth, the invites would have dried up a long time ago. I was able to pull it off for a while, to keep my two worlds from colliding, but I was getting sloppy, and the truth was coming out.

10

NOT A 'REAL DRUG DEALER'

'Self-deception helps us to deceive.'

DAVID LIVINGSTONE

JUNE 2006

Brendan was a gangster, and one of the most dangerous people I've ever known – he also happened to be my drug dealer. Even the police were afraid of him. It was a while since I'd seen him – he'd been in hospital after a former associate stabbed him in the neck. That didn't stop him dealing, however; his wife stood in for him in his absence. Now that he was out, it was business as usual, and I met him on a back road near Swords.

After a quick hello, I handed him €600: half was what I owed him; the other half was for a quarter ounce of heroin. Brendan had been my dealer for years, and despite our different backgrounds, we got on great. If I ever crossed him, however, none of that would matter. He made that clear on several occasions. We had a chat about the row with his former associate, how he was a dead man walking, and quickly went our separate ways.

As I drove home, I decided to pop into my mam's. I stopped at the local Spar on the way, and as I got back into the car, my phone rang. It was my friend Jimmy, asking how I was getting on. My addiction was out of control at this stage, and people were concerned. It was a scorcher of a day, and the sun was beating into the car. As I drove out of the car park, one hand on the steering wheel, the other holding my phone, I leaned my elbow out of the open window as I chatted to Jimmy.

I parked by the curb beside my mam's house, but when I went to fix the position of the car, some idiot had pulled in behind me. They were right up my arse, and I nearly reversed into them. With Jimmy still on the line, I put the phone on the passenger seat, jumped out of my car and began shouting: 'What the fuck are ...' Before I could finish my macho bullshit, two big lads jumped out of the car and flung me across the bonnet.

'Drugs squad,' they said.

'Fuck me,' I said to myself. They must have been following me, but for how long I didn't know. I was hoping it was after – not before – I met Brendan. This was already serious, but that would be a disaster.

'Anything in the car?'

'No,' I said.

I wasn't lying. The bag of smack was in my right front pocket. I paid €300 for it, and it was mostly for personal use, but with an exaggerated street value of €1,000, the charge would be intent to supply.

'No seatbelt, talking on the phone, no tax, bald tyres, and I know you have something in the car.'

'I don't, I swear,' I said.

They didn't say anything about Brendan. That was a relief, but they could feel my fear.

'The sweat is dripping off you. You're hiding something.'

I was always sweating because of my drug abuse, which was now near *Trainspotting* levels, but that didn't sound like a clever excuse.

'It's bleedin' roasting out. That's why I'm sweating,' I replied.

'Look, we're going to search the car, so it's best if you tell us now.'

'Go on, search it. You won't find anything,' I said, tentatively.

The other detective, the quiet one, began tearing through my car. He pulled out the ashtrays, popped the panels off the dash and checked places I didn't know existed. They meant business. It was only a matter of time before they searched me. I stood there nervously with my hands in my pockets, my right hand clutching the bag of gear. I thought about flicking it through the railing behind me, but the one doing the talking wouldn't take his eyes off me. I was fucked, and I knew it.

The detective finished searching the car, except for the drawer under the driver's seat, which was stuck.

'Is that broke?' he asked.

'Nah, you have to have the knack for it,' I told him.

Then, without thinking, I pulled my hand out of my pocket, bag in hand, and rolled it under the seat as I opened the drawer. I couldn't believe it. They didn't see a thing. I was instantly excited, and damn fucking proud. I wanted to celebrate, right there and then. There was an empty bottle of methadone in the drawer, but I didn't care. They knew I was an addict. I'd bumped into them before, and you could tell by just looking at me.

They proceeded to search me, like really search me, but my demeanour had changed, and they knew it. They found nothing and were seriously pissed off.

'We know you're hiding something. We'll tow that car off and pull it apart if you don't tell us.'

They had already searched the car and found nothing. 'Empty threats,' I thought.

Then they threatened to seize the car because it had no tax, but detectives can't be arsed with that kind of paperwork – something I knew quite well. Another empty threat.

Several more empty threats later, something about someone ratting on me if I remember correctly, and they conceded defeat.

'Get out of here. We'll be in touch.'

The final empty threat. I knew I wouldn't be hearing from them again.

I sold drugs for twenty years, always to feed my habit, but that was the closest I came to getting charged – for drug dealing, anyway. I've since thought that jail might have been the wake-up call I needed, but from what I heard, there was as much heroin on the inside as there was on the streets.

It turns out I hadn't knocked off my phone, so my friend Jimmy heard the whole thing. He's a real joker, and his version of the story, impressions and all, is bloody hilarious. It wasn't funny at the time – it was too close a call – but that wasn't new. I had many close calls over the years, ever since I began selling drugs as a kid. I don't know how I got away with it for so long – it was a bloody miracle – and I often wonder if someone was watching over me.

* * *

I started selling drugs when I was fifteen, only a year after I began taking them. My first drug was hash, and it quickly became the centre of my world. On Friday nights, my friends and I would pool our pocket money to buy as much as we could. There were about twelve of us, but we didn't know anything about the drug scene. Instead of buying in bulk, we bought loads of ten-pound deals, called ten spots. We thought we were great, at first, but they were so skinny they looked like razor blades, and we soon realised that our dealer was ripping us off.

I saw my first large block of hash not long after that. I quickly decided it would be better if I bought the hash in bulk, sold better deals to my friends and smoked the profit. It was a no-brainer, I thought. I didn't even see it as a problem, and I certainly didn't think of myself as a drug dealer. As long as I just sold hash to my friends, I was being smart. I always fancied myself as an entrepreneur anyway.

I will never forget the first time I chopped up an ounce of hash. John's brother Gerry was a cool dude, and someone we all wanted to impress. He asked us if we knew how to chop up an ounce. As aspiring hardmen and wannabe homeboys, 'Of course we do,' was our immediate response. He handed us the hash and told us to 'Cut it into twenty nice long ten spots.'

'You can keep two for yourselves,' he said.

John and I looked at each other and nervously replied, 'Yeah, no bother.'

We had no idea how to cut up an ounce of hash. No internet back then, either. We thought about asking someone, but we didn't want to look like idiots. We went back to my bedroom and sat there, pondering what to do. 'It can't be that hard,' John said, and I agreed. 'Let's go for it.' We had plenty of experience buying long skinny ten spots, so we planned to work backwards from there.

An ounce of hash is like a little brown brick, about half the size of an iPhone. Once heated, it goes soft. That much we knew from smoking it. We needed to roll it out so we could cut it into long skinny strips. We had a rolling pin and a knife, but we weren't sure how to heat it. We tried to use a lighter but it was only burning the edges. We needed a bigger heat source. We'd heard people say they used ovens, but 'Hey, Ma, just heating a block of hash. I'll be done in a jiffy,' didn't seem appropriate. That's when John had a lightbulb moment. He once heard his brother's friend talk about using a kettle. 'We can steam the hash,' he said. At least I could bring that up to my room.

With nothing to lose, I grabbed the kettle from the kitchen, hoping my mam wouldn't notice it was gone. We boiled the kettle, and held the ounce over the spout with a fork, but it wasn't much better than the lighter. It only heated the edges. We needed to put it in the belly of the kettle. I don't know who thought of it, but we grabbed a sock, popped the ounce inside, and hung it in the kettle as it boiled. We kept our finger on the release button and let it boil for about a minute. The hash still wasn't soft enough, but it looked like it was working. We stuck it in again, and this time waited for a full five minutes.

When we pulled out the sock, it looked droopy, in an ominous kind of way. We didn't say anything, but we were both worried. John slowly rolled down the soggy sock. What emerged is an image I will never forget. The outside of the ounce had dissolved, mashing itself into the material of the sock. It looked like wet sand. In a panic, John grabbed the remainder of the ounce and began rolling it on the table. Brown juice was leaking everywhere.

'That doesn't look right,' I said.

'I fucking know,' he replied nervously.

John kept rolling, frantically trying to salvage the situation, but half of it stuck to the rolling pin, the other half glued itself to the table. We looked at each other, but didn't say a word. John peeled the hash off the pin, and I peeled it off the table, but it all crumbled into little pieces. It was an absolute disaster. Instead of smooth long skinny strips of hash, we had sand, crumbs and odd-shaped nuggets.

It was like a comedy sketch, and when the panic subsided, we started to laugh. Two chumps trying to chop up a lump of hash. What else could we do? It was fucking hilarious. We literally fell around the room at the calamity of it all. When we finally stopped laughing, we surveyed the remnants of the massacre. We were due to meet Gerry by the laneway at the side of the estate. It was funny, but we didn't think Gerry would agree.

It wasn't long before we were panicking again. We began piecing all the fragments together to make twenty little piles. They looked so small. We grabbed some tinfoil, and as best we could, wrapped them into something that resembled ten-pound deals. We ended up with twelve ten spots, two twenty-pound lumps, and a few bizarre-looking shapes that we called fifteens. We packed them into a money bag, and off we went to meet Gerry in the lane.

I vividly remember standing in the laneway waiting for Gerry. It was a typical Irish evening, dreary and dull, with a hazy drizzle hanging in the air. We sheltered under the branches of a bush, trying to act hard, like wannabe drug dealers, but we were shitting ourselves. At the same time, we couldn't stop laughing. Mostly about what had happened, but also because we had the giggles from smoking the hash. Despite butchering Gerry's ounce, we still took our cut and rolled a joint for the walk.

As cool as you like, Gerry strolled down the lane, and John handed him the money bag. I can't remember what John said, but as Gerry opened the bag, I'll never forget his face.

'What the fuck happened?' he asked, eyes wide open in utter disbelief.

'It just broke up,' John said.

'Have you ever …? How did you …?' Gerry was lost for words.

The wreckage was so extreme that it worked in our favour. A random assortment of stars, pyramids and triangles. You couldn't write this stuff.

'Jaysis, lads, I won't be asking you again.' Gerry was laughing now as he surveyed our handiwork. I'm just glad Gerry and John were brothers. I don't like to think of how it would have gone down otherwise.

* * *

I sold small amounts of drugs throughout my teens, mostly hash, but as my heroin addiction grew, so did my need to feed it. In my early twenties, I began selling bigger quantities of hash, but it was a lot of work, and not really worth the hassle. When I was twenty, cocaine start flooding the streets of Dublin. Despite my love affair with heroin, I had a soft spot for cocaine. It was the perfect marriage. Cocaine to go up, heroin to come down. Cocaine was also more socially acceptable, and a far better fit for my non-addict delusions, especially when I decided to sell it.

Before selling cocaine, I never considered myself a drug dealer. Selling hash and E's in Ladyswell was a rite of passage, something many of the kids did, especially the ones who fancied themselves as entrepreneurs. Selling Class A drugs was different. In my mind, real drug dealers sold heroin and cocaine. Then I thought, *'Real drug dealers make money. They don't sell drugs to feed their habit, or to sort their mates out with better deals. And cocaine isn't that bad. It's not as if I'm selling heroin. I'd never sell heroin. Only scumbags do that.'*

This was a story I could live with. As long as I didn't sell heroin, I wasn't a real drug dealer. Even for me, this was a stretch, but strangely enough, I was far more willing to admit I was a drug dealer than an addict, which made my transition into selling cocaine far easier.

Back in 1997, when I started selling coke, an ounce cost £1,000, ten times the price of hash. I was playing in a different league, but it didn't faze me. My friend's brother, Mark, put me in contact with a guy from Finglas. Let's call him Lucas. Lucas was a serious player – even the infamous Westies were wary of him, although I was unaware of that at the time. There were no mobile phones back then, so Mark gave me a landline number for Lucas. The call was brief, all of sixty seconds, and he said he'd start me off with a half ounce. He told me to cut it into eight one-hundred-pound bags, sell five to pay for the coke, and sell three for profit. My plan was to snort it and use it to fund my other drug habits, but he didn't need to know that.

Lucas warned me to come up to his house on my own. There was a laneway near his back garden, and he told me to whistle when I got there. It was a damp, cold, miserable night. I'll never forget that detail, because I soaked the back of my jeans taking a shortcut when I jumped over a railing. It seeped right through, and my arse was freezing. When I got to the laneway, I began whistling, but my attempts were pitiful. Whistling was never my strong suit, but I forgot just how bad I was. I stood there for the next fifteen minutes, ass shivering, not knowing what to do, hopelessly blowing silent air into the dark. My only hope was if Lucas walked out by chance, but even then, I doubt he'd have heard me. I had a decision to make – I could knock on the door or I could go home. Neither was appealing. I knew he might go nuts, but I decided to knock.

The door opened, but I didn't know what Lucas looked like. The guy who answered was not what I was expecting. He was a big, fit, slick-looking dude.

'Is Lucas there?'

'Who wants to know?'

'I'm Pennier, I couldn't …'

He stopped me in my tracks, calmly.

'What did I tell you?'

'Sorry, I tried to whistle but I'm fuckin' brutal at it. I only realised when I was outside.'

He sniggered.

'Come in. I'm Lucas.'

He brought me past the sitting room and into the kitchen. There were a few older lads in the sitting room watching the football. As a football fanatic, that calmed me down.

'Who do you support?' I asked.

'Liverpool,' he said.

'Me too,' I replied.

I've always been a talker – it serves me well – and we had a chat about Liverpool's season. He knew his stuff and was surprisingly sound. Then he asked me if I liked dogs. I told him I love dogs, but it was only a few months later that I realised he was talking about fighting dogs. We got on great, seamlessly chatting for a good ten minutes about all sorts of stuff. Lucas had a serious reputation, and I had heard a few stories, so I was not expecting us to be getting on so well. In hindsight, I think he was scoping me out, but it worked to my advantage in the end.

One of the lads walked into the kitchen. 'How's it going?' I said, feeling comfortable in my new gangster surroundings. He was a scary-looking dude and didn't even bother saying hello. He just stared at me, giving me a silent grunt, if there is such a thing. Not knowing how to respond, I just said, 'Sound.' It might have looked like I was being cheeky – far from it; I just panicked.

I looked at Lucas, who was smiling. He beckoned me to leave, handing me the half ounce on my way out the door.

'You have a week,' he said.

'No problem, I'll have it before that. Can I knock again, or will I bring someone to whistle for me?'

He laughed. 'Just fucking knock.'

'Thanks, man.' And off I went.

Lucas thought I was a brazen, cheeky fucker, and he wasn't far wrong. He liked that, and it would serve me well. Maybe we could even be friends. As a wannabe homeboy, I liked that idea. I walked home that night, delighted with life. Half ounce of coke stuffed down my jocks, and a new gangster friend. Life was kind. Or so I thought.

It was easy selling coke. I caught the market early, and my friends came to me. My biggest problem was keeping my profit. Everyone wanted some. I was selling an ounce a week in no time, making plenty to snort and an extra few quid to fund my growing drug habit.

I got to know Lucas well over the next year. He loved that I had a good job, and that I didn't bring any attention to myself, especially from the police. I was always very careful about that. I even banned baseball caps and flashy tracksuits from my car.

One day he asked me about my heroin use. I denied it at first, but it was obvious he got the information from a reliable source. I told him I was only dabbling, and he just said: 'Be careful with that shite. It catches up on you.' I like to think he was looking out for me, but I'm sure he was more concerned about our business arrangement. Heroin addicts are not very reliable, after all.

As it turns out, Lucas didn't need to worry about my heroin habit. My newfound love of coke was his real concern. I was now snorting all my profits, and then some. As Christmas 1998 came around, I owed him over £1,000. I asked him for two ounces to sell over Christmas, telling him I'd sell the lot to clear my debts. I had every intention of following through, but I don't remember much of that Christmas. I snorted most of it, and any money I did make, I used to buy drink, tablets and smack.

New Year's Day was one of the most depressing days of my life. I had a Christmas hangover from hell, I owed Lucas £3,000, and I had no idea how to pay it back. I went to the bank and the credit union in early January, but I already owed them thousands, and they rejected me on the spot. I was due to go Belgium with my job at the end of January, and I'd be gone for two weeks. Out of options, I decided to forget about my drug debt until I came back.

It was now two months since I'd seen Lucas, and I still had no way of getting his money. I thought about going over to explain what had happened, but I had no idea how he would react. It was far easier to put it on the long finger, so that's what I did. I asked a few people about what he might do, and I didn't like what I heard. A few months earlier, he had chased some guy through his mother's house for £50. When he caught him in the back garden, he slapped the head off him in front of his family. The idea of bringing something like that to my own mother's door terrified me, but for some reason, I couldn't see it happening.

Over the next few months, I continued to sell hash. I also found a new supplier for coke, but it was weak compared to Lucas's stuff. I tried to save up the money I owed him, but my budding addiction was having none of it. This debt wasn't going to go away, so I went back to the credit union with a sob story.

With the help of a guarantor, my dad, they gave me £1,500. This I could work with.

I'll never forget the day I walked over to Lucas's door. I only had half of the £3,000 I owed him, which was bad enough, but I was also over six months late. To make matters worse, I had to ask him for more coke to pay the remainder of the debt. I knew this was risky, but I had no other options. Dano and Kevo came with me, but they stayed out of sight. They could do very little anyway. I was petrified as I walked up to the door, and had no idea what was going to happen.

Knock, knock, knock.

Long silence.

Knock, knock, knock.

Long silence.

I was about to walk away when the door swung open.

It was Lucas.

'Ah, look who it is,' he said with a wide grin.

It wasn't exactly a friendly grin. There was a menace to it. Something I hadn't seen before.

'You're a cheeky little fucker, you know that?'

I began blurting out my excuses, but he stopped me and beckoned me inside.

I continued spluttering, 'I'm really sorry, man. I have half here, but I'll get the rest in a week or two, as soon as I have more coke. That's how I couldn't get the money up.'

'What? You're telling me you haven't got all the money and you're looking for more coke?'

He didn't give me a chance to answer.

'You've some fucking neck, you have,' he said, with a smirk on his face.

He was trying to act intimidating, which usually came easily, I gathered, but his demeanour had changed. It was friendly, just like old times. My cheeky risk had flipped in my favour. He took the money and told me to come back for more coke. But he left me with a warning: 'I could have found you – you know that. And if it happens again ...' The warning trailed away, but it had a sinister undertone. He left me in no doubt, and I never crossed Lucas again.

VODKA BREAD

'You're going to reap just what you sow.'

LOU REED

AUGUST 2006

A crackling noise, like the sound of a campfire on a clear summer night. It usually takes a bulldozer to wake me, especially when I'm stoned, so it was a minor miracle that it stirred me from my sleep. As I lay in bed, wondering where it was coming from, I was happy. Better than happy. I was comfortably numb. I liked waking up stoned, but it didn't happen very often, and like most things in my drug-addicted life, I knew it wouldn't last long. I tried my best to hold on to the feeling, but I was right, my moment of stillness was the calm before the storm.

The crackling got louder, and I could sense that something was wrong. That's when I felt a surge in the pit of my stomach. I knew this feeling. I knew it well. And it only ever meant one thing. Danger was near. I jumped from my bed and looked out into the night. My instincts were right. The noise was coming from my front garden. Both cars, my mother's and my own, were on fire, only inches from our home.

My dad was away, but my two brothers, my sister and my mam were in the house. I ran into their rooms, screaming for them to get up. Then I rushed down the stairs to get a better look. It was worse than I thought. The cars were blazing, pushed right up against the front door. The house wasn't on fire yet, but I could feel the heat on my eyelids, as the intensity of the flames reached into the hallway, stretching their long grasp through the thin porch door.

I ran back upstairs. 'Quick, you have to get up, we have to get out of the house!' I stood on the landing, three steps from the top, nervously peering down the stairs. It was a terrifying sight. Orange flames illuminated the entire hallway, and black smoke began creeping under the front door. The fire was growing before my eyes, melting the porch and windows, with menacing popping sounds reverberating up the stairs. It was only a matter of time before the house went up.

'Come on! We have to go! We have to go right now!'

As I stood there, waiting, everything slowed down. My brothers came out of their room first, as if in slow motion, looking as shocked as you'd expect. My sister, who appeared strangely calm, soon followed. Finally, my mother opened her bedroom door. Her room was at the back of the house and she didn't realise what was going on. When she looked down the stairs, she began crying. Our only escape was the back garden, but we had to pass the front door. Single file, we shuffled down the stairs, the heat building as we got closer to the door. It was terrifying, like a scene from a movie, but we managed to creep by and get to the back door.

We were safe, that was the important thing, but my mam was hysterical. We tried to calm her, before quickly realising that no one had rung the fire brigade. That was the next priority. The house would definitely burn down otherwise. 'Has anyone got their phone?' I asked. Nobody. They were all in the house, most likely upstairs. The only option was the landline, but it was right beside the front door. I'd watched many cars set alight in the fields, and sometimes the petrol tanks would blow. I thought it was too dangerous, but my sister insisted on making the call. She ran into the house, pulling the phone line into the sitting room, which was only a plasterboard wall away from the front door. I stood in the hall, waiting for what felt like an eternity. She finally got through, but a neighbour had already rung them. They were on their way.

Popping, crackling, snapping, sizzling, crunching – the noises continued as we waited in the back garden. We lived in a middle terrace house, with walls on both sides, so we couldn't get out onto to the road. Our cars were burning and our house would soon follow, but we were completely helpless. All we could do was pray, pray that the fire brigade would hurry up. As we stood there, looking at each other in disbelief, my mam, still hysterical, began asking how it might have happened. I had several theories, all related to my addiction, but this wasn't the time, so I blurted out something about random vandalism in the area.

The fire brigade arrived within minutes. We couldn't see them, but we could hear them extinguishing the fire from over the house. A hissing noise soon replaced the crackling, and the orange glow, which had goaded us through the window, began to disappear. I walked into the kitchen and peered down the hall. The house was still intact, but the smell of smoke and burnt plastic flooded the entire house. Several firemen came through the front door and asked if we were okay. They said we were lucky – a few more minutes and the house would have gone up in flames.

I'm not sure what I was expecting, but they didn't hang around. I also expected the police to show up, but they didn't. Not until the following day. It was getting bright outside, and I walked out to the garden to survey the damage. Both cars looked like the remnants of a Hallowe'en bonfire, burned to a cinder, the char saturated by the firemen's hoses. As for the house, I couldn't believe our luck. The fire had scorched the outside walls, the window panels had melted, and there was smoke damage throughout the house, but otherwise it was fine. I felt so relieved. I had a strong sense that my actions were to blame. As it turned out, I was right.

There were several things in the previous few months that could have led to this. Most of them involved buying and selling drugs, but it seemed unlikely. Besides the Lucas incident, I didn't give anyone a reason to do something that extreme.

It turns out that the fire was over a silly spat. Two weeks beforehand, I had parked at the local chipper and some guy I knew asked me for a lift. He was a devious character and we didn't like each other. Besides, it would have taken me miles out of the way with everyone's food going cold, so I said no. He knew I'd say no and used it as an excuse to throw out a threat. 'You'll regret that, Pennier,' he said, in a sinister but casual way. I thought it was an empty threat, but, evidently, I was wrong.

As I sat in the kitchen with my family, trying to come to terms with what had happened, I was completely lost for words. My brothers and sister seemed OK, on the outside anyway, but my mam was a mess. 'Who could have done this?' she asked again, still visibly shaken. Nobody looked at me or said anything, but I knew what they were thinking.

James sat there in silence, not knowing where to look. Kelvin, uncomfortable in the silence, tried to make light of the situation – a common trait in our family. 'Look, it could have been worse. The house could have gone up in flames.' He was right, and usually we'd all agree on stuff like this, but my mam and my sister were not willing to let this one go.

'I can't believe this. We could have all died,' my mam said. Then my sister, who had been surprisingly quiet until now, began to speak.

'What the fuck are yous after doing? That's mam's car and mam's house. One of yous caused this ... I know yous did.'

She was collectively speaking to my brothers and me, but she really meant me. It turns out they were all secretly blaming me, but Anne was afraid to target me directly because I would have reacted with anger. That's what I always did when it came to defending my addiction. But this time I decided to ignore the statement and keep my mouth shut.

My mam, who was traumatised for weeks after the fire, was distraught. I wanted to help, to reassure her that everything would be okay, but my mind was elsewhere. I knew it was my fault, and I didn't like how that made me feel – guilt, shame, remorse and anxiety, all woven together in a disturbing web of lies. I'd love to say I was thinking about my family at this time, but I wasn't. I needed to kill these feelings. That's all I could think about, and as always, I had a solution. I had two bags of smack in my room, and a great excuse for a day off work, so off I went. I told everyone I was going to the shop, but I drove to a nearby industrial estate with only one thing on my mind: kill those feelings, smoke them bags of smack.

* * *

I moved out of my mam's house soon after the fire. It was best for everyone, for obvious reasons, but at twenty-nine years old, it was time I moved on. Kelvin had previously applied for the affordable housing scheme so my two brothers and I found ourselves a house just up the road. Getting your own place is supposed to be one of life's great milestones, and it should have been exciting, but it wasn't. My anxiety levels were off the charts, and so was my drug use. I wasn't fully aware of it, but my life was in freefall, and my addiction was spiralling out of control.

All my memories from this time of my life are the same. Drugs, drugs and more drugs. From the moment I woke up until the moment I went to bed, I devoted every thought, every action, to the pursuit of drugs. It didn't matter which drug, as long as it killed my anxiety. Heroin worked best, so I smoked as much as my finances would allow. But on its own, it wasn't helping as much as it used to. It was also costing me a fortune. Again, I thought about injecting, but for now, my phobia of needles kept me away.

With my drug tolerance and anxiety at an all-time high, I became obsessed with mixing different types of drugs. I was like a curious scientist, testing different combinations to see what would best relieve my symptoms. Some drugs made it worse, especially hash and uppers, but a mixture of heroin, alcohol and sedatives worked best. I still used cocaine at weekends, despite it making me agitated, but otherwise, it was all about downers from here on in.

When money wasn't an issue, my daily drug use was something like one or two grams of heroin, 60–120 millilitres of methadone and between four and ten sedatives – usually Zopiclone. Unlike most heroin addicts, I also drank a lot of alcohol. Chronic heartburn, because of my drug use, prevented me from drinking beer, so I was downing a shoulder of vodka (350ml) a day. That's probably not too shocking. I was an addict, after all, even if I didn't know it. What was unusual was my choice of mixer. I always insisted on Lucozade because I thought it was the healthier option. My diet wasn't much better than my drug use. Heartburn also restricted what I ate, but I'd binge on breakfast rolls and chipper food when I was hungry, and then eat ridiculous amounts of orange-flavoured antacids to help ease the pain.

Over the next few years, my days looked something like this:

Drunk and stoned, I'd go to bed between 1 and 2 a.m. It sounds like a nice way to go to bed, but anxiety was never far away. It loved to pursue me at this time of night. It was during these hours that I'd fight with my own mind. 'Smoke the rest of the smack now and feel shit in work. Or lie in bed feeling anxious until you force yourself to sleep. Then only feel semi-shit in work.' It was a battle I could never win, and it tortured me for years.

To be in work on time, which was rare, I needed to get up at 6 a.m. But despite setting dozens of alarms, I never got up at 6 a.m. My brothers still get shivers when they hear the music I used for my alarm clock. It was a song by Razorlight, called 'In the Morning.' I used it because the lyrics made me snigger: 'In the morning, you know you won't remember a thing.' I remembered very little during those years, so I thought it was hilarious, even during the dark times. The alarm never woke me because I was comatose, but it woke them, every morning, so I can understand their angst.

I'd drag myself out of bed, usually at around 7 a.m., the time I should have been clocking in at work. On waking, I'd take a couple of sedatives, and smoke the rest of my smack, that's if I'd managed to keep it. Half asleep, half stoned, I'd drive into work. I've lost count of how many near misses I had on the road. I fell asleep at the wheel on numerous occasions, often ending up on the path, and once in the middle of a roundabout.

One morning, I gave James a lift because he was working nearby. I hadn't slept all night, was completely out of it and could barely keep my eyes open. I knew it was dangerous, and obviously I shouldn't have driven, but I had a better idea. I opened both windows, turned the music way up and asked him to keep an eye on me, but he fell asleep too. I woke up on a flyover, a road that goes across Dublin's main motorway, the M50. I don't know what snapped me out of it, but when I opened my eyes, I was on the wrong side of the road with a truck coming straight at me. Through pure instinct, I pulled the steering wheel violently to the left. I winced, waiting for the impact. How we missed each other, I'll never know. The truck must have swerved too. I still have nightmares about that one. I got away with murder, so many times, and how I never killed anyone is a miracle.

When I got to work, that's when the torture would begin. I'd have to stay awake – the minimum job requirement – so I'd restrict my drug use just enough to keep the sickness at bay. It would not be enough to kill my anxiety, however, which would be fierce. I'd sit at my computer, intermittently shaking my hands, fighting the agitation throughout my body, and try to just get through the day. When it became unbearable, I'd go for a walk or drive around the industrial estate. But on days when I had a few extra bags in my pocket, I'd smoke them in the toilet, or the dark room, and then come back to my seat. I was still getting work done in bursts, especially after using, which may seem counterintuitive to some people, but I was just as likely to goof off at my desk. At this point, I was becoming a dead weight. It was torture for my work colleagues, who were also my friends.

Coming home from work was one of the only remaining joys in my life. I didn't have to worry about staying awake, and having been so anxious at work made the drugs feel so much better. I'd park behind the shops in my estate, smoke some smack, take a few sedatives and buy a bottle of vodka for when I got home. Taking so many downers, however, was beginning to have a detrimental effect on my body, and in turn, my behaviour. When I got home, I'd pour a double vodka, light a cigarette and, more often than not, fall asleep with both still in my hands. I burned holes all over our sofa, smashed glasses on the floor and accused my brothers of robbing my drink if they tried to take it off me. I was becoming very aggressive, and they didn't know what to do. When a glass fell or smashed, I wouldn't even clean it up. I'd simply make another drink, spilling vodka all over the counter in the process, including the breadboard. Many times, when my brothers made sandwiches later on that night, they'd be eating what we've now christened vodka bread.

I'd carry on like this, drinking vodka, swallowing tablets and smoking more smack until I'd fall into bed. That's if I made it to bed. My brothers were sick of me, and I wasn't a nice person to wake up, so sometimes they'd just leave me in the sitting room. Those mornings were the worst. I'd wake up on the sofa thinking it was time for bed, and then my alarm would go off and the whole day would start again. I rarely went anywhere else at this stage. I was happiest – if you can call it happy – when I was comatose in my sitting room drinking and doing drugs.

* * *

Despite my 'I'm not an addict' delusion, it was obvious, even to me, that I needed to change certain aspects of my life. I didn't go looking for a cure, however; that would mean facing my real demons. Instead, I attempted to patch up my wounds with a plaster. It would never last very long, sometimes only a day, but I'd try to eat more healthily, go jogging and drink sensible amounts of alcohol, relatively speaking. I even bought a treadmill and put it in my tiny sitting room. That was one of my grander attempts at self-trickery. I'd come home from work, go for a run on the treadmill while watching *Friends* and eat a few carrots. I'd then take a shower, smoke a few bags of gear and marvel at my new healthy lifestyle while downing a vodka.

I'd twisted my mind so much that I simply couldn't see straight. One incident in particular still makes me laugh. A year after we moved in, my brother Kelvin went to Australia for a few months. My best mate Gar needed somewhere to stay, so he moved into Kelvin's room while he was away. Gar is one of the most reliable, solid, stand-up human beings I've ever known. He ate healthily, had a good job, exercised regularly and went out with a beautiful girl called Lynsey, who's now his wife. He was even thoughtful and sensitive, but carried it in a very masculine way. Pulling this off is one thing, but doing it in Ladyswell is a minor miracle. I knew Gar had a structured life, but when he moved in, the consistency of his routine blew me away. After work, and always in this order, he'd go to the gym, come home, do whatever chores needed to be done, make his dinner, prep tomorrow's lunch and gym bag, and then iron his shirt and slacks for the following day.

I've always been comfortable in chaos, so this kind of routine was my worst nightmare, and I shuddered just looking at him. As I sat there, smoking gear and drinking vodka one evening, watching him cook and iron, all while waiting for his girlfriend to arrive, I remember thinking: 'Poor Gar. If only he could loosen up. Then he could be more like me.' I fully believed every word in my head. If I had a magic wand, I'd have granted him my wish there and then. In hindsight, I had completely lost touch with reality. Gar, on the other hand, couldn't believe how I lived my life. He knew my addiction was getting worse, and he'd seen me tear it up on holidays, more than once, but he had no idea it was an everyday thing. Astonished by how far I'd fallen, he tried so many times to make me see sense, to help me to see reality, but I had an addiction to protect, a story to believe, and I was having none of it.

I did once try to address my drug issues, or so I thought. In January 2007, I remember smoking an eighth of heroin (three and a half grams) in one day. That's a lot of smoking, and I barely got a hit. I was becoming immune to the stuff, and I was sick of it. Injection was again a tempting option, but I was still terrified of needles, and I knew it would only be a short-term fix. That's when I hatched my plan. But as usual, I was up to my self-deception tricks, keeping myself well away from the end game.

I decided to stop using heroin and slowly wean myself off methadone. Over the course of six months, I dropped 5ml per week. It worked, and for the last 10ml, I used a syringe (not the injecting kind) to drop 1ml per week. In July 2007, without going through sickness because I'd done it so slowly, I was finally clean. Or so I thought.

Valium and Zopiclone were now my go-to drugs for anxiety, and I was taking them by the bus load. I'd become so obsessed with my opiate addiction that I didn't consider them an issue. I was taking up to thirty tablets a day and drinking twice the amount of vodka. The crazy thing is, I thought I was clean.

It came to a head when I went on holiday. My brother Kelvin, my sister Anne, her boyfriend Barry and I went summer skiing on a glacier in France, in a resort called Les Deux Alpes. I was only two weeks 'clean', and I was on a mission. I loved European pharmacies because they sold Zopiclone over the counter, but that didn't bode well for my body and mind, especially on that holiday. I'm quite a good skier – I've always been good at sports – but on our first morning on the slopes, my skills deserted me. I'd taken six sleeping tablets before breakfast, and when I went to make my first turn, my body refused to respond. My sister was behind me, and she said it was the strangest looking thing: 'Stiff as a board, you bounced down the mountain like pogo stick.' That holiday was a disaster. In every photo, including the ones on the slopes, I've a bottle of Club Orange in my hand. It was actually full of vodka, and the haversack on my back was full of tablets. But, hey, at least I was 'clean'.

I ruined that holiday for everyone, but they were thankful for my antics on one occasion. After a heavy night for all of us, we were late – four hours late – getting up to the slopes. Halfway up, the gondola stopped. A message came over the intercom telling us we'd be stuck for at least an hour. Everyone was hungover and parched from the night before. No one even had water. The plan was to buy some up there. I thought they'd give out, but I didn't care. Not only did I have my vodka, I whipped a two-litre bottle of Baileys out of my haversack. Not a naggin, not a shoulder, a feckin' two-litre bottle.

It was a dark kind of funny, but everyone thought it was hilarious that I was carrying a two-litre bottle of Baileys around with me. There were just the four of us in the gondola, and we ended up sitting on the floor swigging from the Baileys for the next hour. We had a great laugh, and it turned out to be one of the best moments of the holiday.

When we came home from France, it was time to implement the final part of my plan – the one I didn't know about. I was now one month 'clean', just about long enough to liberate myself from my dreaded opiate tolerance. I wondered why I found it so easy to stop using heroin, and this was the reason – my plan was never about stopping. It was about reducing my tolerance. Heroin had stopped working, and I missed her. I longed for the touch of my soft warm blanket, the one that protected me from my demons. I missed her with every fibre of my being. When I realised what I had done, that I had actually hidden my true reason for getting clean from myself, it frightened me, but then the voice spoke: *'Do you remember our first time together? Go. Go get some. It will be just like it was in the beginning.'* In the blink of an eye, I had three bags in my hand. I was so excited, but it wasn't like the first time – not even close. Within a few days, it was as if I had never stopped. Two months after that, I was walking up those dreaded metal stairs, back into the clinic.

***

My last ski trip before I entered recovery for real was a big turning point for my relationship with many of my family and friends. My body was weak and my mind was tired, and until that point, I had never felt more lost in my life. I was a shambles on that holiday, and I ruined everyone's fun. There were several key incidents. One evening I fell down a marble staircase at least fifteen steps high. Everyone got a fright, especially Anne, who was walking right behind me. But I jumped straight up with a smile on my face, proud as Punch that I had held on to my glass of vodka. I felt perfectly fine, until I woke up the next day.

The following night, we were in the chalet getting ready to go out for dinner. I don't know how I had managed to ski that day, but I somehow pulled it off. Separated by a wooden floor, Gar and Lynsey were sitting on one side of the sitting room, and I was on the other. With great difficulty, I pulled off my wet ski socks. It wasn't my most well-mannered moment, but they'd seen me do a lot worse. As I stood up and lurched across the room, they heard a strange noise. Gar said it reminded him of the velociraptors from *Jurassic Park*, but there were no dinosaurs in the Alps. It was the sound of my toenails clicking off the hardwood floor. I hadn't clipped them in over a year.

Despite my antics on previous ski holidays, we always had fun, but this trip was a step too far. I don't know when everyone decided it would be our last, but I sealed the deal on the final day. Because I'm a good skier, when I wanted a sly morning drink, I'd tell everyone I'd ski ahead and meet them at the end of the run.

I'd usually finish my drink before they got down, but this time the shakes were far worse than usual, so I ordered a triple vodka and Coke. I sat there, staring at the drink, and finally took a sip, but physically, I couldn't get it into me. I remember thinking how much easier this would be if alcohol came in tablet form, like most other drugs.

I was sitting outside at a table when everyone else made it down. They sat around waiting for me at first, but their patience was wearing thin. They were moaning, 'Just leave the fucking drink,' but I needed it. I asked them to give me a few minutes and lit a cigarette. I felt like I was going to pass out when my cigarette butt dropped into the vodka. I could hear the relief: 'Come on, let's go, you can't drink it now.' Without thinking, I picked up the glass and downed its entire contents in one shot. I then spat out the butt and said, 'Right, let's go.'

I honestly didn't realise how problematic I was for people on that ski holiday. It was a classic example of my unawareness, in its most complete form.

12

I DON'T CARE

'Be bad, but at least don't be a liar, a deceiver!'

LEO TOLSTOY

JANUARY 2010

was thirty-one when I finally admitted I was an addict. I didn't want to believe I was a normal addict, so I did what I do best. I told myself a story, and decided I was the best addict ever. 'I always have money and I always get my drugs,' I'd tell myself proudly. I used to laugh about with my family and friends, the ones who still tolerated me, but I didn't find it funny. It was a mask. In reality, I was dying inside. That's why I needed a new story. If I was going to survive, if I was going to be able to live with myself, I had to believe in something positive, something to boost me, and this was the best I had. In fairness, I did always have money, and somehow I always found a way to get drugs, so it wasn't a complete lie. It was actually part of the problem. But all of that was changing. It was the start of the end, and deep down, I knew it.

I spent the whole of my twenties and my early thirties selling cocaine. I snorted my profits in the early days, but as time went by, it was simply a way of funding my growing heroin habit. My ability to sell cocaine was now on the slide, however. I did not look well – mentally or physically. When I first started selling coke, dealers loved how I held down a job, drove a nice car and didn't draw any attention to myself, especially Lucas, who often commented on it. But now I looked like an addict, and for many people, that meant I couldn't be trusted. In my case, they were right. In the past, I had always paid my bills. I used to pride myself on it. But not any more. I was now in serious debt. I owed money to dealers, banks, the credit union and moneylenders. The cost of my heroin habit was also out of control – €100 per day just to feel normal.

For the first time in my life, I seriously considered treatment, but I didn't see it as a realistic option. My wages were paying most of my debts, now over €500 per week, and I thought I'd lose my job if I told them the truth. It never occurred to me that I would lose it anyway.

In my eyes, it was clear – I needed to make more money. That meant only one thing: sell more coke. Getting dealers to trust me was an issue, but there was another problem. I only sold coke to friends and acquaintances, mostly at parties, but I was now living like a hermit. The only time I left my house was to go to work, drop into my parents, go to the shops or get drugs. Parties were my worst nightmare, and the invitations had dried up anyway – for good reason. I could only see one solution. I needed to sell larger quantities of coke.

It wasn't long before I found a supplier, and I was soon getting nine-ounce bars of cocaine. Trust wasn't an issue there – high-level dealers use fear for that. I was now selling ounces to friends who would sell smaller bags to their friends. There was a huge upside to this: I didn't have to go to parties; I made more money; and I had fewer transactions to make. However, the potential downside was huge. Nine-ounce bars cost thousands of euros, and if anything went wrong, I was in serious shit. The police were another big concern. In the past, I had only sold small amounts to friends, so I wasn't on their radar. That could soon change, however, especially considering the people I was now playing with. The thing I was most worried about, however, was that my new pals were dangerous individuals. I'd dealt with such people before, some I even called friends, but this was different. We were playing for bigger stakes, and if I fucked up, friendship was out the window. The game had changed.

My cheery new venture seemed to be working. I never had huge sums of money, but it provided me with a great cash flow. I was easily able to feed my heroin habit, and I stuffed my face to my heart's content. My tolerance levels went through the roof, of course, but I didn't care. 'I don't care' was fast becoming a problem in every aspect of my life. I didn't care about anything any more. Not my family. Not my friends. Not my job. Not my health. Nothing. It wasn't a conscious decision. I wanted to care, but my pain consumed me. More accurately, my pursuit of a way to soothe this pain consumed me. From here on in, I directed every thought and every action towards that goal.

* * *

Blinded by my obsession to kill anxiety, I was now taking bigger risks, and people in my life began to suffer, especially my family. I was fine with drink and drug driving – I never even saw it as an issue – but when it came to selling drugs, I always made sure I looked sober. I liked to put on a good show for the Guards, thinking I was clever. In the early days, I even carried a Garda vetting form in the glovebox in case I stumbled upon a checkpoint. I had a whole story prepared. Instead of waiting for them to talk to me, I'd roll down the window and pester them with questions about my vision to help others:

'How's it going, officer? I was wondering if you could help me with something. I have to complete this vetting form [now in my hand] for a project I'm passionate about [I'd keep the charity aspect subtle to avoid suspicion]. Someone told me it can take several months to process, but I need it in a few weeks. Do you know if there's a way to push it through quickly?'

I obviously didn't give a shit about their answer. It was simply a distraction to throw them off the scent. I'd seen many people in such situations, trying to play it cool, but they always stuck out like a sore thumb. They might as well be waving drugs out the window. Having a plan, on the other hand, made me feel calm. It was also highly unlikely that someone hiding drugs would approach the Guards with such questions. I only had to use my ploy twice – and, to be honest, I was far from calm – but the act of approaching, rather than avoiding, seemed to make a difference.

This tactic may have worked in the early days, when I looked relatively healthy, but it wasn't going to work any more. I was too rough around the edges, and I'd lost my bottle anyway.

That's when I made one of the worst decisions of my life: I dragged my family along for the ride.

My sister Anne was first. She had never done anything illegal in her life, and apart from dealing with me, she was completely naive about the world of drugs. Using emotional blackmail, pity tactics and a veiled threat that I'd be forced to drive under the influence, I asked her to ferry me around Dublin.

She wasn't stupid – she knew I was up to no good – but she thought I was buying drugs, not selling them. She drove me all round the city, mostly to Tallaght, Ballymun and Clondalkin, completely unaware of the danger I was putting her in.

Well, that's what I thought. Anne soon realised what I was doing, and over time, I knew she knew, but I didn't do anything about it. I became desensitised to her presence – she was just another cog in the wheel of the addiction machine. One time she drove me to meet a dealer in the Ikea car park in Ballymun. This guy was dangerous, and he put on the tough guy act that day. I remember my sister telling me how intimidated she felt, but it didn't stop me asking her again.

I have only vague memories of these events, and my heart breaks when my sister talks about how scared she was. I was putting her in serious danger because all I cared about was me, and the money I needed to buy more drugs.

Thankfully, not least for my sister's sake, selling ounces of coke came to an abrupt end. I was spending money that I hadn't even made, putting myself under serious pressure to pay my bill. It also turned out that my friends, the ones I was selling coke to so they could deal it themselves, also liked to snort coke. Who knew? I fucking knew, but I chose to ignore that fact, until it was too late. Some weeks the money would only trickle in, but the other side didn't care about that. They wanted their cash, regardless of my problems. It was intense, and at one stage, I had to ask my dad to guarantee another credit union loan just to keep my head above water. My dad would do anything for me, so he kindly agreed.

A few weeks after that, the shit really hit the fan. I owed them over €7,000, and they wanted €3,000 by the end of the week. I was already struggling to make payment, when everyone who could possibly let me down did let me down. It's part and parcel of the drug game, but not like this, not all at once. The timing was cruel. My anxiety levels were already high, but with this hanging over my head, I was starting to panic.

I had one possible way out. A guy called Anto, who owed me €3,500, was due to pay half his bill. I was going to give him another week, but that luxury had passed. I didn't know him well, but on the strength of a friend's word, a friend I trusted, I gave him four and a half ounces of coke on slate. I called his number, but his phone was off. I wasn't worried at first, but I called him twenty times over the next two days and his phone was still off. Now I was worried. I rang my friend – the one who put me in touch – and told him what was going on.

'I'm not surprised,' he said, 'he done that before.'

'What the fuck do you mean he done it before? You should have fucking told me,' I snapped.

'I didn't think he'd do it again. The fucking idiot snorted it all last time and nearly got shot.'

'Are you fucking serious? Well, that might happen again. Do you know who the fuck I'm selling for?'

When I told him who, my friend got worried. 'Don't mention my name.'

'I'll have to. I haven't got a dime to pay them, and they're going to ask how I know this fella.'

'Ah, shit, man.'

'Make a few phone calls and try to get word to that fucking eejit so he knows what's going on.'

'I will. I'll be in touch.'

This was bad. No matter how I played it out in my head, it did not end well. If I didn't pay, they'd come after me. If I told them the truth, they'd want to get to him – through me. I'd seen this before, many times, and it always ended violently. Whatever happened, I would have to be there, in person. I didn't know what to do. These boys didn't mess about. They were serious hitters – I knew that when I got into it – but I didn't think it would come to this.

I knew the middleman well – let's call him Baz – so I thought it best to ask him what to do. I'm not sure what I was expecting, but he shocked me with his response:

'Who the fuck does he think he is? Burn his fucking house down. Then he'll pay up.'

'I'm not even sure where he lives, Baz,' I told him, stunned by the response.

'Ye don't know where he lives? Fuck sake, Pennier. That was stupid, wasn't it? Go to your mate, the one who put you in touch with him, and find out where your man's ma lives. Get him to tell that fucking fool that we have the address, and that we'll burn his ma's house down if he doesn't get the money, and quick. He'll pay then. Believe me, he'll pay then.'

I came away from that meeting in total shock. I couldn't think straight. The same words kept going through my head. 'How the fuck am I going to get out of this one?'

Over the next few days, I agonised over what to do. Setting alight Anto's house, or his ma's house, simply wasn't an option. I couldn't do it even if I wanted to. Violence was never my thing.

I had two options, both long shots. I didn't want to think beyond them just yet. The first – tell anyone and everyone who knew Anto that he was putting his family at risk, and that if he didn't come across with the money soon, something serious was going to happen. The second – get a loan, pay the debt myself and pretend that Anto had paid up. I'd be stung financially, but it felt like a far better option than potentially killing someone. The only problem with option two was that I'd have to go to another moneylender. The one I had in mind was dangerous, so with no way of paying the money back, this could come back to haunt me.

I went with option one, and it didn't take long, a few days I think, when word came back that Anto was fearing for his life. He got word to me that he'd have the money within a week. I was relieved, to say the least. I rang Baz to let him know, and he seemed happy enough. I still had no direct contact with Anto, and as the week passed by, this began to worry me. Baz was calling to ask for updates, and when I told him I was waiting for Anto to contact me, he didn't like that one bit: 'He has one more week, and that's it.'

As the days dragged on, I was not confident that Anto would get in touch, or whether he could even get the money. I was freaking out, and thought about ringing the moneylender.

Then, out of the blue, he called. He began apologising about everything, but I didn't give a shit, as long as he had the cash. I was in my mam's car when he called – I think she was giving me a lift to collect my methadone. She was only just coming to terms with the fact that I was a drug addict, never mind a drug dealer.

I should have waited, and met him later, but I didn't. Paranoid that he might go missing again, I arranged to meet him immediately, in a car park on the Navan Road. I could have easily been putting my mam in danger. It was unlikely, but for all I knew, he might have wanted to retaliate for the threats against his mother, and here I was, driving to meet him with my own mother. I never even thought about it at the time, or maybe I didn't care. I honestly don't know.

My mam and I pulled into the car park early. As we waited in the rain, she nervously asked me what was going on, and who I was meeting. Without giving her any details, I told her I had sold a few things to a guy who had let me down and who now finally had the money. With that, through the raindrops on the window, I saw Anto's car pull into the car park. I jumped out, ran over and got into the passenger seat. He was genuinely apologetic, and quite scared. I told him that nothing would happen now that he was paying up. He handed me €4,500 – €1,000 more than he owed – and asked me to give the extra €1,000 to the guys I sold for. With a smile plastered across my face, I said, 'Yeah, of course,' jumped out of the car, and that's the last I ever saw of him.

When I got back into my mam's car, I was so excited about getting the extra money that I stupidly counted it in front of her.

It was a large wad of cash, and it was frightening for her to know that her son was involved in something like this. I wish I had had the sense to hide it from her, but at the time I simply didn't care. Instead of feeling bad about what I was putting my mother through, I was grinning like a Cheshire cat. Not because I had the money to pay my debt, but because of the extra €1,000. I wasn't telling anyone about that. That was for one thing, and one thing only – lots and lots of smack.

As we drove home that day, my mother traumatised, and me happy as a pig in shite, I was completely unaware of the pain I was causing. Emotional scarring was my new MO, and I was oblivious to it. To make matters worse, I was only getting started. My ignorant behaviour had big plans and would be soon leaving many more scars in its wake.

There were two kinds of scarring, and both left their mark. One was relentless and grinding, such as my family watching me throw my life away. The other involved one-off events, such as bringing my family on excursions into the drug world.

I'm not sure which was worse, but the persistent nature of the first certainly took its toll. My dad was in denial, so he pretended everything was fine. My brothers lived with me, and although they were hurt, probably more than I know, they became immune to it. My mam and sister, however, suffered the most. They tried to keep their distance – for their own peace of mind – but I insisted on dragging them into my world. They'd ask me to stay away, but I'd forget, or ignore them, and drop by to show them how well I was doing. I WAS NOT DOING WELL – ANY OF THE TIME. I'd go into my mam's house and within minutes fall asleep with my head on the kitchen table. If

I managed to keep myself awake, I'd sit there talking shite while scratching my face. Sometimes they found me asleep outside in my car, and then I'd tell them I was just resting my eyes. It was horrific, and it went on for years.

On top of that, there were so many flashpoints. One time, when my sister felt sorry for me, she invited me up to her house for a party. It was going well until I slipped while dancing on the wet kitchen floor. I jumped to my feet, laughing. But then, when I was looking straight at my sister, blood began streaming down the side of my face and neck. I'd caught the back of my head on the corner of the skirting board and there was blood everywhere. My sister freaked out and wanted me to go to hospital, but I said I was grand. I was trying to act hard, but in reality, I was afraid to get stitches or staples. These fears, I believe, stem from my operation as an infant, when they stuck needles in my head. It's not surprising that I've always been afraid of needles, which probably all connects back to my fear of bodily sensations, especially my heartbeat and pulse.

I woke up the following morning and my sister took a closer look at my head. When she pulled my hair to one side, matted together with dry blood, there was a big gaping wound. She insisted I go to hospital, but I refused point blank. There was only one thing on my mind – I needed to get some smack. She persisted, so I got angry – which was now my default setting – and I told her I had more important things to do. I left the house, went off to score, and without even changing my bloodstained clothes, I went on a bender with friends. I ended up at a big boxing match at the Point Depot that night, still covered in blood, with a long deep gash in the back of my head. My only memory of that night is the people behind me loudly letting me know how disgusting I was. I never did get stitches, and I still have a groove in the back of my head. Just like the darning needle sliding through my hand as a teenager, how it never got infected I will never know.

One incident above all others pains me most. I needed to get to a nearby estate called Corduff to score some smack. It was only a ten-minute drive, but my brother had my car. I could have walked it in forty minutes, but I decided against that, for two reasons. One was because I was dying sick, and my body was aching all over. The other was because I needed to be there quick. Heroin dealers are unreliable. They won't hold something for you just to be nice, and Gary, the guy I was meeting, was the only one who had anything.

As usual, especially when it came to heroin, I only thought of myself. I rang my sister to ask her for a lift, but she was in work. I rang a few friends – same thing. I couldn't get a lift anywhere. Feeling desperate, I rang my dad, but he was working too. I knew my mam was at home, but there was no way I could ask her for a lift, especially after the coke debt incident when I collected the wad of money off Anto. She never said it to me directly, but I could tell she was still very upset about that.

That's when I came up with a plan. I obviously couldn't ask her for a lift to score smack, but my idea was simple. I'd pretend I needed a lift to the chemist to collect my methadone – which was also in Corduff – and then I could run over to meet Gary for the smack. We usually met near the chemist anyway. I called my mam on the house phone and I knew by her voice that she was uncomfortable with the situation. I told her I'd miss the chemist if I didn't get a lift, and that I wouldn't be able to go to work the following day, so she agreed.

Everything about the situation was wrong. When I got into the car, I could see the horror in my mam's eyes. I had been unwell for a while, but I had never let her see me like this, not when I was dying sick. I was in an awful state. I had a limp from a knee infection, sweat was pouring off me, especially my face, and my voice was tired and drawn. I was oblivious to most things, especially when I was in withdrawal, but even I could see how upset she was.

We drove to the chemist in silence. There was nothing to say, and I knew I'd only make things worse if I spoke. I asked her to pull into the car park and wait for me there. There's a pub, The Corduff Inn, between the chemist and the car park, so I could pop over to Gary without her seeing me. I knew I'd be a lot longer than a few minutes, so I spun a story about how the chemist always makes addicts wait. 'Fifteen minutes max,' I said in a slurred voice.

I climbed out of the car, my mam watching on helplessly as I hobbled off in the direction of the chemist. As soon as I was out of sight, I rang Gary. 'Ten minutes,' he said. 'I'll meet you at the shops.' The chemist was at the shops, which worked out great, but I knew from experience that I could be waiting a lot longer than ten minutes. Slumped against the piss-stained pub wall, I waited for Gary to show up. Ten minutes passed. No sign. Five more minutes. No sign. I knew I'd piss him off if I called, but I rang anyway. 'Yeah, I'll be over in a few minutes,' he moaned. I couldn't blame him. He was waiting for several customers to show up at the same time. It meant less work but it also reduced the risk of getting stopped by the Guards. Another ten minutes. Still no sign. I peered around the corner to see if my mam was still waiting for me, and of course she was.

I was dying sick, worried about Gary pulling a no-show, and with my poor mam waiting around the corner, it was the worst wait of my life. I was about to ring Gary again when I saw him strolling across the road. It's funny what drugs can do to your mind. Without even putting anything into my body, I felt a million times better – physically and mentally.

From a neuroscience perspective, it's similar to the placebo effect, and shows how our mind and body are connected. I saw Gary, realised I was going to get my hit, and my body responded before I even put the drugs into my system. In other words, my brain released dopamine based on a belief, and not from the drugs themselves. Belief is an incredible human attribute, but just like my 'not a real addict' story, it can be as harmful as it is helpful.

I had kept my mam waiting for nearly an hour, and when I got back into the car, I could see she had been crying. I should have felt terrible, but I just felt numb. I wish I cared about the pain I was causing, but all I could think about was the bags in my pocket and how quickly I could get them into me.

13

THE DRUGS DON'T WORK

'The world breaks everyone and afterward many are strong at the broken places. But those that will not break it kills.'

ERNEST HEMINGWAY

JANUARY 2013

My bed. At night. My worst nightmare. Chest tightens. Heart throbs. It's hard to breathe. My hands shake. My limbs quiver. Chills and cold sweats. My mind races. My scalp stiffens. My thoughts will not stop. I want to escape from this nightmare, but there's nowhere to run. My hands go under the pillow, then over the pillow. Roll over, twist, foetal position. Ah, a moment of relief. It does not last.

My muscles contract. My bones ache. I cannot lie still. My skin tingles. It turns to crawling. The shivers will not stop. My body is clammy. It becomes sticky. The covers are drenched in sweat. Back to thinking. It turns to racing. It will not and cannot stop.

My body shakes and my mind pulsates. Anxiety is all-consuming. There's nowhere to run. Twist. Turn. Bend. Roll over. No relief. Foetal position. No relief. I cannot sleep. Run. Run. Run.

My bed. It's morning. The nightmare continues. Have I slept? It's hard to tell. My chest squeezes harder. My heart throbs heavier. Breathing is shallow and strained. My scalp tightens. My thinking quickens. It will not stop.

The morning onslaught is relentless, and only one thing can save me. I pour the brown powder onto the shiny foil tray. I can taste the heroin on my tongue before it even enters my lungs. A sense of release grows as I anticipate a calmness coming over my body and mind. Freedom from torment is within reach.

With the flick of a lighter, a liquid descends on the foil, but something is different. I was once mesmerised by this golden puddle, but not any more. It looks the same, but it feels different. I feel different. I think it's despair. My anticipation turns to hope, but it's an empty hope. I put the tooter in my mouth and inhale a few lines. Maybe it will feed my hungry ghost. Maybe it will heal my pain. It doesn't.

The morning onslaught continues, but there is something else, something new. A darkness has descended, a hopeless darkness. I don't know this darkness. I think it's dread.

Darkness and dread. They are everywhere. In my bed. In my car. In my body. In my mind. Everything I touch. Everyone I meet. In their words. In their actions. In their eyes. It is everywhere.

I once knew life. I once felt alive. But not any more. I wait and I exist, for what I do not know. I should ask, but I'm afraid. The end feels close. I am afraid.

* * *

Fifteen years of addiction had left its mark. Every day was the same. I wanted to run, to jump out of my skin, to escape the nightmare of being me. But I didn't know how. Heroin was my armour, the soft warm blanket that protected me from my demons, but it was failing me. Worse than that, it turned against me. Withdrawal, the sickness, was now eternally present, leaving me more anxious than ever before. I smoked line after line, but it was still there, always lurking beneath the surface. No matter how much I smoked, or what I mixed it with, there was no relief – not any more.

With my mind in overdrive, scurrying for a way out, ideas, bad ideas, began popping into my head. For the first time ever, I thought about boundaries I was never willing to cross. This included silly ideas, like moving to Afghanistan. Heroin in Ireland was weak, for me anyway, so moving to where it came from – Afghanistan produced 93% of the world's heroin – made sense at the time. I even looked up flights and checked out where to stay, but it made for grim reading.

That's when I decided to face one of my biggest phobias. I decided to inject. I had a morbid fear of needles – I still do. The thought of a hollow spike puncturing a hole in my vein makes me weak at the knees. This was the very opposite of what I was trying to achieve. It didn't make sense.

I was hesitant. I was afraid. And I kept changing my mind. Then, out of nowhere, a familiar voice, one I hadn't heard in a while, whispered in my ear: *'It's not that bad. It will be over in seconds. Do it. Once it's in your veins, it will be even better than our first time.'*

The voice was right. I'd seen hundreds of people inject heroin, and every time, almost immediately, they'd be lost in an ocean of bliss. Once I overcame my fear, I'd be floating in that ocean too. I hadn't felt like that for a long time. The temptation was too strong and I made up my mind. Time to inject.

I'd seen it done many times before, but it's a complicated process, and it can be dangerous if you do it wrong. I didn't want to pump air bubbles into my blood. I had heard that they can travel to your heart or brain and cause a heart attack or a stroke. I also needed someone else to stick the spike into my vein. There was no way on earth I could do that myself.

I wondered who to ask. Barry, my childhood pal and former partner in crime, was the obvious choice. We still met up to sell or buy heroin off each other, but also to use together. It was a few months since I'd seen him, which ironically involved a comical incident that resulted from injecting heroin. It certainly wasn't family comedy, it was a little more on the dark side, but it was funny all the same. I collected him in the city centre and we pulled into a car park in the Phoenix Park. Barry needed to inject into his upper leg, so to make space, he opened the passenger door. Barry banged up while I smoked my smack. I also took a card of Zopiclone.

We both goofed off in the car, and when we snapped out of it, over an hour later, Barry said he'd come to Blanchardstown with me. As we drove home through the park, I jerked the car too hard at a roundabout. Barry had forgotten to shut the passenger door. It flew wide open, and Barry soon followed. Luckily for him, he had his seat belt on, and it stopped him hitting the road. He vividly remembers watching the tarmac zoom by at over 50kmph. I suppose that's something you wouldn't forget, even if you were stoned. He hauled himself back into the car and pulled the door shut. 'What the fuck, Pen!', he shouted, in total shock, but I'd barely even noticed what happened. I was slumped forward, hanging on to the steering wheel, with a look of 'What the fuck are you talking about?' on my face. As I said, funny – in a dark kind of way.

Despite Barry being the obvious choice, I decided against calling him. I didn't want to make injection a daily habit, and I knew that would make it too easy. I decided to call Terry instead. Terry was a friend, the one Barry and I had asked to help us inject a few years ago – the time when I backed out – so he was the next obvious choice.

Terry tried to convince me not to inject, but he knew I wasn't letting it go, not this time. He was reluctant, but agreed to help me. I needed somewhere to do it, somewhere safe, and Terry said I could do it in his house. I got all the paraphernalia from the needle exchange the week before, including spikes, citric acid and sterile water.

It was finally time, but the thoughts of it were giving me a near panic attack. I was so anxious that I needed to get stoned before I could do it. The irony was not lost on me.

I didn't want to inject into my arm because I wore T-shirts in work, and also because it freaked me out the most, so we decided my foot would be the next best option. Terry did everything, and just like when I smoked heroin for the first time, I was captivated by the ritual. Looking at the heroin melt on the spoon, seeing how the filter from the cigarette captured the impurities, watching the syringe fill up with the brown liquid was hypnotic. I'd seen it before, but somehow it was different, maybe because this time it was for me.

It was time, and I began to feel extremely anxious, even though I was stoned. With sweat streaming off my forehead, I told Terry to do what he had to while I looked away. I soon discovered that I didn't mind the needle piercing my vein, or the injection of the heroin. It's the idea of blood being drawn from my body that makes me feel so anxious, which is what you have to do before you inject the heroin. That's to make sure you have a vein instead of an artery, which can be quite dangerous. The thought of this process still unsettles me.

The rush from injecting heroin was very nice, incredible even. It felt like falling into an abyss, leaving my pain behind, but it didn't last long, and it wasn't nearly as powerful as I expected. My fifteen-year tolerance to opiates must have taken its potency away, and I had built it up so much that it could never have lived up to my expectations either way.

Combined with my needle phobia, the fear of overdosing and the fact that I couldn't do it on my own, injecting heroin was not as appealing as I thought it would be. I can never be sure, but my needle phobia might have even saved my life. I injected three more times after that, but in truth, my injecting days were over before they even began.

* * *

Despite an increasing tolerance to my drugs of choice, more of everything was my default setting. More, more, more. I always wanted more. The goal, as always, was to numb my anxiety.

I used heroin, methadone and Zopiclone to get me through work, but a combination of sedatives and alcohol now worked best. I'd buy a shoulder of vodka on the way home from work, sometimes two, and swallow up to twenty sedatives for the rest of the night. I would drink triple and quadruple shots of vodka, which, combined with the tablets, would send me into oblivion. I would goof off to sleep without a second's notice, usually on an armchair in my sitting room. It wasn't a comfortable sleep, however; far from it. It was more like an agitated stupor.

My new method of numbing came with a whole new set of problems, far worse than before. This included serious issues with my job, my family, my friends, my health and my hygiene.

I'd vomit daily, sometimes several times a day. I'd been doing that for years, so it wasn't that big a deal. But because I wasn't eating any more, the vomit now consisted of bile and other odd-coloured liquids that have me baffled to this day. It was horrible to look at, but it tasted far worse, always bitter and always vile.

Opiates also make you horrifically constipated, and I could go days, sometimes a week or two, without going to the toilet. When I did eventually go, well, let's just say it was painful.

Many of my everyday habits, things that normal people take for granted, were falling by the wayside. I had stopped brushing my teeth sometime in 2011, but now I wasn't even washing myself. That's when I read an article about Brad Pitt. It said he used baby wipes to clean himself on set. Taking only what I wanted to hear, I stopped showering from here on in. 'If baby wipes are good enough for Brad, they're good enough for me,' I told myself, completely disregarding the fact that maybe, just maybe, he might also take the odd shower. Anyone who challenged me on my hygiene got the same rant. My sister once said that, even from a distance, I smelled like orange-flavoured vodka – orange from the antacid – with a hint of ashtray and a tinge of musk. It might sound like I was being lazy, but I just hadn't got the strength, or will, to wash myself any more. The basics were beyond me.

My appearance wasn't far behind. When I was younger, I was proud of how I dressed, but now I just didn't care. I wore anything that was in the wardrobe, and when I did go shopping, usually because I had no choice, I must have closed my eyes. One collared T-shirt I bought can only be described as a muumuu. That's the dress/robe Homer wore in *The Simpsons* for anyone struggling with a visual. It was maroon, three sizes too big, and it looked like a tent. I still wore it, though, even though I looked like a freak, and especially because my sister said I shouldn't. Added to my sinful fashion sense, there were holes all over my clothes, mostly from falling asleep with cigarettes in my hand. It wasn't just my clothes – my car, the sofa, the table, the floor and pretty much everything in my house had burn holes in it.

My world was falling apart. I was struggling – emotionally, physically and most of all psychologically. Life was pushing me in directions I didn't want to go, and I started doing things I said I'd never do. I was crossing all boundaries, which included selling heroin – the one drug I swore I'd never sell. 'Only scumbags sell heroin,' was something I used to tell myself, most likely trying to vindicate my own drug-dealing endeavours. Then one day I found myself selling heroin to a guy who I thought was a dirt-ball, for many reasons, one of which was selling smack. In a rare moment of awareness, I caught myself thinking, 'Wow, when the fuck did that switch happen?' I couldn't believe I'd missed it.

I'd stopped selling cocaine and hash at this point – no one would trust me to sell it, nor would they buy it from me. That's why I started selling heroin, to fund my habit, but I didn't sell it the way I sold hash and cocaine, which involved more thought. I simply bought heroin in larger amounts and sold smaller bags, called cues, when the opportunity presented itself. That would allow me to buy more heroin, but even then, I was unwilling to part with it because I feared I wouldn't be able to buy more. The crazy thing was, heroin didn't help my anxiety any more – nothing did – so the whole merry-go-round was pointless.

I was now spending all my time around heroin addicts. I was scoring with them, selling with them, buying with them, using with them and hanging out with them. Just to be clear, I've nothing against heroin addicts. I was one myself. Most of them, like me, only use drugs to cope with something else in their life, usually trauma. I was just surprised that it crept up on me. One minute I was a self-proclaimed non-addict; the next I was the perfect stereotype.

Surprisingly, I quickly accepted my lofty new status, and it wasn't long before I found myself in situations I thought I'd never experience. It wasn't so much the places as the things I saw that really left their mark. On one occasion, another addict and I went to Ballyfermot to buy heroin. I wasn't keen on the idea, but he insisted on sticking it up his ass to hide it from the Guards. When we got to his house, he couldn't get it out. As I sat in his sitting room while he was doing his thing in the toilet, a pungent smell of – for the want of a better word – shite drifted through the air. It hit me so hard and so quickly that I nearly threw up. That was bad enough, but when he walked back into his dingy sitting room, moaning about our problem, there was excrement all over his fingers. I can't even remember the guy's name, but I have never been able to get that image out of my head.

I was quickly learning that addiction and bodily orifices go hand in hand, especially when heroin's involved. This was something I was able to avoid in the past, but I was making up for lost time. One incident, above all others, sticks out most. I was buying heroin from a guy in Ballyfermot. Without hesitation, he pulled down his tracksuit bottoms, and plucked the bags from beneath his foreskin. That was grim in itself, but when he put them in my hand, I literally gagged. Unfortunately for me, things were about to get a whole lot worse. The bags were greasy, and my hands began to sweat, so all I could think about was my own bodily fluids mixing with whatever was on the bags. And that's when it happened. The Guards pulled up as I was about to walk away. I had no other choice, unless I was willing to throw them away, but that was never going to happen. Heroin was my master, so I put them in the only place I knew they'd be safe – my mouth.

* * *

As I descended deeper into the murky world of addiction, as always I dragged my family and friends along for the ride. They tried to keep their distance, for their own wellbeing, but I wouldn't let them. They didn't blank me, far from it, but my mam and sister both asked me to stay away from their homes. Unfortunately, for them, I had other plans.

Although I now admitted I was a real addict, I was miles away from realising the full extent of my problems. For my family in particular, as I filled them full of lies about my plans to get clean, this was the most problematic issue. I had always believed my own lies – mostly so I could live with myself – but the tide was turning. What I believed and what I wanted other people to believe were now miles apart. But this realisation didn't stop me lying.

In early spring 2013, I was on a mission, my last mission, to convince myself, and to convince my family, that I was going to be okay. I told my mam and sister I needed to chat with them. They were sick of my bullshit, but agreed to meet me, and told me they were going for a walk in the Phoenix Park. My goal was to show them I was trying to get clean, or more specifically, that I was weening myself off methadone and quitting tablets for good – the source of my current woes. I had already lied about being off heroin, so I just left that part out.

I intended to put on a good show, and genuinely thought I could pull it off. But when I arrived at the park, it was the worst they had ever seen me. I bounced the rim of the wheel off the curb when I pulled up in the car. Not a great start. Then, when I stepped out, I could barely stay upright or keep my eyes open. Still limping from a knee infection, I eventually stumbled across with a bag over my shoulder. It was my Jack Bauer bag – that's what I called it – an army green denim satchel like the one Jack Bauer used in the hit TV series 24. It was full to the brim, so they asked me what was in it. With a look of confusion on my face, I told them I didn't know and proceeded to empty the contents onto the ground. Out poured a 48 pack of Weetabix, a porcelain bowl, a spoon, a carrot and a DVD box set of 24. It must have been part of my plan, the one that proved my healthy new lifestyle. But I was so messed up, I forgot all about it.

They were both getting upset, and that's when I handed my mam a card of Xanax. I promised her it was my last ever pack, and that I was handing them over to show her how serious I was. I also showed her a methadone label which said I was down to 60 millilitres. But they had heard it all before, and as I stood there, stoned and confused, I was only making things worse. My mam's upset quickly turned to anger and she told me to go home, but as I stumbled over to the car, her thoughts turned to other motorists. I was in no state to drive, so she asked my sister to take me home. I insisted I was okay, so my sister said she'd come with me. When she opened the passenger door, the evidence of my lies lay before her: twenty packs (two hundred tablets) of Xanax lying on the seat. She didn't say much – there was nothing much to say – but she still came with me. As I pulled away, I hit the curb again. She lost it. 'Get the fuck out, and let me fucking drive, you fucking prick.' My sister doesn't usually curse, so it caught me off guard and I sheepishly agreed. I fell asleep on the drive home, ending yet another glorious day with the family.

The madness of that day didn't end there. Later that week, when my Xanax were gone – all two hundred of them – I went to buy more, but everyone had sold out. Not only did I have the neck to ask my mam for the ones I gave her, but when she told me she'd thrown them out, I accused her of taking them herself.

My mam never took anything like that in her life. I'd completely lost my senses. It was a step too far for my mam. She had had enough, and I rarely saw her over the following few months. It was the same for everyone in my life. They had to distance themselves for their own wellbeing, except for my two brothers, who unfortunately still had to live with me.

* * *

I was very close to my nanny. We had visited her house every week since I was a baby, and I continued to visit as I got older, although less often as my addiction grew stronger. She lived in Cabra, right around the corner from my secondary school, so every school day for five years I spent my lunch hour in her house. She would not only make my dinner, she'd mash my potatoes, butter my bread, pour my lemonade, and put salt and pepper on my food. It would be waiting for me on the kitchen table when I walked in from school. We'd have a great chat while I ate my dinner and then we'd watch *Neighbours* together. I was proper spoiled, and it was wonderful.

My nanny always had faith in me, and always said I looked great, even when I clearly didn't. She wouldn't let anyone say a bad word about me, and one of my biggest regrets is that she died when I was deep in addiction. She passed away unexpectedly on 5 March 2013. It hit everyone hard, especially my mam. I wish I could say I helped during this difficult time, but I didn't. I was a hindrance on the day, and my nanny's funeral was another black mark during this phase of my life.

My mam hadn't seen me since the Phoenix Park incident, and when I showed up at the funeral I was even worse – fragile, weak and barely able to talk. Everyone thought I was stoned, that's what it looked like, but it was the exact opposite. The drugs didn't work any more – not how I wanted them to. They just helped me to function, barely. I've only learned in hindsight that in situations like this, when I restricted my drug use in order to look better, it only made things worse.

My aunt Tess suggested that the grandchildren should carry the coffin, and of course, I wanted to help. On orders from my mam, my sister said I shouldn't, but I insisted. I only have one vivid memory from the funeral, and that's when they placed the corner of the coffin on my shoulder. I nearly collapsed. I hadn't got the strength to walk, never mind carry a coffin, so one of my uncles had to step in.

I should have felt embarrassed, guilty, apologetic, ashamed, or something along those lines. I obviously cared – I wouldn't have been there otherwise – but I felt nothing. Not for my nanny. Not for my mother. Not for my family. Not for anyone. I just felt numb.

As I stumbled around causing havoc, oblivious to everyone's feelings, including my own, my sister remembers watching my nanny's coffin move down the aisle. At the exact moment it passed her, my face came into view, and she thought, 'You're next'.

***

My sister's thought was an omen. The end was close, I could feel it, but the end of what? In hindsight, it was quite simple. I was going to get off drugs and live, or keep doing drugs and die. There was no in between, not any longer. But, for me at the time, getting off drugs wasn't even an option. As far as I was concerned, it was impossible.

I felt like a caged animal, and when my best mate asked me to be groomsman at his wedding, I didn't know what to do. I knew it would be a disaster, but Gar hadn't seen me for about a year, and had no idea how far I'd fallen. He would have invited me anyway, but at least we would have avoided the disaster that was about to happen – me being groomsman.

Methadone aside, I promised Gar that I wouldn't take any drugs on the day. I keep my promises, so that's what I did. This was a big mistake. I felt ten times worse than I would have done, and doubled down on vodka to help me cope. That set the stage.

I don't remember much about the wedding, but various people have told me about my antics. I missed most of the big moments – the dinner, speeches, first dance. I'm sure my partnered bridesmaid was happy that I missed the dance, but it was brutal all the same. I also went missing for the photos at the hotel. When they went looking for me, someone found me asleep in the garden and thought it best to leave me there.

I woke up in a corridor the following morning, and all I could think about was the drugs I had in my room. I had told Gar I wouldn't take drugs on the day of the wedding, but in my mind, the following day was fair game – even though it was a two-day event. When I went to my room I soon realised that I hadn't completely kept my promise. Half of the drugs were gone, though I couldn't even remember taking them, but I still had a card of Xanax and a bag of smack left – thank God. I took a few Xanax, smoked the smack and then went down to the bar.

That's when the problems really started. I downed vodka after vodka over the next few hours, and combined with the tablets, I was in a bad way. It came to a head when I took my shoes and socks off and started picking at my toenails – right in front of everyone in the lobby.

This was Gar's wedding, and he had had enough. He asked me to go home and rang my sister to collect me. With my suit still on, I went up to get changed. The suits were in his name, so when I came back down, he asked me where mine was. I told him it was in the bag. 'What bag?' he asked. 'This bag,' I said, pointing to my Jack Bauer satchel, which was hanging off my shoulder. It's not a big bag, so I had balled up the expensive suit and stuffed it inside.

In fairness, it was better than the previous time I rented a suit in his name. It was for a black tie New Year's Eve party, and when he rang me four days later asking where it was, I still had it on – dickie bow and all.

* * *

How I held on to my job for so long is one of life's minor miracles. In reality, I put several of my work colleagues, my manager included, in a very difficult position. Kim, my old manager, had left a few years earlier. Wayne was my new manager, and he was also a friend. I was a problem he inherited, so getting rid of me wasn't as straightforward as it seemed. For starters, I had mountains of experience, I was very good at my job and I rarely made mistakes, although part of that was because I didn't get much done any more. We were also a close-knit group – we had worked together for seventeen years – so getting rid of me would be tough from a human perspective. In hindsight, the reason I lasted so long was because my decline was so slow that it was difficult to see, even for my family.

In the summer of 2013, however, things had changed. My life was falling to pieces, and it was only a matter of time before I lost my job. Several key incidents sealed my fate. Crazy as it sounds, keeping my eyes open in work was my biggest challenge. Without realising, I'd take micro sleeps in the middle of meetings, often in front of senior management.

It was becoming more and more obvious that I had a serious drug problem. One time, on a late shift, I was smoking heroin in a small toilet near reception. Unbeknownst to myself, I set off a silent fire alarm, triggering an automatic callout from the fire brigade and setting off an alarm in the production office. One of the managers saw it and came bursting in like a hero looking to put out the fire. With heroin smoke everywhere, I walked out of the cubicle wondering what the hell was going on. He asked me where the smoke was coming from, and without missing a beat, I told him I was burning the loose threads on my jeans while taking a dump. I had previously burned the threads on my jeans in anticipation of such an event, so there was little he could say.

In August 2013, however, the game was finally up. After several complaints, senior management began asking questions. They were not happy with what they found, and I was becoming more and more difficult to manage. They made all the right legal moves, and I received several warnings in quick succession. It was only a matter of time before they sacked me.

We had a strong union at the company, however, and in a final attempt to save my job, they called a meeting with senior management. At the meeting were me, Larry, Barry, Wayne and Mick. Wayne and Mick were the union representatives. They were also my work colleagues and close friends, and Wayne was my manager. Barry was the managing director, and Larry was the factory manager.

The union advised me to say nothing. 'Just listen,' they said, but I had other plans. Without giving away too much, I tried to tell everyone how I was getting my life back on track. When I walked out of the meeting, I looked at Wayne and Mick and said: 'I think that went well, lads. What do you think?' I'll never forget the looks on their faces – jaw on floor comes to mind.

Wayne spoke first. 'Brian, you fell asleep – in the middle of the meeting. Mid-sentence actually. You were talking shite anyway, but then your eyes glazed over, your head drooped to the side, and you fell asleep.'

'Shit, man. That's fucked-up,' I muttered. My usual default was denial, but there were too many witnesses for that.

'I know it's fucked-up,' Mick said, raising his voice, 'We were all left looking at ye, not knowing what to say.'

'This is serious, Brian,' Wayne interrupted. 'We'll ring the union, but I can't see how you can come back from this.'

Wayne was right. The union couldn't see a way back either. I met with them anyway and told them everything. They advised me to seek professional help for my addiction, but under no circumstances was I to go back into work. My employers had ticked all the right boxes, and if I went back, it was just a matter of saying 'You're sacked,' and that would be it. In fairness, it would have been the right call, but I had to look after my own ass. The only option, it seemed, was to seek professional help, and if I got myself clean, I might even get a redundancy package.

I should have been devastated; I was losing my job after seventeen years. But all I could think about was drugs, and how I wouldn't have money to pay for them. I hadn't sold cocaine in well over a year – no one trusted me – and apart from selling the odd bit of heroin, my only income came from my job. I also owed a fortune: €30,000 to banks and the credit union – most of which were loans for drugs – and over €5,000 to drug dealers and moneylenders. The banks and credit union could wait, but the dealers and the moneylenders wouldn't be so forgiving. I was in serious trouble.

As clear as day, images of my new life began crashing into my head. Dressed in rags. Living in a squat. Begging on the streets. Drug dealers slapping the head off me because I couldn't pay my debts. Moneylenders threatening my parents because I was a waste of space. So much for the best addict ever. I'd be an addict on welfare, dying sick all week, living only for labour day. Nothing was off the table, not any more. I used to pity people like that, but never in my wildest dreams did I think it could be me.

As I lay in bed that night, my mind began racing, faster and faster than ever before. The voices, those dreaded voices, wouldn't stop. I longed for the soft whispers of heroin, but they were gone, long gone. In their place were piercing, angry voices, like sheet metal scraping on the ground. So many voices, arguing, berating and fighting with one another.

'You have to get clean. I can't get clean. The drugs don't work. I'll find some that do. You don't have any money. I'll get money. You've run out of options. I'll ask my family for help. They all hate you. I'll do whatever it takes. Anxiety will stop you. I'll fight it. You'll fail.'

It was relentless. It was torture. It would not stop. The voices fed anxiety. Anxiety fed the voices. My chest tightened. I could not breathe. My body trembled. I could not lie still. My body and mind were screaming for drugs. Every fibre of my being was screaming for drugs. But they didn't work any more. I was trapped in a body that was afraid and a mind that had become a stranger. There was nowhere to go, nowhere to run. For the first time in my life, it was hopeless. Everything was hopeless. The end was close.

14

COCKROACH

'One day, in retrospect, the years of struggle will strike you as the most beautiful.'

SIGMUND FREUD

AUGUST 2013

wanted to live again, but only on my terms. I still couldn't see a future without drugs. I needed drugs. All I wanted was drugs. But no one else seemed to agree. Anyone who cared about me said the same thing: 'You need professional help. You need to go to treatment. You need to get clean.'

'Maybe they're right,' I wondered. Drugs didn't work any more – that was a fact – so perhaps treatment was my only option.

Apart from what I saw on TV, I had no idea what was involved in treatment. I never asked in the clinic, and no one ever talked about it, the addicts included. I thought it was some kind of secret. This turned out to be another story I told myself, a story I believed for one reason: I wouldn't let anyone talk to me about it. I had a talent for side-stepping these discussions. Any time it was mentioned, especially by a key worker, I'd bring out my machine gun, a relentless onslaught of verbal diarrhoea. It wasn't aggressive, just a barrage of bullshit to keep them off my case. I was hard work.

Those days had long passed. I was sick, exhausted and confused, and for the first time in my life I considered treatment. The day after my work fiasco, I rang the clinic. Hugh, my methadone doctor for the last twelve years, was away on holidays, so I arranged to meet Austin, the senior key worker.

I met Austin at the clinic the following day. My sister came with me for support, despite the harm I was causing her and the family. I don't remember much from the meeting, except Austin telling me, 'If you want to get clean you need to go to detox.' At this stage, I thought detox was treatment, but as I found out later, it was far from it. He suggested a place called The Lantern. Hugh was the resident doctor there, so that sealed it for me.

Unfortunately, it wasn't that simple. Besides methadone, I would have to give a clean urine test before they took me in, and that was a big problem. Most drugs come out of your system in days, but not benzodiazepines (e.g. Xanax). They can take up to a month, and I was taking heaps of them.

'Benzo withdrawal can cause seizures,' Austin told me, 'especially with the amount you've been taking.' It was twenty to thirty tablets per day. For safety reasons, the detox facility wouldn't be able to take me in until the benzos were out of my system. There were other facilities, but the waiting lists were long.

I was pissed off when I heard this. I was finally looking for help, possibly to save my life, but they were refusing me because

I had benzos in my system. It was a bloody detox centre. I thought that was the point. I could feel the anger building.

'That's fucking stupid,' I said. 'What am I supposed to do, then?'

'Slowly wean yourself off the benzos and when your urine is clean, we'll try get you in. You'll also need to get down to forty millilitres of methadone.'

'Jesus, they don't make it easy, do they? I don't think I can wait, Austin. I need to do this before I change my mind. I don't trust myself.'

'There's no other way,' Austin said.

With a hint of anger, I said, 'Look, I haven't got time to wean myself off benzos, so I'm just gonna go cold turkey on my own. I need to get them out of my system as soon as I can.'

I'll never forget our next exchange of words.

'I strongly advise you not to do that. You'll have a seizure if you don't wean yourself off them,' warned Austin.

'As if I'll have a seizure. Shit like that doesn't happen to me,' said the special addict, and off I went.

* * *

I asked for help, but I didn't want help. I was ready to give up drugs, but only some drugs. I was willing to go to AA meetings, but only if I was drunk and stoned. I was willing to go to detox, but only because I didn't have a choice. I was going to stop taking benzos, but only until I got clean.

I didn't have a chance of recovery – not with that mindset. I hadn't even started, and I'd already failed.

I needed a kick up the arse ...

I needed a jolt of reality ...

I needed a miracle ...

And that's when it happened.

Two days into my benzo detox, I woke up on my sitting room floor, covered in blood and cloaked in misery. I'd been to dark places, I'd experienced pain, but nothing quite like this. My skin felt raw. My muscles ached. Even my bones felt angry. I tried to get up, but my arms crumpled beneath me. I tried to focus, but my brain wouldn't work. The room began spinning, faster and faster, and I felt like I was going to throw up.

Suddenly, everything drifted into the background, as I became acutely aware of a piercing, stabbing pain in my mouth. It was my tongue. The force of the seizure had pushed my teeth through the centre of it, and it had split. It felt like it was growing inside of my mouth, as if it was ready to explode. I couldn't breathe. And I began to panic.

Out of nowhere, someone loomed over me, shaking me, frantically screaming: 'No, please ... no, shit, don't die, Brian ... wake up, Brian ... wake up ... will you wake fucking up!' It was my younger brother, James. He had witnessed the whole thing. He was in a panic too, but his frenzied screams shocked me back into the moment, and in what seemed like an instant, everything slowed down.

I was still on the floor, now face up, with my left elbow propping my head off the ground. I tried to gather my thoughts, to get my bearings, but my body wouldn't let me. It was doing things that it clearly should not have been doing. As I looked around the room, I could hear a clicking noise in my head, like the sound of my old mountain bike slipping into gear. It was coming from the back of my eyes, maybe an inch deeper, towards the centre of my head. When I looked to the right – 'click'. When I looked to the left – 'click'. It was terrifying, so I kept my eyeballs centred firmly in their sockets, and stiffened my neck to scan around the room.

Next there was the twitching, the violent twitching. I'm not a naturally calm person, I never was, but my body was jolting in a way that clearly wasn't normal. I'd experienced twitchy eyes before, even twitchy legs, but this was entirely different. It was internal: in my stomach, neck and chest. It had a twisting, pulling feel to it, like there was something alive in my body, desperately trying to escape. I was afraid to move, in case I made it worse, but it had an agenda of its own, regardless of how I felt.

Despite these disturbing bodily sensations, and the searing pain in my mouth, it was an overwhelming sense of emptiness that took centre stage. Everything in the room was lifeless and dull, as if the world had lost its pigment. It wasn't just my vision, however – everything was different. Bad different. My brother was frantically making phone calls, but all I could hear were dampened muffles. There was a strange artificial taste in my mouth. Everything felt wrong – unnatural and synthetic. Even the familiar stink of my smoky sitting room was peculiar. 'Maybe this is permanent,' I thought, and with that, emptiness turned to fear and, again, I began to panic.

I wanted to jump out of my skin, anything to avoid these terrifying bodily experiences. I tried to lift myself up off the floor, but I didn't have the strength – or the will, I'm not sure. My brother helped me to my feet. 'I neeth a dhink ov whather,' I said. He helped me over to the sink, my limp legs dragging along the floor. I tentatively filled a glass of water, hands trembling, and put the glass to my lips. It was like acid in my mouth and made me feel nauseous. I put the glass down, blood smeared along the edges, and began vomiting into the sink. It was not pretty. Congealed lumps of blood clung to the corn snacks I had eaten an hour earlier, and there was a bright yellow liquid, which looked strangely out of place.

I coughed, spat and retched into the sink for what felt like an eternity. Out of breath, and seemingly out of time, I hugged the sink as if my life depended on it. My brother helped me back into the sitting room, and like a bag of wet sand, I plunged into the armchair. I sat there for several minutes, and that's when it hit me. I was two days into a drug detox, my first after fifteen years of chronic addiction. A wave of relief swept over me. I wasn't in the twilight zone any more. Maybe there was a logical reason for what had just happened.

I had experienced a convulsive seizure. Only twenty minutes earlier I had been watching TV, albeit in the depths of a drug detox, when, as my brother told me, my eyes began rolling in the back of my head and my body went stiff. I slipped off the armchair and started slapping off the ground like a fish on wet concrete. I shook uncontrollably for three or four minutes, and then slumped on the ground. There was a long silence, my brother recalls, as my pale, sweaty, lifeless body lay motionless on the hardwood floor. A dripping sound broke the silence. It was blood coming from my tongue, where I'd bitten through it. My brother thought I was dead and rang my dad in a panic. It must have been quite a scene.

My dad and the emergency services arrived at the house, and my sister was on her way. She had received a call from my mother, one she'd been expecting. 'It's Brian. Something serious has happened.'

Thinking the worst, my sister assumed I was dead. She was trembling so much she couldn't drive, so she asked her boyfriend, Wayne, to drop her to my house. It was a fifteen-minute drive, and all the way she was agonising over my death and how it would play out for the family.

'Mam will be devastated,' she thought, 'but it was breaking her heart, so she'll be better off in the long run. Dad will struggle, and possibly blame himself. I'm not sure if he'll get over it. The two lads will miss him terribly – I don't know why – but they'll be much better off without him.'

As they got closer to the house, they could see the blue lights of the ambulance flashing in the distance. Still shaken, and terrified of what she was about to see, my sister walked into the house. She expected to see my dead body lying on the floor, but there I was, sitting on the couch, with the emergency services all around me. I looked like shit, but I was still alive.

Dazed and confused, I looked at my sister. 'Howya,' I muttered, the sweat streaming off my face. Anne doesn't often curse, but in that moment, only one thought crossed her mind: 'How is that cockroach cunt not dead?'

I have no memory of what I looked like, but my sister paints quite a picture. I was sitting there, talking nonsense, with no idea of where I was. What she remembers most was my skin. My primary organs were screaming for blood. I was like a figure from the wax museum, pale and translucent, with a greasy layer of sweat sticking to my skin. She wanted to kill me, but she also wanted to give me a hug, to comfort me, but my skin looked so fragile. It was like soft grey putty, and she was afraid she would hurt me if she touched it, or that it would break away from my body.

The next thing I remember is the hospital. It was several hours later. I was lying on a trolley, and when I woke up I was physically, mentally and emotionally broken. I was also on my own. As I opened my eyes the room gradually came into focus. Dimly lit, with a yellowish hue, a fluorescent white light flickered intermittently from the corridor. The walls were orange, but not a happy orange. They had a mature, stained feel to them, and I could have sworn that they were taunting me. The tiles on the floor were also orange, but they seemed a little happier. What I remember most, however, was the smell. The stink of vomit, combined with the sickly sweet, disinfectant-like odour of the hospital, made me feel nauseous, and the taste of puke in my mouth didn't help.

I should have felt worried, or scared, but I didn't. It's hard to describe, but if I had to put words on it, I'd say I felt vacant or flat. Broken also comes to mind, but in an empty kind of way. I slowly pulled myself into a seated position, and then came the moment that changed my life. As I sat on the edge of the trolley, bewildered and confused, that's when my eyes landed on the red fire extinguisher.

I thought I was brain damaged, but I didn't care. I thought I might not recover, but I didn't care. I thought my life was over, but I didn't care.

I should have been terrified, but I wasn't. I didn't flinch. I was unmoved. Not out of bravery or courage, but because I accepted my fate. For the first time in my life, I stopped fighting with my own mind. For the first time in my life, I surrendered. A sense of peace replaced dread and panic, and the darkness lifted. It was the start of my new life. It was my first taste of bonus time.

* * *

I got my miracle in the form of a seizure and a fire extinguisher. Without thinking rationally about it, I knew I couldn't use drugs again. I'd been smothering my survival instincts for as long as I could remember, but that night they woke up. That night, they screamed loud and clear: 'DRUGS DON'T WORK.'

I had just experienced peace for the first time in years. I had just tasted bonus time. However, despite the significance of this night, my war against drugs was not over. I had several more seizures over the next four weeks, including one that landed me back in hospital, but the worst was yet to come. As I lay on my couch, waiting to go to detox, the relentless nature of benzo and alcohol withdrawal hit me like a train. It was, by far, the most difficult month of my life.

I camped on my couch this entire time. Was I too weak to go upstairs? Possibly. Was I afraid of my bed? Definitely. Was it because I couldn't sleep? Maybe. Confusion and uncertainty were my dominant states, so it's difficult to know for sure. I was certain about one thing, though: the condition of my body and mind. Shaking and trembling from the after-shocks of the seizures, I was a fragile shell of my former self, even the one that struggled in addiction.

Withdrawal is a reversal of what drugs originally offer. I used benzos to soothe anxiety, so my nemesis came back with a vengeance. Tight chest. Stiff scalp. Cold sweats. Twitching. Heart and mind racing. All the usual suspects, but with a lot more bite.

My dad visited the house every day, and my brothers were ever present. My mam and sister popped by too, but there was little anyone could do, so I asked to be left alone.

Several days after the second seizure, withdrawal peaked. It was night-time. It was dark. It was quiet. And as I lay on the couch, something different, something powerful came over me. It started as a pulsing sensation inside the top of my head. I tried to fight it, to avoid it, but the more I resisted, the stronger it became. The pulsing began moving down my body, getting angrier on the way. Through my ears and towards my chest. Through my chest and towards my hands.

The room was silent and calm, but my body, loud and frenzied, was the complete opposite. I could hear my heart pounding. I could hear my head pulsating. I could even hear my hands throbbing. It was terrifying. It was too much. I wanted to cry. I wanted to die. I wanted to disappear. Then, for the first time in years, I felt emotional, and tears began streaming down my face.

'What is happening to me?' I asked, begging the universe for an answer.

I looked for answers within, but they weren't there. I was too fucked-up to think straight. There was nothing to do except wait. Nothing to do except endure. So I lay there, waiting and enduring, begging for time to pass, pleading for the benzos to leave my body.

It was morning. I had not slept. I was still enduring, still waiting, but there was something else. I had to do something I was trying to avoid. The union had been in touch. I was too unwell to speak to them myself, but they left messages with my family. They said I had to go to the company's doctor to give a urine sample, and if I didn't, I'd lose my job without getting a pay-out. This was crazy. My system was still full of drugs. I would be giving them the evidence they needed. I'd been putting it off for days, so today I had to call them.

My body was throbbing, my mind was a mess, and I'd spoken only in whispers since the seizure. 'How am I supposed to make a phone call?' I thought.

The union had been speaking to my dad, so he came to my house to listen in on the call. I was lying on the couch when he arrived.

I try to sit up and I cannot sit up. My dad looks at me. He sees my pain. I try to speak and I am unable to speak. He tells me I don't have to make the call, but I insist. He types in the number and hands me the phone. My grip is too weak. I readjust and let it lie in my hand. I press the call button, and the phone rings. Someone answers. I can only speak in whispers. It takes a while, but I explain who I am. I struggle to tell them my concerns about the urine test, but they assure me it is simply protocol and that the company doctor will not divulge my information. I was too weary to argue, so I agreed to go the following day.

I went to the company doctor as promised. It was my first time out of the house since leaving hospital. I was incredibly weak, and it was a horrible experience, but it was nothing in comparison to what followed.

I hadn't eaten solid food since my first seizure. That's why I felt so frail. I didn't feel hungry, mostly because of the split in my tongue caused by the first seizure. The doctor said there was nothing they could do, and that it would heal itself, but the pain was excruciating. Pulsing day and night, it felt like it had developed its own heartbeat.

I didn't want to eat, but I knew I had to. My brother Kelvin made me two boiled eggs and two slices of toast. I looked at my food and squirmed. To test the water, I rubbed my tongue off the edges of my mouth. It was worse than I thought. A sharp, stinging pain shot through the root of my tongue, running straight up the back of my head.

I was about to back out, when suddenly, without thinking, I shoved a piece of the soft egg white down the side of my mouth. I winced, sharply pulling my shoulders back from the pain. But it wasn't nearly as bad as I expected. The recoil was more in anticipation of pain rather than a response to actual pain.

I continued eating and soon realised I was starving. When I finished the eggs, I broke off a piece of toast and used my fingers to stuff it down the side of my mouth. Big mistake. In comparison to the soft eggs, the coarse texture of the toast felt like hot needles. Instead of sliding down my throat, it crumbled into tiny pieces, spreading across my mouth.

Like glue, the tiny fragments of toast stuck to the wound on my tongue. It was agony. My face contorted, my eyes welled and tears began streaming down my face. Not from sadness, but from the searing, stinging pain. I just sat there, sipping water, trying not to move, as I waited for the crumbs to dissolve.

Just when I thought it couldn't get any worse, I began to feel nauseous. I hadn't eaten in nearly a week, and my stomach was not happy with this sudden change of events. My hands became clammy and I could feel my body temperature rise. I was going to vomit, no doubt about it, so I quickly made my way to the sink. I tried to stop it, but I couldn't. Most of the food came up, as did some bile and blood. I didn't mind that, but the force of the undigested toast scraping off my tongue was torture.

I stuck to softer food for the next few weeks, but a merry-go-round of eating and vomiting was my new daily routine, at least until I got to detox.

* * *

Four weeks into my home detox, and the benzos were finally out of my system. I had also weaned myself down to 40 millilitres of methadone, a requirement for The Lantern, and I had stayed away from all other drugs. I was tempted to use on several occasions, and I couldn't get it out of my head, especially when I was in the depths of withdrawal. However, my fragile state, combined with my moment of clarity in hospital, prevented me going out to score.

On 10 September 2013, nearly five weeks after I inquired about going to detox, The Lantern agreed to give me a bed. The hardship was worth it. Now there was just the minor issue of getting off methadone, supposedly the toughest withdrawal of them all.

The clinic told me to meet someone from the detox centre on the outskirts of Dublin – for security reasons, they don't give out their location to friends or family. They gave me an exact time and place, and like something out of an IRA film, they picked me up and drove me to an unknown location about twenty kilometres away.

As I sat in the front seat of a beat-up minivan, I reflected on my predicament. I was entering the unknown, in more ways than one, but my new journey was strangely exciting. I'd come through a lot in the last few months, and I felt like I could handle anything.

The detox facility was a little farm in the countryside. The long tree-lined driveway led up to an old house which sat in the middle of eight acres of land – four football pitches to you and me. Huge blackberry bushes lined the entire perimeter, and a tranquil little stream cut across the far right corner. Under different circumstances, it might have been a lovely little retreat, but it didn't feel that way. I couldn't put my finger on it, but there was something about the place, something haunting, that seemed to hang in the air.

Peter, the van driver, introduced me to the staff and several other addicts on my arrival. Everyone seemed nice, and over the next few weeks, we'd cook, clean, talk, cry and look after the farm together. We grew our own vegetables and went for walks around the grounds. There were pigs, cats, donkeys and chickens on the farm. I loved being around the animals, and I grew particularly affectionate with a cat called Mollie.

Unlike the life of an addict, detox was highly structured. We'd have breakfast at 8 a.m. and the staff would give us our medication at 9 a.m., which for me was methadone and Mirtazapine, a drug the doctor gave me after my seizures. We'd then have to do our chores, which included cleaning the house and preparing food, before going to our group sessions with Natalie, the psychologist at the centre. These sessions included casual chats about our feelings, self-improvement techniques and psychological issues related to addiction. We'd also meditate, and it was here that I first heard of mindfulness. That would take us up to lunch, and we'd have another group session in the afternoon. Our evenings included dinner and a few hours of free time where we watched TV, read books, or played games. It was far from what I was used to, but I was happy to have some structure back in my life. I also didn't have to worry about where my next fix was coming from, and not having access to a phone felt so freeing.

Detoxing off methadone was a weaning process, so, anxiety aside, the early days weren't that bad. After three weeks, I was down to a dribble of methadone – 10ml. This was tiny compared to my usual 60–100ml dose, but I felt okay, which shocked me. I became convinced that withdrawal had given me a pass; biology be damned. The 'special addict' – the one who thought he couldn't have a seizure – reared his ugly head again. This is a common thread in many addicts. Some people without addiction issues might think that they're special; some might feel worthless, like sad little worms; most fall somewhere in the middle. Addicts, on the other hand, are very different. We think we're special little worms, and that's exactly what I thought I was. But I was wrong; I didn't get a pass. A few days later, 'the sickness' hit hard, and every bit of 'specialness' was kicked right out of me.

It is difficult to describe what opiate withdrawal feels like. Many people compare it to flu, which is close, but with several key omissions. It's a roller-coaster of emotions, feelings and bodily sensations, many of which have not been felt for a long time. My gums were throbbing, my feet were on fire and my digestive system was a mess. I was also terrified of the strangest things, like the wardrobe. A broken panel at the back reminded me of something from my past, something haunting. There were times when I wore the same clothes for days because I was afraid to look in the wardrobe.

I would also well up at the silliest little things. They allowed us to watch TV for a few hours each evening, and we'd all sit there, bawling our eyes out watching programmes like *The X Factor*. They also let us have a fifteen-minute phone call to our family each week. On one occasion, the nurse was talking loudly during my call and I got so angry that I ended up in tears. I struggle to cry at the worst of times, so it was very confusing.

The most intense physical symptom was the fever. The sharp shivering sensations cut to the centre of my bones. I vividly remember one night lying in bed, trembling for hours, as the loneliness of the morning seemed to taunt me. I put on as many clothes as I could, including my jeans, jacket and a thick grey bathrobe. I even put on my shoes. I got back under the covers, but it was no use, I was freezing. I soon realised that time would be my only salvation. As I lay there shaking, cold sweat streaming off my body, it finally dawned on me why the mattress smelled so vile. I wasn't the first one sweating in the bed.

As the last of the methadone left my system, my senses began turning back on. This was great, except for one thing: my sense of smell. As the days passed, the stink of the mattress got worse. It was one of those plastic sheet mattresses so I decided to clean it with bleach. After two hours of furious scrubbing, it was sparkling, and I put clean sheets on the entire bed.

That night, despite the lavender I stuffed in my pillow to help me sleep, I could still get the vile smell of human odour. I pulled off the sheets the following morning and smelled the mattress. Bleach. Nothing but bleach. It had to be something else. I began sniffing around the bed, and after a few minutes, I picked up the scent, that nasty scent. It was hanging in the air, just beneath the lavender. I grabbed the pillow, pulled off the pillowcase, and pressed my face into it, inhaling deeply. My whole body quivered in disgust. I sprang back, flinging the pillow across the room. It was revolting. Buckets of head sweat from hundreds of addicts, all concentrated in this little pillow.

In a fit of rage, I grabbed all the pillows from the room and ran up to the back of the farm, far away from the house so no one could see me. I was like a madman, two pillows in each hand, and I set light to them all. Insanely happy as I watched them burn, I felt like I'd conquered my greatest enemy.

The physical symptoms of withdrawal were bad, but manageable in comparison to what came next. Combined with chronic insomnia, the biggest challenge was coping with the intense waves of anxiety.

Having spent most of my life pumping drugs into my body, I'd transformed my brain into a pleasure monster, devouring as much dopamine as it could find. Now that the drugs were gone, there was no more dopamine, and my body was screaming for more. That's the essence of withdrawal, but now that I was near the end of my methadone detox, the monster wasn't just hungry, he was ravenous, and he took it out on me in the form of anxiety.

Amplified to levels I'd never experienced before, it felt like electricity rippling up and down my body, or insects crawling under my skin. I wanted to run, but there was nowhere to go. One night I thought about climbing out of the window, but I was afraid of the bloody wardrobe, never mind the pitch-black night of the countryside.

I was now in the depths of withdrawal, and I couldn't face my bedroom any longer. I hadn't slept in days, and I spent the next six nights sitting at the kitchen table – all of the other rooms were locked. It was a small kitchen, about twelve feet by twenty, and although it was homely, it was stained, worn and old. Sitting at the end of the table, I wanted to run away from myself, escape the relentless anxiety, but there was nowhere to go. I must have done ten thousand laps of that little kitchen, but I couldn't outrun my demons.

The nights stretched for miles, and I still remember the clock tick-tocking in slow motion. Again, it seemed like time would be my only saviour, but for the first time in my life, I didn't think I would make it. I didn't specifically think of suicide, but there was no end in sight; I couldn't see a way out. In that instant, I realised why they locked the knives up at night.

I'm not even mildly religious, but that's when I decided to pray. I'm not sure if I was going crazy, but after losing my nanny only a few months earlier, I could have sworn I felt her presence. She was a devout Catholic, so I just sat in the kitchen and asked her for strength. I'm still not religious, but maybe I should be, because I firmly believe my nanny got me through those nights.

15

THE END OF THE RACE

'We cannot change what we are not aware of, and once we are aware, we cannot help but change.'

SHERYL SANDBERG

8 OCTOBER 2013

I woke up in the detox centre and the world felt different. I was still in the depths of withdrawal, but it was my first day clean in fifteen years, and a sense of possibility filled the morning air. I went down for breakfast and sat at the kitchen table. It was early, and I was the only one there. As I drank my tea, I noticed that the room felt a little unfamiliar. Not in a bad way, but in a soft, joyful way. It had a caring shimmer to it – one I hadn't noticed before.

I gazed out the window and the beautiful autumn morning beckoned me outside. I finished my tea and walked out to the farm. The skies were clear. The sun was beginning to rise. And a misty chill filled the fresh morning air.

As I strolled around the farm, everything felt different, magically different: the sun didn't just shine, it danced; the wind didn't just blow, it kissed my skin. I was in a state of euphoria. I had spent the last fifteen years dulling my senses, but now, the normal, everyday things that others take for granted felt like a gift.

I could see, smell and hear everything – louder, deeper and brighter than ever before. I could even feel the mist on my skin, as if nature herself was breathing on me.

I inhaled deeply, as if drinking the crisp morning air, when the mood was broken. It suddenly dawned on me: 'This is your first sunrise in over fifteen years.' I jumped to the realisation that I'd missed more than sunrises. I had thrown away a huge chunk of my life – some would say my prime. I should have been upset, but I wasn't. I finally understood why I lost those years, and I didn't want to lose any more.

* * *

Something was happening to me, something big, and deep down, I knew it. I'm not a religious person, but in the days that followed, I felt an intense shift, as if my spirit or soul were awoken from a deep sleep. It is difficult to describe – it's more of a feeling – but in what seemed like an instant, everything seemed to glow. Colours were more colourful. Sounds were more cheerful. Things that were once hollow were now full of depth. Life was everywhere. I could feel it floating around me, through me, I could even see it in those close to me. It was hypnotic, suffocating even, but in the most spellbinding way.

I chatted to Natalie, the psychologist at The Lantern, about what I was experiencing, and she directed me towards several books that they had in the centre. One of them was grounded in Eastern philosophy and I was drawn to its concepts. I began reading many more books on this topic and for the first time in my life, I started to meditate. I quickly became enchanted by this philosophy of life. You might even say I had switched addictions.

'Addictive personality' is not a term I like to use, but if you practise anything long enough, it will become a habit, and addiction is the same. When I think about this in terms of my brain, I created a pleasure monster who was hungry for more dopamine. I needed to fill that void in order to feel better, and lucky for me, I got it from my newfound love of Eastern philosophy. This makes me wonder if people in recovery found a newer, more positive addiction, perhaps at a later date they could find balance in their lives. It was certainly working for me.

I was still at the height of withdrawal, but it didn't matter. I was awestruck by this new way of being. Even the agony of the sleepless nights disappeared. I still couldn't sleep, and the physical symptoms remained, but they were the most enthralling experiences of my life. I would sit in my bed until the early hours, passionately scribbling in my diary, more alive than ever before.

9 October, 3.00 a.m.: 'First day clean, first day living. And today, I lived.'
9 October, 3.30 a.m.: 'If you're not completely open on this journey, you lose.'

9 October, 4:00 a.m.: 'To savour the good, one must know the bad.'

9 October, 5.00 a.m.: 'Your mind is like a garden. What you put in is what you get back. Worrying is like poison for the garden ... so stay in the moment.'

I was fascinated by this way of thinking. I was also shocked. How had I never heard about it before? But I didn't care – I knew about it now. Life had given me a second chance, and I was going to devour every second of it.

The books nourished my mind, and meditation fuelled my soul, but the biggest difference was how I felt. I was happy, bursting with energy and completely carefree. But why? I had lost everything, and I had many obstacles to overcome. By all accounts, I should have been struggling, tormented even.

I started to question why I felt so alive. Then it hit me. How did I miss it? It had tortured me my entire life. The voices in my head, the stories that I told myself – the ones that drove my anxiety and, in turn, my addiction – they were gone. For as long as I could remember, thinking had consumed me – my mind racing about what I needed to do – but the voices were silent, and my anxiety was gone. There were no more lies, no more stories. The race was over. Bonus time had truly begun.

* * *

Emotionally and mentally, I felt amazing, but the physical symptoms of withdrawal endured. One minute I'd feel great; the next, fever would hit hard. The bone-chills were the worst, dulling my bursts of energy in a flash. But underneath the physical torment, my spirit never dropped.

Whenever I noticed my mind wandering, 'I have a life again' was the tune I heard. 'I have a life again.' How was this even possible? Seven weeks ago, I was staring death in the face, and now I was full of hope. I couldn't believe my luck, and I began to dream about my new future.

One week before my first day clean, Professor Jo-Hanna Ivers came to the detox centre. She was studying the impact of long-term methadone use on the human brain. The counsellors asked those of us on methadone if we wanted to take part in the study. If we agreed, we would have to do a psychological assessment at the detox centre, and then go to St James's Hospital for an MRI scan. There was only one problem – they needed to test everyone as soon as they finished detox, when withdrawal was at its peak.

They asked me if I wanted to take part in the study, and without hesitation, I said yes. Jo-Hanna arrived to do my psych assessment on 9 October, one day after my last ever dose of methadone. I was excited about the test, strangely excited for someone going through detox. I did have one concern, however. It was less than two months since my first seizure, and I hadn't forgotten about the fire extinguisher incident. I wasn't dwelling on it, but I often wondered if I had damaged my brain.

Natalie called me into the sitting room and formally introduced me to Jo-Hanna. She was very friendly, but bemused by my excitement. I was supposed to be going through hell, but instead I was like a little kid at Christmas, bursting to open his presents. In this case, the present was a psychological test, so I can see why she was a little confused.

The assessment involved a series of questions. I don't remember the specifics, but I remember how they delved into the nature of human suffering and how people feel. They also related to what I was reading in the books. It was just like my first time doing heroin, and I was like a sponge trying to suck it all in.

As we went through the questions, I began expanding on my own answers, frequently answering the questions that followed. That's when Jo-Hanna said something I'll never forget: 'You have a very sharp mind, Brian. It's like you've studied this stuff before.'

It's always nice to get a compliment, but I only heard one thing: 'You're not brain damaged.' I couldn't be, not if a scientist thinks I'm sharp. Maybe I could even go to college?

In one simple and kind-hearted observation, Jo-Hanna planted a seed. That night, in huge letters, I wrote in my diary: 'Find your passion and live it.' For me, that only meant one thing: go to college and study the human mind. It was just a matter of figuring out how.

I was due to go to St James's Hospital for my MRI scan the following day, but I didn't want to miss our group sessions with Natalie. I loved these sessions, especially when we meditated and discussed self-improvement techniques.

The day before, we'd touched on a topic that fascinated me. Natalie called it the Johari window. She said it helps people to build self-awareness and understand themselves better. We were supposed to cover it the day I was getting my MRI, but I didn't want to miss it. Ironically, Natalie was only covering the Johari window because of me, but I was completely unaware of this at the time. After a quick chat, she told me she'd do it another day.

I was happy with this arrangement, but on the day of my scan, I began wondering what else I might miss. I called Natalie aside and asked her what was on today's curriculum.

'Brian, there is no curriculum. You're here to get off heroin, to save your life,' she told me. 'I've only been discussing these topics because you asked about them, so don't worry, we'll wait until you come back.'

I conceded, but just in case I missed anything interesting, I asked one of the clients to take notes. They all thought I was mad, and maybe they were right. We were there to get off heroin, not to learn about life. In hindsight, however, I believe this is the very thing that saved me – my new-found addiction to learning, which in the non-addicted world we simply call drive.

I stepped into the minivan, the one that had brought me to the detox centre, and off I went to St James's Hospital. It was bizarre being back in Dublin with my new perspective on the world. Besides being brighter, everything looked the same, but it felt completely different. We met Jo-Hanna outside the MRI room and she went through the procedure with me. I hadn't slept for days and I was still shivering, but I got through it.

When testing was over, Jo-Hanna and I had a great chat. We spoke about meditation, Buddhism, human suffering and much more. She highly recommended a book she was reading called *Buddha's Brain*. It's about the power of meditation and how it can physically change your brain. This book, and meeting Jo-Hanna, would have a huge impact on my life, but I wasn't yet out of the woods. I thought I'd be home in two weeks, but they still hadn't told me about treatment, which was another facility I would have to attend after detox.

* * *

Over the next two weeks, the acute symptoms of withdrawal retreated. I continued to meditate, I read more books, and I harassed Natalie for more self-improvement techniques. I also learned how to bake bread and make vegetable soup – not bad for a man in his thirties. When I had time to myself, I'd stroll around the farm and spend time in nature. It was one of the most magical times of my life.

My mind was clear, and my body was getting stronger by the day. With that, big dreams were looming. I began talking about my future, planning for life after detox, but the staff thought I was going too fast.

They tried to slow me down, but I disagreed. They didn't know how good I was feeling or how much belief I had in myself. They couldn't get into my mind. How could they possibly know what was best for me? The fact was, they didn't know. No one did, and in my opinion it's the same for most people entering recovery. They were right about one thing, though: I was going too fast.

The race was over, and I felt amazing, but years of delusion had left its mark. Yes, I was stronger than I'd been in years. Yes, I was seeing the world more clearly than ever before. But my new-found clarity was lopsided. I had spent the last fifteen years thinking about me. I need drugs now. I need to soothe my anxiety. I need to avoid how I feel. I need help. Me, me, me, me, me. I never thought about anyone else, so I couldn't take other people's perspective – not in a normal fashion, anyway. I hadn't developed that crucial skill and didn't fully realise that other people didn't know how I felt. Nor did I think about how other people felt. It simply wasn't in my repertoire.

That's when I began writing letters to my family. The only one that survived was the letter I sent to my aunt Tess. As I write this section, Tess is in the final stages of cancer. But before she passed, she wanted to give back to the people she loved the items that she held most dear. For me, it was my letter.

At first, she was afraid to give it back in case it upset me, but I was delighted to get it. My first surprise was when I sent it. It was dated 8 October, my first day clean. The second surprise was how closely the words reflect how I felt. Here is a passage that really stood out:

'It's crazy Tess ... my mind has come back to life, like when I was 16. I'm just feeling full of life, as if I can take on the whole world – on my own. It's hard to explain.'

When I got out of treatment, I popped over to see Tess. I'll never forget the first words that came out of her mouth: 'Oh my God ... we have our Brian back.' She let out such a loud scream that a neighbour thought I was robbing her.

Unfortunately for my sister, she got a letter too. I had spent fifteen years addicted to heroin, the final few living like a tramp, so the last thing she expected was life advice from me. I had only been in detox four weeks, so maybe, just maybe, it was a little cheeky to tell her how to live her life.

The letter didn't survive – I think she burned it – but this is how she remembers the self-help section:

'Hey sis, I have a secret. When I get out of here, I'll tell you and the family all about it. It's a different way of thinking that will help you to change your life. It's hard to explain in a letter, so I'll tell you all about it when I get out.'

She was shaking with anger when she read it, and admits that she would have killed me if I had been standing in front of her. I didn't think about her perspective. It was a sign that I was rushing towards recovery. I thought I had discovered the secret of life, but I was still in a detox centre, barely a day clean.

Despite my inability to see other people's perspectives, I was seeing the world more clearly on several fronts. I don't know exactly what happened to me, but my mind went quiet, I was more present, and life made sense. More accurately, it was clear what didn't make sense: worrying about the future. Regretting my lost youth. Overthinking. Over-reacting. Comparing myself to others. Talking without acting. Not working on myself. Not reading. Doing drugs. Not exercising. Eating junk food.

I didn't just approach this new philosophy intellectually. I embodied it. It became part of me. It was how I felt, and going forward, it was how I was going to act. Living any other way seemed like madness. Whereas this way of living felt so light, easy and effortless.

When I look back now, I can see why others were worried about me. There was a hyper, even manic, aspect to my behaviour. My introduction to affirmations highlights this best. I was deep in withdrawal when I read about them, and the power of these repetitive statements blew me away. I stole one from a book I was reading, and I'd repeat it about thirty times before getting out of bed:

'I am more than I appear to be. All the world's strength and power lie within me.'

'I am more than I appear to be. All the world's strength and power lie within me.'

'I am more than I appear to be. All the world's strength and power lie within me.'

As soon as I finished, I'd leap up from the bed, ready to attack the day. I couldn't believe how well it worked. Not everyone was a fan of my affirmations, though. Sean, my roommate while I was in detox, struggled badly with withdrawal. He didn't know what to make of my random behaviour. My morning affirmations were especially traumatising for him, as I chanted them aloud on waking.

One morning in particular, I dived out of bed telling Sean he should give it a shot. He had just experienced one of his worst nights, and I genuinely thought it might help him. Like a boxer before a fight, I was bouncing around the bedroom telling him to try it:

'Sean, you've got to do this, man. It fucking works. You'll have loads of energy. We can go out and do the gardening and try to forget about the sickness.'

Sean was shivering, curled up in the bed with his jacket on beneath the covers. He was facing the wall, but twisted his head around to speak to me. I'll never forget the look of anguish on his face.

'You're really freaking me out, Brian. I think it's fucking weird. Can ye please just leave me alone?'

Poor Sean was in tears. Withdrawal is bad enough, but I was turning it into an episode of *The Twilight Zone*. That was the first time I stepped in someone else's shoes for years, and I stopped reciting my affirmations out loud after that.

My outlandish behaviour didn't end there. At one point, I thought I might be a sage. 'Maybe I'm like one of the Zen monks from the books I'm reading,' I thought to myself, 'and detox is where my journey starts.'

This led me to believe – well, consider – that I might be able to communicate with animals. I didn't think I was Doctor Dolittle – nothing like that. But I believed there might be some kind of shared presence. I even acted on it. I went down to the stream one day, the one near the back of the farm, and silently stood there for about fifteen minutes with my eyes closed. I thought if I could quieten my mind enough, the wild animals would gather around me. When I opened my eyes, I was the only one there. Much to my disappointment, my sage dreams fizzled out before they had begun. I think it was for the best.

* * *

I made friends with many of the clients in detox. Shared experiences, especially difficult ones, tend to bring people closer together. I was now one week clean, and as my new friends were leaving, the counsellors arranged for them to go to treatment.

I still didn't know what happened in treatment, but I didn't care. I didn't need to go – I thought. One of the clients, a girl we'll call Melanie, told me that the counsellors would talk to me about it soon. She'd been through this process before and seemed to know what she was talking about. It's not that I didn't believe her – I just thought everyone knew that I didn't need treatment.

With energy coursing through my body, and a ferocious appetite to learn, I wanted to take on the world, not go to treatment. So I began getting a little defensive about it. I was ready to hit them with my excuses when Melanie said something that completely changed my mind.

'I hate treatment,' she said. 'That's where they really start getting into your head. They challenge you about everything.'

If I was a dog, my ears would have pricked up. I wanted people to challenge me. I wanted to go into the depths of my psyche, to figure out what was going on. And just like that, I made up my mind. I *was* going to treatment. They didn't even have to ask me.

Everyone was going to different treatment centres. I asked the counsellors which one would suit me, and we decided on a place in Wexford called Aiséirí. It was a twenty-eight-day programme and I couldn't wait to go. 'Bring it on,' I thought. 'Let's see what challenges you have for me.' It was obviously the wrong attitude, but it came from a place of belief and curiosity. It held me back in treatment, but it has pushed me forward in life, so I don't regret it.

People are supposed to be nervous going to treatment – I wasn't. I was like a six-year-old going to Lapland for Christmas. I was so excited on the drive down, and as I walked through the doors of the centre, I vividly remember humming one of my favourite songs:

'Cause I'm leaving
On a jet plane
Don't know when I'll be back again …

I wasn't just as excited as a six-year-old, I was acting like one. I'd numbed my feelings for years, and although I was willing to feel again, I had an almighty preference for positive emotions.

When I reflect back now, it wasn't possible for me to feel negative emotions – not back then. I was on cloud nine from my shift in detox, and I was far too high on life. This has been my biggest challenge in recovery, and it has taken six years, and this book, to fully feel my pain, which came mostly from the harm that I caused to my family.

It didn't take long for them to realise I was going to be a problem. In my first group session, two hours after arriving, I was jumping off the edge of my seat, willing them on to pick me to share. I loved talking in group – or, more accurately, my ego did. With Melanie's words ringing in my ears, my whole body was screaming, 'Pick me! Challenge me!' They could see it from a mile off, however, and picked someone else.

This was the trend of my first three weeks in Aiséirí. I did everything they asked of me, and more – except feel my pain. I tried, but I just didn't know how. Even on family days, which were every Wednesday, I'd sit there like a stone as my mother cried her eyes out. These events included group sessions where the whole family would talk about the problems I had caused. My mother tried to talk, but she couldn't get the words out. She just kept crying, and I just sat there completely detached.

I wasn't smiling during these sessions – numb probably best describes it – but as soon as my family were gone, I was back in fun mode. It was the first time in years that I felt joy in my life. That was part of the problem. I just wanted to have fun. I turned everything into a joke, and the staff even accused me of making meal time feel like pub banter. It wasn't just me – there were a few of us in on it – but I was at the heart of it all.

I turned the serious stuff into jokes, too. In most treatment centres, people have to write out their life story and read it out loud in front of the entire group. This terrifies most people, as they are disclosing some of their darkest moments, but I couldn't wait to have my spot in the limelight. I took the writing part very seriously, not leaving any details out. But then I thought it would be fun to give it a title, so I called it 'The Life of Brian'. In fairness, I still think it's funny, but the counsellors weren't amused.

On my last week in Aiséirí, they hit me with a curveball.

'Brian, we're giving you a silent contract.'

'What the hell is a silent contract?' I asked.

'Besides saying "thank you" and "pass the salt", you're not allowed to talk.'

They hit a nerve – a big fat one.

'That's fucking stupid,' I moaned. 'How I am I supposed get better if I can't talk? I don't agree to that.'

'If you break the contract, you have to leave.'

'Well I'll save you the fucking hassle. I'm outta here.'

I stormed up to my room and started packing my stuff. 'How dare they tell me not to talk?' I was enraged. Suddenly I realised how ridiculous I was being. I was having a tantrum, just like the spoiled six-year-old when his parents tell him he can't go to Lapland for being bold. I also thought about how it would affect my family, so I stopped packing and sheepishly walked back downstairs.

I agreed to the contract, for the most part, and over the next few days, I sat quietly during group and mealtimes. I've since wondered what the point of it was. They said they wanted me to sit with myself, but I was already meditating for over an hour a day. In hindsight, maybe they just wanted to shut me up, which I can also understand.

I'm not sure what good the silent contract did, or treatment for that matter. It wasn't their fault, or mine. Addiction is complex, and so is recovery – one glove doesn't fit all. Their methods do work, for many addicts, but they didn't work for me. I wasn't supposed to be so happy and joyful, and they didn't know what to do with me. They told me it was just a phase and that reality would soon kick in. But I knew they were wrong. I couldn't explain why, but every fibre in my being believed I was starting a wonderful new journey.

Despite my ill fit for the programme, I learned several huge lessons while I was in Aiséirí. There was a priest in the centre called Father Jim. After five minutes in his company, I knew I had to spend more time with him. He called Aiséirí an awareness centre, not a treatment centre. He was right. Recovery is about building self-awareness. We had several great chats during my stay. He didn't say much, but what he did say was powerful. Following his advice, building self-awareness has become not only the cornerstone of my recovery, but the foundation for my new life.

Before detox, I had never thought about the idea of self-awareness. You could say, I was unaware of self-awareness, which is more than a little ironic. I now understand it to be the 'aha moment', the 'lightbulb moment', when you realise the truth of your ways. Like many addicts, I had the knowledge that drugs were killing me, but I did not have the awareness. As soon as I became aware, everything changed.

The most important lesson I learned in Wexford came from the last family day. All of my family came down, including my brother James. I told him to bring my phone because they let you have it for the last few days – a lie, of course.

From my family's perspective, it looked like I wasn't taking the programme seriously. I was like a stone during group sessions, while they were all in tears. Then they'd have to drive back to Dublin, emotionally exhausted, while I had fun with my new treatment pals in a beautiful big house by the sea.

On a client's final week, family days were celebratory affairs. Happy tears would flow as family members would tell them how brave they were. It was my turn, and I couldn't wait. 'Well done, Brian. We're so proud.' That's what I had in my head. So it came as a surprise when my family went on the attack. My sister, who had found out about my phone lie, was livid. 'We don't want him coming home,' she said. 'He hasn't learned a fucking thing.' It was the only time I felt emotional during group, but not for my family – I felt sorry for myself because I didn't get my pat on the back.

I didn't see it immediately, but this was the wake-up call I needed, and I began to think about everything from my family's perspective. I remember feeling shaken as we said our goodbyes in the car park. That was until one of the counsellors asked to speak to me after they'd left. We went into one of the therapy rooms and he asked me about the phone. I played dumb, as if I didn't know what he was talking about.

'What phone?' I asked, a puzzled look on my face.

'You told your brother to bring your phone down. You said we let you have it for the last few days. James didn't know what to do so he told your sister and she told me.'

Without skipping a beat, I went on an epic rant: 'No way. I can't believe she said that. She obviously knew this was her last chance to twist the knife in, so she made up this lie. I don't know what to say. I'm shocked. Sure what the hell would I want my phone for in here?'

He knew I was lying, but I was delighted with how I played it. I walked out of the room with a big grin on my face, but it soon turned to anger as I said to myself, 'I can't believe she did that to me.'

As I walked down the hallway cursing my sister, it hit me. 'Holy fucking shit. That's not what happened. I lied, not Anne.' I was in shock. In the space of a few seconds, I made up a lie, believed it and acted as if it was true. Stunned into silence, I went for a walk and tried to make sense of what I'd done.

'How did I do that without even realising it?' I wondered. 'Is this what I've been doing my entire life?'

It suddenly became clear. I *had* been doing this for as long as I could remember. Whenever I didn't like a situation, or if I felt uncomfortable, I'd tell myself a lie so I would feel okay. I thought I was too clever to be a drug addict, so I told myself I wasn't one. I felt terrible about being a drug-dealer, so I found a way around that too.

My whole life was a lie, a story I fabricated because I was afraid of the truth. That's why my family and my job believed my bullshit for so long. In my head, it was true.

Aiséirí wasn't for me, but thanks to my sister, I learned one of my biggest lessons there. The counsellors had been telling me to stop lying from the moment I arrived, but after my self-lie realisation, I began calling everything out. As usual, I was taking things to the extreme, so the day before I left they said: 'Brian, it's important to be honest, but be careful, you can't be brutally honest either.'

16

THE LIFE OF BRIAN

'Show up in every moment like you're meant to be there, because your energy precedes anything you could possibly say.'

MARIE FORLEO

NOVEMBER 2013

Seven jet streams blazed across the blue morning sky, fading into the distance as the planes raced out to sea. Aiséirí was situated directly under the transatlantic corridor, so on a clear day, which was most mornings in Wexford, that was the view that greeted me. I was going home today, so I walked out to the garden to see it one last time.

It was a crisp morning, my breath clearly visible in the frosty air. The birds were strangely quiet, but a crunching sound broke the silence as I trudged on the grass. At the bottom of the garden, a small tree looked out to sea. I climbed up, as I did most days, and as I reached my spot – a thick horizontal branch about ten feet from the ground – the birds began to sing.

Aiséirí is located at the back of a huge bay, with Rosslare to the right and the Raven to the left. Several lighthouses, I counted seven, line the bay. It was early morning, so the beacons were still visible, flashing in sequence across the sea.

A field of long wispy grass, about the width of a football pitch, separated the house from the bay. The distance made it difficult to hear the waves, but when I listened carefully, I could hear the ocean, its soft hum filling the morning air.

I sat there for fifteen minutes, sucking it all in, when suddenly, I realised how much I was going to miss this place. The people, the garden, the view, the group sessions, the house, the laughs, everything. Just like detox – well, parts of detox – it felt like I was losing a limb. I didn't need treatment to stay clean, and I certainly didn't need a contract of silence, but I had so much fun, and I learned plenty of lessons along the way, especially from Father Jim.

However, the next leg of my journey was about to begin, and I couldn't have been more excited. My dad came to collect me at 11 a.m. I said goodbye to the staff and the clients, and off we drove to Dublin to start my new life.

* * *

When I came home from Aiséirí, my family didn't know what to expect. I was hyper aware in one sense, and intensely present, but slightly deluded in another. I was also full of ego – wrapped up in me, and still unable to take other people's perspective.

Nobody knew what I'd been through, and some of my friends didn't even know I was clean. Yet I still thought everyone would understand me in a sentence, as if they had experienced it too.

It didn't take long for my family to start worrying about me – about ten seconds to be precise. My dad and I drove straight to my parents' house. This had been my home for many years, and I knew it inside out, but when I walked in, it felt different. It even looked different – brighter. Besides saying hello, as I stepped into the kitchen, the first words I spoke were a cause for concern.

'Wow, is that a new washing machine?' I asked.

In my head, it looked like a fancy washing machine from a dry cleaner's, like something you'd see on an American TV show. The glass door looked huge.

'No ... no, we've had that for years,' my mam replied, a little confused.

'Huh, it looks new. Either way, it's a beautiful washing machine.'

As I crouched down, gazing into the window of this magnificent washing machine, my parents stood behind me, looking at each other in utter disbelief. We laugh about it now, but when I ran out the back with our dog, Frankie, my mam turned to my dad and said: 'I think he's on drugs.'

It was scary for my family at the time. I don't know why – they never said – but Aiséirí were certain I was going to relapse. They said my only hope was to spend another few months in a secondary facility in Navan. I went for a few days in December, but it wasn't for me. I had big plans, and I wanted to put them into action.

After Aiséirí, I spent my first few days adjusting to life and reconnecting with family and close friends. The first thing that struck me was how small our house was, the one I owned with my brothers. 'This house is like a matchbox,' I kept saying. 'How the fuck did I not notice this before?' I was even angry about it, blaming my brothers for not telling me. It was a little manic, and my brothers thought I was being a bit weird.

At the same time, my brothers weren't too smart either. There was nothing malicious in it – they had their own issues – but on my first night back in the house, they both smoked weed in front of me and Kelvin drank a six-pack.

That same night James handed me back my phone – the one I had given him while I was in treatment. The lads threw several parties while I was in Wexford. Nothing wrong with that. But with a fridge full to the brim with Heineken, James thought it would make a cool photo. He also used my phone to take a picture of a pile of cocaine that had accidentally spilled on the floor.

So there I was, my first night home in over ten weeks. Clean for the first time in fifteen years. And I was surrounded by drink and drugs. It wasn't what I was expecting, but what could I do? I decided to flick through my phone, and that's when I saw the photos of the cocaine and Heineken.

I'm not sure how I was supposed to react, but I just broke my heart laughing. I was never more grateful for my shift in perspective. Instead of wanting to use, I felt sorry for my brothers. When I tried to explain how stupid their behaviour was, they just sat there looking at me. As I said, the lads had their own issues, and in hindsight, they were probably afraid of losing me. They knew the old Brian, and we got on, despite my madness, but the new me freaked them out.

'Seeing the world through new eyes' came in many forms. It started with food. I was obsessed with healthy eating after my time on the farm. We grew our own vegetables in the fields and got our eggs straight from the chicken coop. I also picked fresh strawberries from the polytunnels every morning. They tasted amazing, as if I was eating food for the very first time.

Now that I was back in the real world, I wanted everyone to taste strawberries as I had experienced them in detox. To do this, my Jack Bauer bag came back with a vengeance. The more I retell this story, the crazier it sounds. I went up to the shops and bought three large boxes of strawberries. Each day, I put one of the boxes into my bag and continued on my rounds visiting family and friends.

Anyone I met got the same line: 'I'm sure you've tasted strawberries before, but have you ever really tasted them? You need to forget about your worries, or whatever is going on in your head, and focus on the strawberry.'

This is actually sound advice. I was asking them to get out of their head and into the moment. But these people had watched me destroy myself for fifteen years. Who was I to give them lessons on life? How I said it didn't help either. People described me as excited, enthusiastic and bouncy during this time. A former manager even used the word 'evangelical'. Positivity is a powerful thing, but it made me look a little manic, and without the right language to describe my experience, 'Seriously, have you ever "really" tasted a strawberry?' came across a bit twisted.

A combination of worry and bewilderment were the expressions on people's faces. I couldn't see it at the time, though. I thought they were confused and simply misunderstood me.

My brothers got the worst of the new me. I was reading ferociously about subjects such as awareness and self, and I was dying to talk about it. So every evening, I'd corner them in the house and tell them everything I had learned. It wasn't all about me, though. They were struggling with their own demons, and I wanted to help, but this was not the way to do it. As I later found out, it only made them reject what I was trying to explain.

No one in my family escaped the onslaught. My parents were delighted I was happy, but they also thought I was mad. My sister got it too, but she wasn't willing to listen to my latest insights, especially after the letter. She was also the only person to challenge me about my behaviour. This included the strawberries incident, but also my bizarre realisation about scarves.

I bought a new scarf to match my Jack Bauer bag – God, I loved that bag. Like everything after treatment, if I liked it, I wanted more, and I soon became obsessed with scarves. My sister's issue had nothing to do with the scarves, but more with my realisation that scarves *actually* keep your neck warm. 'Scarves are great, aren't they? Do you know they keep your neck warm?' To this day, I've no idea what was going through my mind. I've struggled to live that one down, and my sister, in particular, loves to remind me about it.

* * *

I was excited to chat to all my friends when I got out of treatment. But it turned out I didn't have many friends. So much for being popular. Another little story I told myself. I was blessed with the friends I did have, however. Despite the wedding incident, and several other scenes that haven't made the book, my best mate Gar stuck with me throughout my addiction. Bridges had to be built, and he was definitely weirded out by the new me, but we've grown very close over the last few years. In December 2018, Gar and his wife Lynsey even asked me to be godfather to their beautiful daughter Penny.

Dano, another close friend, was in recovery when I got clean. When he quit his own madness in 2006, we went our separate ways, so it was great to catch up with him. I thought he was crazy when he got clean so we had a good laugh about that. Barry, my partner in crime, was still in the depths of addiction. We met up a few times, but we live in different worlds. I tried to talk to him about getting clean, but he was just like me when I was deep in addiction. Anytime my family and friends tried to talk to me about getting help, I was having none of it. I've since found out that everyone has to walk their own path.

People often ask me how I stayed away from my addict friends, but besides Barry, and Dano in the early days, I didn't have any. I had many acquaintances, but the gift of delusion – thinking I wasn't a real addict – stopped me getting too close.

Another one of my close friends, Clarky, now lived in Australia. We chatted on the phone quite a bit, which was great, but Australia is a long way away. That's when I realised that the world didn't stop while I was falling deeper into my hole. And it didn't really care now that I was clean. Apart from Barry, all my friends were married with kids, or planning to have kids. They had got on with their lives. What else were they supposed to do? It would have been the same if addiction had killed me. It was quite a shock for my ego. The world didn't revolve around me. There was no 'Life of Brian'.

This realisation didn't faze me, however. If anything, it fascinated me. I had so many questions. How did I twist my mind to believe these things? Why did I think the world revolved around me? Why did I feel so alive, but at the same time not be able to see other people's perspective? Why do people suffer? How can I help others escape their suffering?

These questions drove me forward. I was obsessed. I was on a mission. But I was also starved of social interaction. I'm a people person at heart, and I'd spent so many years alone. Even when I was around people, I felt alone, disconnected and completely detached from other people's reality. This made my desire to be around others even stronger.

The problem was, everyone was busy, and I was going to have lots of time on my hands. I had no job – not officially, anyway. I was still technically employed by Kenilworth Products, but they weren't paying me, and they had no plans to take me back. The union advised me to go back to them when I sorted myself out, to see if I could secure a pay-out, so that was the plan.

So, fuelled by my desire to be around people, and to work on myself, I decided to take Aiséirí's advice and I began attending Narcotics Anonymous and Alcoholics Anonymous meetings.

I spent the next few months going to meetings, reading books in coffee shops and rebuilding shattered relationships. I continued with my meditation practice and constantly worked on myself, always digging deeper into my mind and always trying to grow as a human being.

I also joined the gym at the National Sports Centre. I wanted to improve every aspect of my life, and exercise was a key feature of that. I began going to the gym at six every morning. This was a masterstroke for several reasons. To go to the gym that early, you need to have a certain mindset, so I ended up meeting a fantastic group of people there, many of whom I now consider friends. We work out from six to seven, and then have the craic in the Jacuzzi for half an hour. What a way to start the day.

Of all the books I was reading, two were life-changing for me. *The Power of Now* by Eckhart Tolle left a mark that will never fade. Perspective shifts are more common than you might think, and that's what happened to him too. His was much grander, however, and he didn't have the delusion of addiction following him around.

The story at the start of his book was particularly striking. One night, not long after his twenty-ninth birthday, he woke up in the early hours with a feeling of absolute dread. He had previously battled with anxiety and depression, but it was more intense than ever before, and he began to question his reason for living. As he played with the idea of suicide, the same thought kept repeating itself in his mind: 'I cannot live with myself any longer.'

He suddenly became aware of what a peculiar thought this was. 'Am I one or two? If I cannot live with myself, there must be two of me: the "I" and the "self" … maybe only one of them is real.'

Stunned by this bizarre realisation, his mind went quiet. He was fully conscious, but there were no more thoughts. Upon waking the following day, the world seemed different. Although he recognised the room, he had never truly seen it. Everything looked fresh and alive as if it had just come into existence. He knew that something profound had occurred, but didn't understand what it was. It wasn't until several years later that he realised what had happened. The intense suffering of that night had forced a split in his consciousness, and his deeply fearful 'self' fell away.

Three lessons from this book, which I've since called my pillars for life, hit me so hard that I inscribed them on a medal around my neck as a daily reminder.

The first lesson, and possibly the most important practice in my life, involves objectively observing my own body and mind. I struggled terribly with overthinking when I was younger, always worrying about my family dying and fearing my own heartbeat. These negative thoughts would fuel my anxiety, which drove me towards a life of addiction. I don't struggle with negative thoughts and feelings any more. Instead, when they do arise, I take a step back and objectively watch them float by, without engaging. Just like clouds floating through the sky – I let them pass, without engaging.

The second lesson is tricky to explain. It's related to the one above, in that instead of becoming entangled with your thoughts, you just be. Think about it this way. Have you ever heard of a jealous racehorse? Or a frog with self-esteem issues? Of course not. Why? Because they are not tormented by their minds – that's a human quality. However, this book showed me that we can let that stuff go, and just be. In other words, if you're sitting on the grass, you just sit on the grass. If you're looking at the stars, you just look at the stars. You take your mind out of the equation, and just *be*.

The third lesson was a complete game-changer for me. It involves *accepting reality*, accepting what is. This might sound obvious, but how often do we regret past mistakes or agonise over missed opportunities? I could have easily tormented myself about losing so many years. 'Oh, I wish I never done heroin'; 'Why was I so stupid?'; 'I wish I seen sense in my twenties.' This is called resisting reality. The past has already happened. It already is the case. I cannot change it, so why dwell on it? I never torment myself with what might have been or agonise over lost years. Fully embracing this lesson is the reason why.

The second book, my favourite of all time, had a profound impact on my life. You cannot put a price on books that change your life, but if forced to pay for this one, I'd be happy to put a mortgage on it – it was that big.

The book, by Anthony de Mello, is called *Awareness*. De Mello believed that the greatest human gift is awareness, to be aware of one's body, feelings, thoughts and sensations. However, he found that most people are unaware; in his words, they are asleep. They live asleep, marry asleep, breed children in their sleep and die in their sleep. Much of his work, therefore, focused on waking people up, to help them to break free from their minds.

The book begins with a powerful parable about a little eagle:

One morning a farmer walked out to his yard and found an eagle's egg. Unsure what to do, he put the egg into his chicken coop. The little eaglet hatched and grew up thinking he was a chicken. He clucked like a chicken, scratched the earth like a chicken, and thrashed his wings like a chicken. Years passed by, and the little eagle continued to believe he was a chicken. One day he saw a magnificent bird soaring through the sky. It glided gracefully, with scarcely a beat of its powerful wings. The eagle looked up to the sky in awe. 'Who's that?' he asked. 'That's the eagle, king of the birds,' said his chicken siblings. 'He belongs to the sky. We belong to the earth – we're chickens – and that's all we'll ever be.' So the eagle lived the rest of his life and died like a chicken, for that's what he thought he was.

What does this parable mean? Anthony de Mello was telling us that most people are eagles living like chickens. They are consumed by their minds, conditioned by society, unaware of their true potential and living their lives without ever truly waking up; and for many people, he is right.

This story slapped me square in the face. All my life, I had been living in a drug-riddled chicken coop, tormented by my mind and not knowing how to escape. But my shift gave me a glimpse of awareness and allowed me to break free. I made a promise to myself that day, one I will never forget: 'I am an eagle, and I'm going to soar as high as I can.'

* * *

Bliss. That's the only way I can describe my first few months after treatment. I'd never felt more alive, energised and present in my entire life. But it was time to make a decision. Life had given me a second chance, and it was time to soar. I just had to decide how.

I considered going to Asia, to study Eastern philosophy first-hand, but it didn't feel right. I also considered travelling, to expand my horizons, but I didn't have the money. Even if I had, something else was calling me. Ever since the fire extinguisher incident, I had a burning curiosity to know what exactly happened to me: what caused my perspective shift? Why did I feel so alive? And how could I share it with others? For me, there was only one place to start. I needed to go to college to study psychology.

My family weren't keen on the college idea. They thought a normal job would be more secure for my sobriety, but my gut was screaming loud and clear, and I felt I had no choice but to listen to it.

I began looking for courses in February, but I was too late, except for one course. Mature students could still apply for a psychology degree at Maynooth University, so that's what I did.

Interviews for college didn't start until July, and the course didn't begin until September, so I had time to kill. First, however, there was the small matter of my job. They couldn't take me back, not after what had happened, but I hadn't officially left either. I was €35,000 in debt, some of it to dangerous people, and I was hoping for a pay-out. If I wanted to go to college, this was the only way.

I had worked in Kenilworth for seventeen years. We were like a family. So going back to see them for the first time in six months was a strange experience. I didn't know what the reaction would be, from my friends or from the management, but I needn't have worried. They were amazing. Everyone, including the management, was delighted that I had turned my life around. I looked completely different, and some people wondered how the staff hadn't noticed. But it happened gradually, over many years, so it was difficult to see.

I negotiated a figure with the management, said my goodbyes, and off I went to start my new journey. I'm still close friends with many of my old work colleagues, and I've since been invited back to speak about mental health awareness. That says it all about the people who work there.

I paid my debts and bought a car – nothing too fancy, which left me with a few quid to keep me going until college. I'd need to get a part-time job to get me through college, but in the meantime I was going to enjoy myself in my little world of bliss.

My first year clean was like a dream. I played lots of golf, mostly on my own, and I even got a hole in one. Thankfully I wasn't playing on my own that day, so I have a witness! It might sound lonely playing golf on your own, but for me it was a form of meditation. Strolling around in nature playing a sport I loved. It was heaven. I continued to meditate and relentlessly worked on myself. I also read many more books, immersing myself in anything to do with the human mind.

In May that year, I decided to go to Portugal on my own for a week. I visited Alvor, a quiet little fishing village in the Algarve. This trip turned out to be one of the most powerful experiences of my life. My plan was to relax, read, meditate and, of course, play a few rounds of golf. I've always wanted to go scuba diving, so that was on the agenda too.

Before I went to Alvor, I kept coming across references to a book called the *Tao Te Ching*, often referred to as the Chinese book of wisdom. I expected a big heavy book with thousands of pages, but what arrived in the post was a slip of a thing, consisting of eighty-one verses, one verse per page.

Every time I read this book, I come away with something different, but to sum it up, it's about lessons in self-awareness. One such lesson from the third verse reads like this: 'Practise not-doing, and everything will fall into place.' Here, the Tao, which literally translates as 'the way', highlights how we might see more clearly if we spent more time in awareness, and less in thinking and doing.

This book is cryptic, reminding me of the famous Zen phrase, 'What is the sound of one hand clapping?' Of course, there is no answer to this. Its purpose is to highlight our compulsive need to answer unanswerable questions, which, according to the Tao, is the mind's greatest dysfunction.

There are over 250 translations of the *Tao Te Ching*, and mine didn't make much sense to me at first, but the more I sat with it, the more I softened.

'The flame that burns twice as bright burns half as long.'

'Do you have the patience to wait until your mud settles and the water is clear?'

'Those who know do not speak. Those who speak do not know.'

One evening, while having dinner at a beach restaurant, I was reflecting on the verses in the Tao. When I finished my food, I began listening to the noises of the night. I could hear the sea in the distance and the crickets chirping in the grass. Over the next few minutes, it felt like the world began moving in slow motion. Not in a scary way, but timelessly, beautiful and pure. I sat there for several minutes, lost in the moment, before strolling down to the ocean.

The cold sand, which squished between my toes, tempered the warm air as I made my way towards the sea. I sat a few metres from the water, gazing up at the stars, as the waves crashed against the shore in the background. As I fell deeper into the moment, the sense of timelessness grew stronger, as if there were no time, or that it simply didn't matter.

My mind was silent, awestruck by the beauty and radiance of nature. Every now and then, a thought would slip in. 'Wow ... I wonder how long this will last,' but then I'd drift back into the moment. I could sense the significance of this experience, so I looked up at the sky and took a mental snapshot of the stars – one I love coming back to.

This was, by far, the most powerful and mesmerising experience of my life. I'd never felt so connected, to what I'm not sure, but in the moment, everything seemed to make sense. I sat on the beach for a few hours, and then walked back up to the hotel. As I went to sleep that night, the sense of timelessness was still there, but its intoxicating effects were fading. I drifted off to sleep, and when I awoke the following morning, it was gone.

This experience left a permanent mark. I've had glimpses of it since, especially during meditation, but I've never reached the level of wholeness that I experienced on that beach. In a strange way, it reminded me of heroin, but better, in every way imaginable. I chased my new high for a time, meditating more in the hope of finding it. It didn't work. I've since come to the conclusion that I need to let it find me, or in the words of the Tao, wait for my muddy water to clear.

17

RELAPSE

'*Those who are unaware they are walking in darkness will never seek the light.*'

BRUCE LEE

MAY 2014

The summer of 2014 presented my first few hurdles in sobriety. First came a strange experience at the dentist. Methadone and heroin destroy most people's teeth, but I was lucky. They still needed a lot of work, but the dentist told me it was a miracle that I had so many left. Some of my teeth were too far gone, however, and I had to get several extractions, including a wisdom tooth. I don't like getting teeth pulled, but after what I'd been through, I wasn't too bothered about it.

My strange experience occurred on the day I got my wisdom tooth pulled. It was embedded deep in my gum, with not much tooth above the surface, and the dentist was struggling to get it out. After ten full minutes, he changed tactics. He made an incision in the gum and then twisted, tugged and yanked at my mouth for another ten minutes. It still wouldn't budge, so he tried some kind of loosening technique. Finally, it came out. I can still hear the crunch.

The next thing I remember is falling, not onto the floor, but into a faceless, formless void, like a dark spinning vortex. It had a timeless quality to it, but not like the beach in Alvor, more like my petrol experience when I thought I had died. I wasn't lucid within the void, but I sensed it was pulling me down.

The movement towards the bottom had a pulsing quality to it, like a short video on repeat. At first I let it happen, in a helpless kind of way; but suddenly, I began fighting back. Every fibre of my being was screaming to get out, and in the blink of an eye, I was back in the dentist's chair. At first I thought I'd fainted. The dentist and his assistant were white as ghosts. They kept asking if I was okay, but I felt more embarrassed than anything else. I left that day, not knowing what had happened, but on my next visit, they told me all about it.

The dentist told me it was the scariest moment of his career. Apparently I stopped breathing for a full two minutes. He thought he had lost me and was in the process of calling an ambulance when I let out a gasp of air and snapped out of it.

Besides the regular numbing injection, I didn't receive any other medication, so I'm not sure what to make of this experience – perhaps my body was simply weak from years of addiction. Its similarity with the petrol incident is what intrigues me most. It was also a stark reminder of what I had put my body through, and that I was not yet out of the woods. I began to wonder what long-term impact the drugs had had on my body, so I went to my doctor. He put it like this: 'It's like you were driving at a hundred miles an hour. You were in grave danger. But now you've slowed down, you're just like everyone else.' It feels like a stretch, but I hope he's right.

That was the start of a bumpy summer, and my next challenge came in the form of the government. Before applying for college, I had to make sure I could afford it. I'd still have to get a part-time job, but with bills to pay, getting the back to education allowance was critical. It also paid for a large portion of my college fees. I'd paid tax for seventeen years, despite my addiction, so I felt I deserved it.

I didn't know how the welfare system worked, so I went to the Citizens Information Centre to see if I was eligible for the allowance. They said I was, and I didn't think too much about it until I had to apply. When I went to the welfare office in June, however, they told me a different story. I won't bore you with the details, but the welfare system is a tricky business, and I had missed the threshold by a few days.

I tried to explain that the Citizens Information Centre had given me the wrong information, but it didn't matter. I arranged a meeting with the guy in charge – maybe he could bend the rules, I thought – but he told me, 'Not even the President of Ireland, or America for that matter, could give you a pass on this one. I'm sorry, but even if I wanted to, there is nothing I can do.'

The concept of luck fascinates me. More specifically, 'who-luck' and 'when-luck'. Sometimes meeting the right person at the right time can make all the difference. I didn't believe the welfare officer's presidential spiel, so I scoured the internet looking for another angle, hoping my who-luck would jump out from the screen – it didn't. I went back to the welfare office to plead my case, and from the most unlikely of places, my who-luck sailed in.

I'd asked to speak to anyone from the back to education department, but the same guy, the boss, my who-luck, was the one who came out to meet me. He looked exasperated when he realised who it was. He was on his way to lunch – my when-luck – and with one glance at his sandwich, he said, 'It's your lucky day. I'm going to push this through for you.' It's strange to think a rumbling stomach had such a big impact on my life, but I was happy to take it.

The summer bumps weren't yet over. I was required to do an interview for the psychology course in Maynooth. I thought it would be a formality, but it wasn't.

It was a scorcher of a day, over 25 degrees. It was my first time to visit the college, or Maynooth for that matter. The interview was in the older part of the college, the South Campus, which reminded me of Hogwarts from *Harry Potter*

I was an hour early, so I located the interview room, then took a stroll around the grounds. I found a lovely lawn at the front of the South Campus, and sat there in the sun until it was time. I wasn't even slightly nervous about the interview, and didn't feel the need to rehearse anything, so I read one of my books, Eckhart Tolle's *Stillness Speaks*.

With ten minutes to spare, I walked back to the interview room, marvelling at the beautiful old hallways on the way. I waited on an antique bench right outside the room. Right on time, a young guy – early thirties I thought – called me into the room. He was tall and trendy and didn't seem to fit the surroundings, but he was very friendly. There was an older woman in the room too, who also seemed nice.

In my naivety, I thought I just had to show up and my passion, energy and willingness to deliver would shine through. 'A mad learner like myself, they'll be begging me to join the ranks,' I figured. But I was wrong. True to form, I completely disregarded their perspective. How could they possibly get to know me in a twenty-minute interview I'd barely prepared for? I can't remember what questions they asked, or how I responded, but at that stage of my recovery, I'm sure my answers were wild, most likely involving something to do with spirituality, self and stillness.

I thought it went well in the moment, but at the end of the interview, the tall guy hit me with something unexpected: 'I don't think you're a good fit right now. It would be best if you were to do an access course and reapply next year.'

'What's an access course?' I asked.

'It's a one-year course that shows mature students how to cope with the challenges of third-level education.'

'*Cope?*' I yelled. 'I'm not here to cope … or just take part, for that matter. I'm here to kick ass, to be the best.'

Delusion is a funny thing. For years, I didn't believe I was a real addict, despite the facts. When forced to face that reality, I decided I wasn't just an addict, but the best addict ever. This belief, if somewhat delusional, carried through to my sobriety, and although it held me back at times, it has provided me with a massive advantage in life: the gift of belief. I genuinely believed I would top a class of three hundred, no matter how big the challenge, and it was this belief that propelled me into college.

The interviewer was a decent guy, and I'm sure he was just following protocol, but he wasn't expecting that response. I'll never forget the look on his face when I finished my rant. He was shocked, but he was also impressed, I think.

'Okay,' he said, 'we hold a four-week writing course over the summer. If you pass that, you don't have to do the access course, and you can join up this year.' I thanked them for their time and for giving me the opportunity and walked out of the room.

The course started two weeks later. It was tough, but I got through it, just. Two weeks after that, the university sent me an official acceptance form. The difficulty of the writing course was a real eye-opener, however. My writing and critical thinking skills were poor, and I had a lot to learn, but I was ready for the challenge.

* * *

Having realised how much I had to learn, I looked for anything that would give me an edge. The university had a specific set of courses in the library to help first-year students with the required critical skills, so I signed up for every single one of them. It was exactly what I needed, and just like detox, I soaked up every bit of information like a sponge.

My first year in college was a year of aggressive learning. Obsessed with psychology, I relentlessly sought out anyone who could help me to understand the human mind. Within the first week, I lined up meetings with every one of the psychology lecturers. I'd been dying to speak to them for months, so on more than one occasion, my enthusiasm spilled over. They didn't know what hit them as I bombarded them with questions about all kinds of topics. I had very little knowledge of psychology at the time, and assumed the course covered concepts such as self, awareness and meditation. This was not the case.

Each of the lecturers gave me great insights about the course, but the degree was only secondary to me. I wanted to go deep into the nature of the human psyche. That's what I was there for, and only two lecturers were willing to go there with me.

Professor Yvonne Barnes-Holmes was the head of the department and a world expert in her field. She is also a wizard of a therapist, has a heart of gold and is one of the most brilliant people I've ever met. More than that, however, Yvonne had answers to many of my questions.

When my mind went quiet, anxiety left me, and I wanted to know why. If I could answer this, I could share it with others. So my question to Yvonne was: 'What is the relationship between our emotions, meditation and the voice in our head?'

This was one of many big questions, but Yvonne was a busy woman. She set aside two hours each Wednesday for consultations, but there were over three hundred students. That's when I struck gold. Yvonne doesn't have time for bullshit, and she's quite blunt. She was my kind of person, but those same traits scared the life out of the other students. Over the next year, for one hour every Wednesday, sometimes more, I'd chat to Yvonne about the nature of human suffering and how best to treat it. These sessions were some of the most important lessons I learned during my degree.

I'll never forget my first meeting with Dr Michelle Kelly, and neither will she. Michelle was our statistics lecturer. She was also quite young and not what I expected. As I had with the other lecturers, I hit Michelle with a barrage of questions about meditation, self and spirituality. Instead of evading the questions, however, Michelle went with me. With that, animated as ever, I launched into a spiel that went on for the next hour. We had a great back and forth, mostly forth, as we delved into many deep topics.

My lasting memory from that meeting is when the conversation ended. I looked at Michelle from across the table, and with her head and shoulders arched back, and a look of astonishment on her face, it looked like a giant blow-dryer had ambushed her in the room.

At the end of our next statistics class, she sought me out. In a class of three hundred, that was quite some feat. She told me she'd been thinking about our conversation and had read something that might interest me. As we walked to her office, I remember feeling dumbfounded that a stranger could be so thoughtful. I'd never experienced anything like it before, and it has shaped how I think about other people ever since.

Over the next three years, I met Michelle once a week. We spoke about many psychological concepts, but more important, she taught me how to write. Michelle was also my final-year supervisor, and with her help, my dissertation, about the nature of wanting more as it happens, became my first academic publication.

Michelle's influence went much further than academia. She was my guiding light as I navigated my new world. She helped me to realise the importance of connection, how to take the perspective of others and, most important, she reminded me to have fun. Despite my light-hearted nature, and the laughs we had during our meetings, I was beginning to take academia very seriously. Michelle was quick to point this out: 'What's the point in anything if you can't have fun?' This has had a huge impact on my life, and I've been having fun ever since.

Michelle also helped me to realise that I'm not fundamentally flawed. Whether it was a side-effect of addiction, or simply who I am, my self-centredness was beginning to bother me. I called this my fundamental human flaw. I convinced myself that I lacked emotional and social intelligence, key human ingredients when interacting with others. Over many conversations, Michelle pointed out how I was always thinking about people, especially my two nephews, and that my ability to get on with others proved I was talking crap.

It took me a while, but I finally believed that I am not fundamentally flawed. I have Michelle to thank for that. She is now one of my closest friends, and one of the most important people in my life.

When one of my best mates, Clarky, came back from Australia to visit his family, he introduced me to his cousin Niamh. Niamh, fresh out of secondary school, was in my psychology class, but she was finding the first year tough. Besides commuting for four hours each day, she was struggling with bouts of anxiety, which included extreme nausea and a tight chest, primarily caused by a traumatic car accident not long before. I'm quite close to Clarky's family, and because of what I'd been through, they thought I might be able to help.

I chatted to Niamh at one of Clarky's 'back to Ireland' parties. I told her about my own battle with anxiety and the tools I used to cope with it. I also gave her tips on what was helping me in college. In hindsight, it seemed cruel that Clarky would unleash me on his young cousin, and, like Michelle, she looked like a giant hairdryer had ambushed her.

We arranged to meet over the following few weeks, but I didn't hold out much hope. Niamh was young and seemed quite timid. I assumed that if I hadn't scared her with my rant, her gentle nature would prevent her from turning up.

I also told her she should meet with Yvonne, but I thought she'd be afraid to do that too. As usual, I met with Yvonne the following week, and I was astonished to see Niamh going in after me. As I've learned over the last few years, many people look for advice, but they rarely act on that advice. Niamh, however, turned out to be a doer – she was all about action.

Our Christmas exams were only a few weeks away, so I booked a room in the library for a study group. There were four of us: Niamh, myself and two other mature students who appeared to be doing well. I thought Niamh might hold the group back, but either way, I had promised Clarky I would help, and that's what I was going to do.

Before the session, we each picked a topic and prepared notes that we planned to share. One of the mature students had done nothing. The other one, Ellen, was the exact opposite, so much so that it was bordering on insanity. It would have taken years to study the content – it was that meticulous. I was somewhere in the middle, but Ellen's notes made me think I hadn't done enough. That's when Niamh showed us what she had prepared. It was clean, sharp and straight to the point. It turned out that Niamh was better than the lot of us.

That study session was a pivotal learning experience for me. It provided the foundations not only for my academic career, but also for how I cut through complexity in many aspects of my life. It also reminded me of my delusional sense of grandeur. Just like the unwelcome life advice I gave my family after detox, I made a judgement of Niamh that wasn't accurate – I had written her off, when in reality, I needed to learn from her.

Niamh and I have since become close friends. We were a tremendous help to each other throughout our degree, and I was able to support her with her anxiety. I have particularly fond memories of our early chats, especially when I gave her a lift home. I was still quite animated back then, and once I had someone trapped in the car, they were getting it with both barrels. We laugh about it now, but Niamh being Niamh, she took it on board, and I was delighted that we were able to help each other.

* * *

I loved college. I spent most of my time studying, but I'm a people person at heart, and despite being a mature student, I got on great with the younger and older students alike. In first year, I mostly chatted with students closer to my own age. But after that, when the class was reduced to sixty full-time psychology students, I found myself spending more time with the younger people in the class. I didn't go out partying or anything like that – it was all about psychology – but I found them easier to connect with and more fun to be around. I think I'm just a kid at heart.

I was living with my brothers throughout my college years. My back to education allowance helped me to cover some of the bills, but I still needed to get a part-time job. I didn't drink, so it made sense to work when everyone else was socialising. I also felt it gave me an edge. I decided to get a job as a delivery driver, and applied at a local Thai takeaway called Camile. On my first day the boss handed me a pink dickie bow and told me to wear it with a white shirt and slacks. I thought it was a joke, but it wasn't. To make matters worse, the job only paid €6 per hour. My ego screamed, 'Hell, no,' but I needed the job, so I reluctantly took it.

I thought about leaving after the first night, mostly because of the dickie bow, but it was a perfect fit – the job, not the dickie bow. I knew I couldn't let a silly uniform mess things up, so I stuck with it. In truth, I never did a delivery wearing the dickie bow, except once, when I forgot to take it off in the car. I don't know why it bothered me so much, I didn't even know the woman I was delivering to, but my stomach sank when I realised.

I worked in Camile for three years, my entire college degree. I was grateful for the job, but I didn't enjoy working five hours per night every Friday, Saturday and Sunday for three years. This experience, however, became one of the biggest lessons of my life, and just like my addiction, taught me how to turn negatives into positives.

Starting off, I tried to study between deliveries, but I was driving eighty per cent of the time, so that didn't work. I felt I was wasting valuable time – fifteen hours a week – and it was really bothering me. I'm not sure if it's a side-effect of fifteen lost years, or my newfound love of learning, but I couldn't let this go.

I began wondering how I could utilise this time. Maybe I could use it as a way to relax or recharge, I thought. I created a playlist with chill-out music, which worked to an extent, but I soon found out that music makes my mind wander. That has its advantages, but it wasn't what I was looking for right then. I considered guided meditations, but dismissed that immediately because it wouldn't be safe. Then it hit me: I could practise mindful driving. Instead of being distracted from the road, I could use it as my object of focus. To this day, mindful driving is a core practice of mine. I simply put my entire focus on the driving experience, and when I catch my mind wandering, I bring it back to the road.

It suddenly occurred to me that I could flip any undesirable situation into a positive one. I'm not saying you can make every negative situation better, but if you focus on the positive, it's far more productive than crying about what you cannot change. This would become one of my most important life lessons, but before that, it nearly became my undoing.

Second-year psychology was a big step up. The assignments were coming thick and fast, and the Christmas exams were looming. I wanted to get top marks, so I began utilising all of my time to make sure I stayed ahead of the game.

Anything that wasn't helping my new obsession was killing it, so I flipped it into something that did help. I'd recall my exam answers while I exercised in the mornings. I pushed every lunch conversation towards what we were studying. I'd read my notes while I was eating my dinner. If I couldn't sleep at night, which was rare, I'd use it as an opportunity to reflect on my assignments.

Mindful driving and chill-out music also became a hindrance to my academic aspirations. So when I found out I could download YouTube videos to my phone, I decided to flip that too. I downloaded any videos relating to my course material and played them while delivering food at weekends.

I was now spending every minute of every day in my pursuit of top grades. I had a winning formula, and it was working, but I was forgetting why I went to college in the first place. I was there to learn about the human mind, not get lost in it.

I'd come a long way since my days as a heroin addict, but my newfound obsession with college was taking its toll. I was losing that light beautiful feeling I'd been gifted in detox, but I couldn't see it. It was happening in unawareness. Life had given me a second chance, a shot at bonus time, but I was throwing it away.

* * *

We always went to my nanny's house for Christmas Day. She had since passed, but two of my aunts and my uncle still lived in the house, so Christmas 2015 was no different. My nephew Ollie, my sister's first-born and my parent's first grandchild, had been born the year before. Like every Christmas, the adults were getting drunk downstairs. I didn't drink any more, and I don't like being around drunk people, especially family, so I played with Ollie up in my uncle John's bedroom.

Since the age of twenty-one, John had suffered with serious health problems. Now in his sixties, his issues were a lot worse. I felt for John, but in truth, I was always more obsessed about the medication on his locker. I knew he'd have powerful pain meds, and I used to dream about being in the room on my own. But John rarely left his room, so I never got a chance, until tonight.

John was downstairs, but my obsession had since lifted, so I didn't even notice my opportunity at first. That's until I realised that the meds could be dangerous for Ollie. I wish I could say I thought about what happened next – at least I'd have a chance next time – but I didn't. Without thinking, or even hesitating, I walked over to the locker and checked the meds. Lots of people were floating around the house, so I quickly grabbed a few tablets I recognised – my old pal Zopiclone – and stuck two of them in my back pocket.

There was no fear in my actions, no feelings whatsoever. I was like a robot. I continued to play with Ollie, but there was only one thing on my mind. 'When will I go home?' Within a few minutes, I was downstairs. 'I'm going to make a move, guys. Happy Christmas,' and off I went.

I was still like a robot when I arrived home. Again, I didn't think about it – I swallowed both tablets immediately. I sat down on the sofa and waited for them to hit me. I was excited, but in a gentle, calm way. After a few minutes, I could feel them kicking in. The excitement grew, but it soon turned to disappointment. The buzz was nice, I suppose, but nothing like I remembered.

When I woke up the following morning, I was exhausted. It wasn't physical, more of a drowsy stupor. It was the exact opposite of my new energetic self, and I hated it. All of my Stephen's Day study plans went out the window. Instead, I sat around eating junk food all day, disgusted at myself for falling behind on my schedule. I tried to take the positives out of it, realising that drugs no longer served me, and although I was still pissed off, I found this fascinating.

I had used drugs to soothe anxiety. That's why they felt so good – the contrast. But I didn't suffer with anxiety any more, so all they did was make me drowsy. This was a refreshing realisation.

I didn't think much about my mini-relapse until the following summer. A few months before that, around March 2016, I was still blindly obsessed with chasing top grades. With assignments coming thick and fast, and the summer exams looming, I wanted to turn the screw. I couldn't afford to lose time, so I wasn't impressed when I felt ill while doing deliveries one evening. It was nothing serious, but I don't do well with colds and flus. In reality, it was barely the sniffles. It was more of an excuse.

Maybe it was the realisation that drugs no longer served me, or maybe it was heroin waiting for its chance to pounce, but I became obsessed about Solpadeine. Solpadeine are opioid-based, but because my tolerance levels had always been sky-high, they had never been on my radar. I soon began justifying the actions I was about to take. 'Sure, it's only Solpadeine. You can buy them over the counter. They can't be that bad.' The fact was, I had met many people in Narcotics Anonymous meetings who were addicted to Solpadeine, including pharmacists, so just like the old days, when I thought I wasn't a real addict, I was only fooling myself. Unlike the Christmas incident, however, I began thinking about potential consequences.

'What am I doing?'

'This could be a slippery slope.'

'Maybe I shouldn't.'

But I'd already made up my mind, and I quickly justified my decision by prioritising college. *'You need to take them so you can study properly – that's all,'* said a voice from the past, one I hadn't heard in years. It was both seductive and soothing, and within minutes, I was driving around looking for a pharmacy.

It was late, however, and none of the pharmacies were open. Like a man possessed, I began frantically searching my phone for one that was open. Jackpot. The Roselawn pharmacy was only a few minutes away and it was open until 9 p.m.

'One small box of soluble Solpadeine please.'

'Are they for you?'

'Nah. They're for my dad. He usually takes Difene for his back but he's none left.'

Pharmacists usually ask who and what you're buying Solpadeine for, so I'd rehearsed that little sketch on my way in. I sat in my car looking at the box of Solpadeine. I should have been concerned, but just like at Christmas when I took the Zopiclone, there was no emotion. I put three tablets into my bottle of water, waited for them to dissolve and swallowed it before I changed my mind.

Zopiclone didn't serve me any more, but opiates were a different animal. As I drove back to the takeaway, I could feel the opiates surge through my body. The immediate high faded quickly, but there was a lasting sense of ease. They didn't make me drowsy either – the caffeine actually gave me a boost.

I took four tablets the following night and the remaining five the night after that. What surprised me was how quickly my tolerance built. The five tablets gave me an opiate itch – an actual physical itch – and I felt a little more at peace, but there was no surge like the first night. When I reflect back now, that's what I was chasing – the high – but I wasn't going to get it from Solpadeine. I needed a stronger drug.

18

A PROGRAMME FOR LIFE

'When it is dark enough, you can see the stars.'
RALPH WALDO EMERSON

JUNE 2016

My body felt heavy as I shuffled out of the library. I wasn't aware of it at first, but as I walked past the giant sequoias on the South Campus of Maynooth University, it suddenly hit me. The trees weren't vibrant and alive, as they had been in my early days in recovery – nothing was. Life had lost its colour, its energy, its soul. That light, joyful feeling I was gifted back in detox was gone. What shocked me most, however, was that I hadn't even noticed.

How did I not see it? How did I lose the most profound thing that had ever happened to me without even realising? Stunned into stillness, I just stood there, gazing at the trees, when out of nowhere, the last two and a half years came into sharp focus.

My experience in detox forced me into a state of present moment awareness. That's why my mind went quiet. That's why anxiety left me. And that's why I felt so alive. I was deliriously happy, but in this state of hyper awareness, I had no rudder. I'd lived my life as an addict, so I didn't have the skills to navigate my new world. It worked for a while, but when I went to college, I was seduced by achievement. My competitive nature led me astray, and to cope with my new demands, I over-committed – I was back in the rat race.

Instead of being present, I projected into the future. Instead of feeling light and easy, my body felt tight and heavy. Instead of meditating, I spent all my time studying. I even stopped reading the books I had found in detox, the ones that reminded me how to live.

That's when I thought about my relapse. Until then, I hadn't even considered it a relapse. I belittled it in comparison to my old habit, but over the past four months it had been building momentum. I was taking up to three boxes a week, switching between Solpadeine and Nurofen Plus. I had even set up a system to buy them from different pharmacies so they wouldn't get suspicious. I had a list of about twenty, and I'd alternate between them so I didn't look like an addict.

I was back to my old tricks, too, taking tablets from Friday to Sunday, then skipping a few days to avoid physical addiction – sound familiar? How did I miss this? I was shocked. I visited pharmacies all over Dublin and even memorised their opening hours. Several pharmacies had stopped serving me, including Roselawn, the one where I bought my first box. They saw right through me, but I refused to see the truth and cursed them for what they were implying.

The reality was, I hadn't relapsed on drugs. I had relapsed on anxiety and overthinking. That was the real problem. Just like before, the tablets were just a symptom – my mind was the real issue.

Floored by this sudden realisation, I felt a deep sense of loss and fear. I was still gazing at the giant sequoias, but in that moment, a sense of purpose, resolve and determination surged through my body. I needed to act and my response was swift.

I was top of my class at the time, with a promising career in academia ahead of me, but I didn't care. In my mind, college was the problem, and even though I had stopped taking the tablets with relative ease, I felt I had no choice but to leave. My initial plan was to go to Asia, possibly Nepal, to meditate for a few months. However, I quickly realised that chasing what I had lost was not the solution. That was addict behaviour. I had to leave college, though, to protect myself from my competitive nature – of that I was sure.

I had all but made up my mind, and I began looking at alternatives, but something was telling me to slow down. I couldn't trust myself any more. I needed a second opinion. I chatted to friends and family, without telling them about the tablets – I didn't want to worry them. Everyone told me to stay in college. However, they were the ones who thought I shouldn't have gone to college in the first place. I needed an objective opinion, from someone who wasn't so close.

I'd read a book the previous year by a guy called Steve Taylor. Steve, whose book was about perspective shifts, was a senior psychology lecturer at Leeds Beckett University. He was also associated with Eckhart Tolle, whose books touched me deeply when I found recovery.

I don't know what possessed me – maybe it was my good old ego again, or the fear of falling back into addiction – but I decided to reach out to Steve. I found his email address on his college website and sent him a message seeking advice for my situation. I'd kept my addiction and anxiety hidden for years. At times, I even kept it from myself. I never sought help because I was afraid of what people might think, but I didn't feel like that any more. I recognised the loop I was in, even if it had taken a little longer than I expected, and I told Steve everything.

I fully believed Steve would get back to me, and sure enough, he did. He suggested I should stay in college, as long as I put my wellbeing first. In his experience, academia can provide a great balance between life and career, and he was a shining example of that. It made me think that college might not be the problem – maybe it was something else.

As I reflected on Steve's email, it suddenly became clear. 'The only Zen you'll find at the top of a mountain is the Zen you bring up with you.' This quote, by Robert M. Pirsig, is one of my favourites. It resonated with me deeply, but until now I didn't know why. It was trying to speak to me, to tell me I could not run away from my problems. If I ran off to Asia, I'd be bringing those issues with me. College was not the problem – the problem was in me. Just like that, my mind was made up. I would stay in college, but my mental health would come first.

After the summer exams, I directed all my focus towards my mental, spiritual and emotional wellbeing. I began reading again, all my old favourites. I developed a consistent meditation practice, with a focus on self-observation because of my keen talent for self-deception. I spent more time in nature and more quality time with family and friends. I didn't want to worry my family about my relapse, but I told them how I was feeling, and how I had lost sight of what was important – just so they'd keep me in check. I also started journalling, regularly writing about my thoughts, feelings and behaviours.

My new journalling practice helped me to become more reflective, and I began wondering what other habits might help me to navigate my life better. I kept coming across books and podcasts on personal growth and self-development, but if they weren't Zen-related, or based on something I had learned in detox, I usually glossed over them. That's when I realised I wasn't practising open-mindedness, something I placed great value on. Maybe it was time to start reading further afield?

That's when Tim Ferriss popped up on my radar. Tim is an author and self-development guru from the US, but his podcast is what caught my attention first. The aim of the podcast is to tease out the habits and tactics of world-class performers so you can apply them in your own life. I couldn't believe my luck. It was exactly what I was looking for.

As well as topics I was familiar with, such as meditation and self-awareness, the podcast covered subjects such as happiness, productivity and decision-making. It opened up a whole new world to me. Meditation was a popular topic, and I was amazed by how many of his guests – about eight per cent – practised it regularly.

Over the following year, I devoured these podcasts as if my life depended on it. I noticed my obsessive nature kicking in again, so I kept a watchful eye on that. Tim would ask guests about their favourite books, so that was my new addiction – I began consuming self-development books by the truckload, and these would direct me towards other books. I could live with this addiction.

From these books, I began taking notes on the tools and tactics that resonated most. I would then implement them in my own life, and if they worked, they made it into a programme I was developing. I also reflected on the practices I learned in early recovery, and these provided the foundations for the programme.

At first, I was developing this programme for myself, to help me navigate my own life, but the more tools I collected, and the more the programme took shape, I began to realise that it could be of huge value to others.

The programme is vast, but several threads run consistently through it. The first part centres on why we suffer and how to break free, with a focus on building self-awareness. The second part focuses on reducing stress and anxiety by simplifying life. It includes a variety of tools, such as self-observation techniques, mindfulness and mindset change strategies, as well as tactics to boost your energy, find your life purpose, recognise negative thought patterns and successfully navigate the relationships in your life.

The programme also highlights the importance of goals, purpose and values, and how they can guide our decisions. I've developed several tactics for making better decisions, which have had a tremendous impact on my life. I put all of these tools together like pieces of a jigsaw puzzle and kept the shapes that fit, and soon enough, they formed a complete picture: my new 'programme for life'.

* * *

Before my second-year summer exams, and my realisation that I was back in the rat race, Yvonne told me she was moving to Ghent University in Belgium. I was still obsessed with academia at this stage, and I could see my life going in only one direction. I wanted to do my PhD with Yvonne, for both personal and professional reasons, so this threw a spanner in the works. She told me it was possible for me to do a PhD in Ghent, but I needed to get my master's first.

That same month, Professor Rob Whelan, a former student of Maynooth who worked with Yvonne, came to the college to give a talk. Rob was based in Trinity College Dublin, and his work centred on addiction. He was very impressive, so after the talk I asked him if I could be his research assistant for the summer. He was a little surprised by my brazenness, but he gave me an interview and agreed to take me on.

I worked with Rob for two days a week during the summer of 2016. I must have done a good job, because he asked me if I wanted to do my PhD with him. I told him about my plans for Ghent, so he was happy to take me on for a research master's. It was a perfect fit, except for one thing: it cost €10,000. I didn't have that kind of money, and a master's in the Netherlands was only €2,000, so that looked like my only option.

I told Rob I couldn't afford it, so he suggested I should apply for a scholarship with the Irish Research Council. It would cover the €10,000 for the course, and pay a further €16,000 so I wouldn't have to work and I could focus on my research. There was a catch, of course. These scholarships are prestigious and highly difficult to attain. It would require a lot of work, which wouldn't usually put me off, but after recent events, I needed to focus on my wellbeing.

That's when Paul, one of my gym buddies, told me to forget about the Netherlands. He said: 'Apply for the scholarship, and if you don't get it, I'll look after it.' I couldn't believe it, and I'll be forever grateful for this act of kindness. I thought, 'Why not?' and applied for the scholarship.

The final year of my degree was a fine balance between acquiring the grades I wanted and keeping myself mentally fit. My wellbeing was top priority, always. But my grades didn't get worse, they got better. I was calmer, more focused and more driven than ever before. But unlike the previous year, when I had over-committed, there was a flow to it. I was calm and stress-free. I was back on bonus time.

The year flew by, light and easy, and I loved helping other students who were struggling with their degree. Despite my competitive nature, I had helped others from day one (mostly because I prefer to compete with myself rather than other people), but now I was really enjoying it.

On 27 March 2017, I was working on an assignment in the library. When I checked my email, there was a message from the Irish Research Council. This was it, the results of my scholarship application, the moment of truth. I was far more nervous than I thought I would be, and my heart began pounding out of my chest. The email was short and to the point. 'That can't be good,' I thought.

Dear Brian,

This email is to notify you that your application (GOIPG/2017/21) to the 2017 Government of Ireland Postgraduate Scholarship Programme **has been recommended for funding**.

I had scored 92.5, way above the required cut-off. I couldn't believe it – I was ecstatic. Then, out of nowhere, came a warning from within: 'Be careful. What makes you happy, the lack of it will make you sad.'

You've got to celebrate your wins in life, but this was a wise message. I'd read about the pendulum effect – what goes up must come down – in several books, especially the *Tao Te Ching*. I'd been up and down my entire life. I began to wonder how I might have felt if the email was bad news. As much as I'd like to deny it, I would have been devastated. My pounding heart was proof of that. I was sick of swinging on the pendulum, and finally wanted balance in my life, so I was delighted to see my practice paying dividends. In the end, catching my reaction in full flow made me happier than winning the award.

I finished college in the summer of 2017, winning several awards, including the W.J. Smyth Prize for finishing top of my class, the Carmel Staunton award for best dissertation, and, best of all, a fully funded IRC scholarship for my master's. I'm proud of these awards, but I'm more proud of how I achieved them. I wasn't the most intelligent in the class, not by a long shot, but I was strategic, passionate, hardworking and driven, and to see these traits pay off was rewarding. More than that, however, it was my mindset – positive mental wellbeing – that allowed me to perform at such a level.

I had gone from falling asleep mid-sentence at an important work meeting to achieving something that I would have thought impossible in my heroin days. Instead of numbing my mind with opiates, I was focusing on expanding it. Instead of spending my evenings drinking vodka, I was focusing on self-care. Instead of trembling with anxiety in bed, I was launching myself into the world. The detox, the seizures and the hardship – it felt like they were all worth it to get to where I was now.

* * *

I officially started in Trinity College Dublin on 1 October 2017. Within a month, I was presenting my research to a room full of professors, doctors and PhD students. Like most people, I was terrified of public speaking. Apart from a one-off mock session in my second year of college, I had no experience whatsoever. There were only four other students in the room for the mock session, and I failed miserably. It was the closest I had come to panic since my days as an addict. That's why I was surprised to find myself enjoying this speaking experience – another perk of my practice, I realised.

The meeting was challenging, with lots of difficult questions, but I handled it well. Again, it was down to my practice. As luck would have it, Louise McHugh, a professor from University College Dublin (UCD), was also in the room. She seemed impressed with my knowledge of the neuroscience of mindfulness, and offered me a chance to lecture in UCD. After pinching myself to see if it was real, I immediately agreed. Although it paid ten times the amount I got for doing deliveries, I didn't care about the money. I would be a university lecturer, and that's what appealed to me most – plus I wouldn't have to wear a dickie bow!

Around the same time, a friend from college, Ciara, asked if I'd be interested in doing a talk at St Aidan's, an all-boys secondary school where she now worked. I'd never spoken to a group about my programme before, but I immediately said yes. If I could plant a seed with even one kid, it would be worth it.

There were hundreds of kids in the room, and despite my fear of public speaking, and the fact that it was my first public talk, it went well. But the response is what I remember most. A few of the kids, as well as several teachers, sought me out after the talk and told me it was a message they needed to hear. But there was one young kid in particular – a second-year student – who made a huge impact on me. Full of excitement, he walked straight up to me and said: 'I'm going to do that. I'm going to do that. I'm definitely going to do that. Thank you so much.' He reminded me of how I felt when I stumbled across these tools, and the energy of his appreciation told me that he would put them into action.

The fulfilment I felt from that interaction has never left me, and I've been trying to share my message ever since. In that very moment, I found my purpose in life – to show people that change is possible. For that, I owe that kid a debt of gratitude.

I soon wanted to share my message in schools everywhere, but there was one big problem – nobody knew who I was. I sent emails to several schools and colleges around Dublin, but I didn't get a response. Without a profile, for all they knew I could have been recruiting for a cult.

That's when Michelle, my former supervisor, asked me to speak to her students. She was now lecturing at the National College of Ireland (NCI) and believed they would benefit from my message.

With two talks under my belt, UCD and St Aidan's, I felt like a seasoned pro. I've always been a big believer in myself, regardless of the task, so I strolled into the college that day, cocky as hell.

Michelle brought me to the room ten minutes before the talk. It was a large auditorium, nothing like I'd experienced before, and I began feeling quite anxious. 'What's going on?' I thought. 'This doesn't happen to me any more.' I tried to calm myself with breathing techniques, but it felt like my body and mind were singing different tunes. I then tried a few positive affirmations, telling myself to relax. Unfortunately for me, my body wasn't interested.

Michelle had told everyone, including other psychology lecturers, about my talk, and as they filed into the room, the anxiety began building. I tried every tool I could think of, but the fear had taken hold. I couldn't get my bearings, and I started to panic.

It was nearly time, and as Michelle was introducing me, it suddenly dawned on me: I could have a panic attack while talking about mindfulness and tools to cope with anxiety. With that, Michelle said my name and I took to the stage. The auditorium was packed, and as I scanned around me, trying to look relaxed, every eyeball in the room was glaring into mine.

Like lasers, they shredded my carefree persona, as the truth was beginning to unravel right before their eyes.

My worst fears were about to come true. I tried to focus on my intro, but my mind went blank. I tried to speak anyway, but my mouth felt like sandpaper. I looked for my bottle of water, but I had left it in Michelle's office. My body began to shake. Beads of sweat were forming on my forehead. I hadn't experienced one in years, but I could feel it coming – I was about to have a panic attack.

I'm not sure what happened next, but suddenly I was looking at myself from above, as if I had physically stepped outside my own body. I don't know where the voice came from, but the words were wise: 'Wow, you're about to have a panic attack. But don't worry. You'll be okay. You just need to name it and own it. Tell everyone exactly what's going on, and ask Michelle to get you some water.'

With that, I came back into my body. I asked Michelle to get me some water and began telling everyone about what I'd just experienced, how my daily self-observation practice had helped me, right before their eyes. Instead of getting overwhelmed, I went into observer mode, and I was able to pull myself out of it. I also spoke about my fears, how I was afraid that Mr Mindfulness was going to have a panic attack on stage. It was one of my most authentic and powerful talks, and one of Michelle's students later described it as life-changing. Just like the kid in St Aidan's, it was thrilling to hear that my message was having such a positive impact.

I've done far bigger venues in the years that followed, but ever since that day, my fear of public speaking has disappeared.

Not because I don't get anxious – I still do; it's natural, after all. But now, if it does happen, I know I can observe it and let it pass. And if it does take hold, I can use it as an opportunity to teach a lesson in action.

***

Later that year, I received a grant from Trinity College to present my master's research at a world conference in Montreal. It was a big deal at the time, and I was super excited to speak at the event. I hadn't been to Canada since the authorities deported my family over thirty years earlier, but I didn't think they'd hold a grudge against a five-year-old, so I wasn't expecting any issues.

It was a four-day event, and I was set to do two talks. I was ecstatic when I set out that morning, but when I arrived at the airport, they asked me for my Electronic Travel Authorization (eTA). 'My what?' I said. 'You can't travel to Canada without an eTA,' the guy at the check-in told me, 'but don't worry, it's an automated service. It only takes twenty minutes to get approved.'

Luckily for me, I was early for the flight, so I went to a coffee shop and completed the form on my laptop. I waited thirty minutes and went back up to the desk. The guy seemed surprised that the approval hadn't come through. He told me to give it another twenty minutes. I waited patiently, but when he checked it again, it was still the same. I was expecting him to give me another option, but he just said, 'Sorry, you can't get on the plane without an eTA.'

I was stunned, and I could feel the anger building inside of me. But then something amazing happened: I observed it rising before it got out of control. In that moment, I quickly realised that no amount of anger or whining would change the situation. Instead of exploding, I stood there smiling at my ability to catch my negative energy in full flight. I thanked the guy for his help, jumped into a taxi and made my way home. I was disappointed, of course, so when I got home, I sent a few emails to the Canadian authorities. I also contacted my professor as I was supposed to meet him over there.

I waited for the authorities to get back to me, but there were no emails that night. I was definitely going to miss my first talk, but I was hoping for better luck in the morning. There were two emails in my inbox when I woke up. The first said that my eTA was approved, but the second, from the Canadian government, said something very different. Apparently, they did hold grudges against five-year-old children:

> Your application does not meet the requirements of the Immigration and Refugee Protection Regulations (IRPR), and as per A52(1), because a removal order has been enforced, a foreign national shall not return to Canada unless authorized by an officer.

I decided to ignore the second email and get another flight to Montreal, hoping my eTA approval would get me through. I could still catch my second talk if I got a flight that day. I got a loan of €1,300 off my parents for a new flight, and five hours later I was in the air. I was so happy when I landed in Montreal, but my ordeal was not yet over. As I went through passport control, an immigration officer pulled me aside. She brought me to a small room and began asking questions. There was no point in lying, so I told her about my deportation as a five-year-old, joking about the dangers I must have presented to the state. She was very nice, and we had a laugh about it, but she was also blunt: 'I'm afraid you don't have many options here. We're going to have to send you straight back to Ireland.'

As we waited for her colleague, she asked me why I was so calm. I told her about my experience in Dublin airport. I then told her about my life in addiction, how meditation had provided the foundations of my recovery and how I was in Montreal to speak about these topics at a world conference. 'If I get stressed out about it, what does that say about my beliefs?' I said with a smile. She smiled back and, to my astonishment, replied: 'I shouldn't be doing this, so make sure you keep a low profile.' With that, she stamped my ticket and told me to go through the gate. I couldn't believe it. The fruits of my practice, the ability to observe and respond instead of reacting emotionally, got me into Canada. I thanked her profusely and went on my merry way.

When I put my neuroscience hat on and think about what happened in Montreal, it blows my mind. Our brains are like plastic, or playdough, and they are constantly being shaped by new experiences. I spent my youth scanning the environment for threats, so I turned my brain into a well-oiled anxiety machine. It's the same for any negative feelings, thoughts and emotions. Whatever you rest your mind upon, be it anger, self-doubt or fear, your brain will eventually take that shape.

I was easily overwhelmed before I got clean – it was my default. Daniel Goleman calls this emotional hijacking, where the fear centre of my brain screamed like a siren. That's what was happening on the stage in NCI. That's what was happening when I was first told I couldn't get onto the plane for Montreal.

However, the plastic brain can also work for you. Thanks to meditation, I have literally shrunk the fear centre of my brain. Stressful events still challenge me, but I am no longer hijacked by my emotions. Instead of having a panic attack in NCI, or losing the plot in Dublin airport, I was able to catch these negative emotions in full flight. That's how I nailed the talk in NCI. That's why the immigration officer let me into Montreal for my talk. I'm now more aware, focused and calmer than ever before, and through consistent meditation practice, it's not even a struggle – it's my new default.

*** *** ***

As 2017 ended, I was growing disillusioned with the world of academia. There were many reasons for this, but the big one was how the system that governs science is riddled with political and ego-driven problems. Not to mention the issues around methods and statistics. I naively believed it would make more sense over time, but it didn't. The more I learned, the worse it became.

My own master's research didn't help matters. It was part of a larger study, so Rob set me up with a more experienced researcher to help me with the finer details. This turned out to be more of a hindrance than a help, and at Christmas that year I had to start my project again. I'd lost three full months, but at least now I was the master of my own fate, and things began moving quickly.

In hindsight, that experience played a key role in my disillusionment with academia. With my hands tied, it gave me time to reflect on the nature of my project. Instead of studying the human mind, which is what I had set out to do, I was spending my time creating code and analysing data. It was good science, and highly informative research, but it didn't translate to the real world or my own experiences, which was my original reason for going to college.

I started to question where my future lay, and it seemed clear. Combined with my newfound love of public speaking, I wanted to help others with their suffering, especially young people. For me, academia was not the way to do it. Sharing my programme was.

I had a big decision to make. The previous summer, I'd given up on Ghent and applied for another IRC scholarship to do my PhD in Trinity College with Rob. The question was: did I want to do a PhD? The results of the scholarship wouldn't be available until April, four months away, so I decided to delay my decision until then.

I'd been dreaming of a life in academia since detox, but with my interest now waning, 2018 was full of uncertainty. I should have been concerned, but I wasn't. In fact, I was incredibly excited. An energy was building, a beautiful energy. I could feel it in my bones. This was going to be my year.

WONDERFULLY WEIRD

'In the end, we only regret the chances we didn't take.'

LEWIS CARROLL

19 FEBRUARY 2018

was both excited and nervous as I drove to Dundalk. I was meeting John Boyle, one of the wealthiest and most successful men in Ireland, but this was uncharted territory for me, and I had no idea how it was going to go.

My research told me little about John. He was the founder of BoyleSports, a self-made millionaire and he didn't drink, but that's all I knew. When I arrived at the company's headquarters, my excitement grew, but so did my apprehension.

I'd met another successful businessman two weeks before, one of the wealthiest in Ireland, and based on that meeting, I'd be lucky to get twenty minutes with John. I wanted to make a good impression, but I also wanted to make it count – hence my unease. The receptionist was expecting me, and we had a lovely chat while I was waiting. 'You'll love John,' she said. 'He's a wonderful human being.' Her kind words helped me to relax.

John appeared a few minutes later. He was composed, confident and self-assured – what you'd expect from a leader – but there was something else. He had a serenity and a stillness about him, which immediately put me at ease.

'Come on,' he said, 'I know a nice place for coffee.' I felt strangely relaxed as I jumped into his car, and quickly realised I was getting more than twenty minutes. I began thinking of more good questions to ask, but before I got a chance, John jumped in:

'What date is your birthday?'

'April the sixth,' I told him, a little confused.

'No, your new birthday,' he said.

I instinctively knew what he meant. 'The eighth of October,' I told him proudly.

'Mine is September the twenty-third,' he said.

I couldn't believe my luck. John was in recovery too, and had been for thirty-seven years. This was going to be a great chat.

Ten minutes later, we arrived at a large, homely café, parked ourselves in a quiet corner and began chatting about recovery. John is a spiritual man, and I quickly realised we had a lot in common. He was big into meditation and personal development. We read all the same books. And it was clear that he took care of his physical health.

The next few hours gave me some of the most insightful moments of my life. John was keen to answer my questions, so I bombarded him with everything I had. Gems of wisdom came flying back, and I soaked them up like a sponge. Several things he said resonated deeply, but the main message I took was this:

'If you keep it simple, anything is possible.' I have carried that lesson with me ever since.

Before we left, John said something that I will never forget. 'Do you know what you're doing, Brian? Do you know why you're sitting here right now?' I shook my head. 'You've been given a gift, a second chance at life. You're living on bonus time.'

* * *

During one school talk, I noticed that only some of the students were listening to me. I figured that the ones who were listening were the students who struggled with anxiety or who were impacted by addiction. But the others, the ones who switched off, must have wondered what some former heroin addict could teach them about life.

I wanted to grab everyone's attention, because whether they knew it or not, they would all experience challenges at some stage in life, especially in today's crazy world.

When I was speaking at Blackrock College on their addiction awareness day, it dawned on me. If I was a famous rugby player giving tips on life, everyone would be listening, even – or especially – the sports jocks. That got me thinking. If I could share my own tools for life, as well as those from high performers in areas such as business and sport, it would make my talks far more powerful, especially to impressionable young teenagers.

That's when I remembered Tim Ferriss's book *Tribe of Mentors*. Struggling with his own issues, Tim reached out to his dream list of interviewees and asked them the questions he couldn't answer himself. My situation was a little different, but the idea provided me with a solution to my problem: I needed a tribe of my own.

So I set out to interview Ireland's top performers with the aim of bringing their life advice to the kids in the classrooms. I didn't know where to begin or how to contact them, so I started with people in the corporate world, guessing their email addresses based on their corresponding company websites.

I wasn't sure what to write either, so I simply wrote from the heart. Over eighty per cent of these corporate leaders responded to the email, and I got interviews with each and every one.

I wasn't concerned about those who didn't respond – another perk of bonus time. The way I figured, if they saw the email and weren't interested, it was a good thing. It stopped me wasting their time and them wasting mine. One of my favourite life lessons came about as I reflected on this: 'Be true to your wonderfully weird self. You'll attract what you need and repel what you don't.'

John Boyle was my second interviewee, and he set the tone for what followed. Anne Heraty, founder of Cpl, Ireland's largest recruitment agency, was the next. She was incredibly welcoming and invited me to a leadership conference several weeks later. Carolan Lennon, CEO of Eir, Ireland's largest communications company, was equally amazing, inviting me to speak to her staff at the company headquarters.

As a thank you, I told each of my interviewees that I'd love to share my message at their local school. Corporate talks weren't even on my radar at the time, so I was quite surprised when several of the CEOs asked me to speak to their staff. Eir was my first big corporate talk; little did I know that it was the start of a new career.

My initial reason for reaching out – to capture the attention of switched-off kids – was still the primary goal, but this bold move grew legs of its own.

***

In April 2018, the results of my new IRC scholarship application landed in my inbox. Although the application was far superior to my successful master's application, the selection process can be finicky, so I was still nervous. This was a three-year scholarship worth €76,000, so that didn't help my nerves. As I opened the email, it looked familiar: 'You have been recommended for funding ...' They had awarded me another scholarship.

It's a great achievement in itself, and I was delighted that the hard work had paid off, but I still wasn't sure if I wanted to do a PhD. My research would explore the impact of mindfulness on people in early recovery from addiction. This was real-world stuff, and something that excited me, but there was a huge downside. Rob's lab, where I planned to do my PhD, put a huge emphasis on advanced statistical analysis. I'd be sitting in an office creating code and crunching data for the best part of three years. It didn't inspire me.

In contrast, sharing my programme with people made me feel alive. The dilemma was that completing a PhD would provide me with amazing opportunities to share my programme in the long run. People listen to those in authority, and 'Dr Pennie' carries a lot more weight than 'Brian, the former heroin addict who went back to college'.

I had a big decision to make, a life-changing decision. I battled with it for several months, and I was coming up with different answers several times a day. My heart was telling me to go all in on the talks, but my head was telling me to do the PhD.

Upon deep reflection, and some sound advice from others, I decided to do my PhD, but it had to be something that inspired me, not drain me. I also needed the freedom to continue with my school talks, so I needed to be strategic.

I couldn't do that with my current PhD proposal, so there was only one thing to do. I couldn't believe I was even considering it. I was going to reject my scholarship and do a PhD on my own. My friends and family thought I was mad, but my gut was screaming 'Do it!', and I knew it was the right call.

Without funding, however, I'd have to pay for the PhD myself – €30,000 over three years. That meant I'd have to get a part-time job. The thought of doing deliveries again was even more unappealing than sitting in a lab crunching data.

I was seriously conflicted, and in all the confusion, I began to doubt myself. 'Maybe I should just do what everyone says,' I thought. 'They can't all be wrong.' With the acceptance date looming, I was out of time, and I decided to accept the scholarship.

It felt like I was betraying myself. Every fibre of my being was telling me I was wrong. Accepting the scholarship was going against everything I stood for. Bonus time allowed me to take risks, embrace failure and act boldly, but this felt like I was taking the easy way out.

That's when I had a stroke of luck. There were about twenty people in Rob's lab, including research assistants, PhD students and doctors from a variety of disciplines, mostly neuroscience and psychology. Based in the Lloyd building, we were moving to a brand new office space. With no expense spared, the move felt exciting. 'Maybe three years here won't be that bad,' I thought.

My luck came in the form of a lab meeting to discuss the rules of the new office. There was nothing out of the ordinary until somebody proposed that the room should be non-speaking. I thought it was a joke at first, but it wasn't, and several others thought it was a good idea too. I jokingly asked: 'So can we not say hello to each other in the morning?' I was expecting a 'don't be silly', but instead someone asked me, 'What do you want to do, say hello to everyone?' I was blown away and simply responded, 'No, I just want to be human.' Here I was, post-Aiséirí, nearly five years into recovery, and I was being asked to sign another silent contract. But this time I had a choice, and I wasn't going to sign on the dotted line.

Although I got on great with the people in the lab, I never felt I belonged. I was too loud, I loved to talk, and I'm not one to shy away from a good distraction. In truth, this kind of behaviour doesn't belong in an academic office, and neither did I. This was the confirmation I needed, but it only made things worse. How could I stay in an office where I felt I didn't belong? In the end, it was simple.

In the months before this, I had come across a line by an American writer called Derek Sivers: 'If it's not a hell yeah, it's a no.' As soon as I heard it, it became one of my mantras for making decisions. Generally speaking, if I have a decision to make and my gut is screaming 'hell yeah', I do it. If it's not, I don't. Working in a non-speaking office wasn't a hell yeah, it was a hell no.

As well as reflecting on this, I used another decision-making tool from my programme. It's based on a mantra first used by the Great Britain rowing team at the 2000 Sydney Olympics. In the run-up to the games, when faced with a decision, they asked themselves: 'Will this make our boat go faster?' The answer to their question determined their decision. For example, if they were asked to go out for drinks, they would use this mantra to guide their decision. In this case, it's unlikely that a few drinks would have made their boat go faster – so the answer would be 'No'.

Taking this mantra, I developed a metaphorical boat of my own. It helps me to make decisions based on my values, purpose and goals. My goals were my PhD, speaking in schools and sharing my programme. My purpose was to show people, through my programme, that change is possible. My values are extensive, but they include boldness, having fun, compassion, sharing and inner peace.

I asked myself: 'Does taking the scholarship and working in a silent office make my boat go faster?' Besides helping me with my PhD, the answer was a big fat no. There was only one thing to do – reject the scholarship.

I met with Rob the following week and told him I was turning down the scholarship. Understandably, he wasn't happy, but Rob is an amazing supervisor, and a great human being, so he understood my concerns.

It wasn't going to be easy, but I would find a way to fund my PhD. The research part was not a problem, however. I was going to stick with the primary study of my previous proposal – a mindfulness intervention for people in early recovery. The Rutland Centre, a treatment facility for addiction, kindly agreed to host the study, and Barry Costello, an addiction specialist and mindfulness trainer who worked in the Rutland Centre, generously agreed to conduct the interventions. This was an amazing opportunity to conduct real-life research, so I wanted to keep this as the main part of my new PhD.

I was still working with Rob to complete my master's, and when I told him about my other new ideas for the PhD, ones that were close to my heart, his interest surprised me. Rob is a hard-core neuroscientist, a statistical genius and a brilliant researcher, so I knew he was interested in the Rutland study – he helped me design it, after all – but I thought my new ideas would be too fluffy and personal for him. I was wrong. 'You can still take the scholarship and do those studies with me if you want,' he said. 'You're still doing the primary section of the proposal, so it won't be an issue.'

I was shocked. I didn't even realise this was an option. I told him I'd be delighted to do it with him, but I had huge reservations over the non-speaking office. I needed to work outside the lab, and he was fine with that too. I'd put a tremendous amount of work into my master's, and never let him down, so he knew I could deliver. This arrangement also gave me the freedom to work on other projects, such as my talks in schools. This was important – it was my mission. My PhD was simply a small piece of that puzzle.

I couldn't believe my luck. By following my heart, sticking to my guns and using the tools in my programme, everything fell into place. I was doing a PhD that I loved. I wasn't going to be crunching data for the next three years. And I had the freedom to work on other projects that were part of my life purpose. The risk paid off, boldness paid off, and as a result, extraordinary opportunities began falling at my feet, including a chance to write this book and an amazing opportunity to teach in Trinity College Dublin.

Professor Jo-Hanna Ivers, the researcher I met in detox, and the one who helped me to believe I might not be brain damaged, was developing a new course in Trinity College. Jo-Hanna was also the person who helped me to realise my college dreams, and now, five years after handing me one of my favourite books, *Buddha's Brain*, she was asking me to teach the neuroscience section of her new addiction course. I had to pinch myself. I'd come full circle and it felt amazing.

* * *

My determination to make the most of bonus time led to many connections, and although putting myself out there was both exciting and terrifying, it paid off in spades. One such connection was Mick Slein, founder of ROBUS LED Group.

I met Mick for the first time in Clontarf Castle and we hit it off immediately. Mick was fascinated by my mission, but he also wanted to help me on a personal level. He invited me to speak at his company, connected me with so many people that I've lost count and regularly offers advice as I strive to build my career.

Mick also introduced me to Bernard Byrne, who at the time was CEO of AIB, one of Ireland's largest banks. Like all my interviews, it was a brilliant experience, but there was something else about our conversation. As it turned out, Bernard loved how I took full accountability for my life. He felt strongly about this topic. When the interview was over, I told him I'd like to speak at a school of his choice as a thank you. He said he'd think about it, and off I went.

I had a feeling we'd be talking again soon, and I was right. Within a few weeks, Bernard invited me back for another meeting. Like Mick, he believed in my mission. He also wanted to help me with my career and invited me to speak to his team at AIB headquarters. It would be my third corporate talk, but a far different proposition from the others. His team included all the leading executives at the bank. Having never seen me speak, he was also putting huge faith in me. I didn't want to let him down, and the thought of it was nerve-racking, but I jumped at the opportunity.

I asked Bernard what topics I should cover, and he simply replied, 'Just be your usual uncensored self.' I took that as a huge compliment, and that's what I aimed to do. He loved my message of taking full responsibility for your actions, so I thought it best to base the talk around that.

A week before the event, I met with his staff to discuss details of the talk. It was far bigger than I thought. I knew the leading executives would be attending, but there were over a hundred people expected on the day. On top of that, they were recording it to make it available to all ten thousand employees.

My anxiety was building as I spoke to Susan, the person who was organising the event. I don't know whether it was belief, stupidity or delusion – I think they are all closely related – but I felt I could pull it off. That was until I did a full dress rehearsal the night before the talk. The room was intimidating, and there was even a proper stage. Susan advised me to rehearse the entire thing, word for word, but it was a disaster. I kept forgetting my lines, and I felt completely out of my comfort zone. Susan was amazing, though; she must have been worried, but she didn't show it, and just kept telling me I'd be great on the day.

Despite the dress rehearsal fiasco, I still felt confident about nailing the talk. Yes, I was out of my comfort zone. Yes, I was under pressure. But unlike my degree, when I relapsed, or my talk in NCI, when I had a near panic attack, this pressure was different. With the help of my programme, I had tools at my disposal that could catch anxiety before it took hold. This gave me an incredible sense of self-belief, as well as the confidence to know I could pull it off.

On 13 February 2019, I arrived at AIB HQ for my big talk. I got there twenty minutes early, and as I sat in my car, my nerves began to jangle. I practised my self-observation techniques, which worked to an extent, but this was their biggest challenge by far. Waves of anxiety flowed through my body, and my chest began to tighten – my old adversary.

I tried to observe these bodily sensations, without letting them consume me, but they were powerful. 'Can I really do this?' I asked myself. Thank goodness for my practice, because I caught my self-doubt in full flight and immediately fought back. 'Of course you can do this, and if you do forget your lines, so what?

You shouldn't even be alive, never mind getting an opportunity like this. You're living on bonus time – embrace it.' With that, the nerves lifted, and I walked into AIB HQ.

Apparently, Bernard was not in the habit of inviting staff members to talks, so there was a sense of intrigue in the air. He sought me out before the talk, and told me they had kept the topic under wraps. No one knew who I was or what I would be talking about. They'd advertised it as 'Change Is Possible' and that's all anyone knew. 'People are quite excited,' he told me. Should this have made me nervous? I'm not sure. But it didn't. It was thrilling. And Bernard's confidence in me was energising.

It was finally time. Bernard took to the stage first. He addressed the crowd, talking about future events at AIB, and then introduced me. 'I now want to introduce Brian. He has a fascinating story and a powerful message. I think we can all learn something from it.'

By now, my heart was pounding a million miles an hour, but there was no backing out. In my flat Dublin accent, I began: 'You might be wondering what I do, what I'm about or, more important, how the hell I got the opportunity to speak here today. As I stand here, especially now, I'm wondering the very same thing myself. The fact is, I know nothing about banking. I know very little about the corporate world. But what I do have is a unique set of experiences and life skills, and that's what I want to talk about today.'

It was a nervy start, but I didn't forget my lines, and it wasn't long before I got into a flow. I quickly told the audience how I boldly reached out to the top CEOs in the country, and that's how I was here today. Before I knew it, I was cracking jokes about stalking Russell Brand for an interview. I even looked into the camera to tell him I was coming after him. I couldn't believe it. I was in my element, cracking jokes in front of all these top execs, and not only were they laughing, I felt completely at home.

Ten minutes into the talk, just when they didn't expect it, I hit the clicker to reveal my before and after addiction pictures on a huge screen behind me. 'That's me on the left,' I said, 'two years before I hit rock bottom after fifteen years of chronic heroin addiction.' You could have heard a pin drop. The energy in the room was intense. I proceeded to tell them about the fire extinguisher incident, how it helped me to break free from my demons, and then I told them about the tools I've since used to thrive in recovery. When I finished the talk, I got an incredible ovation, and from that very moment, I knew this was something I wanted to do for the rest of my life.

Maybe it was my before and after pictures that triggered me, but as I sat in my sitting room that evening, the same room where I'd spat blood onto the wooden floor, I began reflecting on how far I'd come.

Addiction stole my spirit, but now I had never felt more alive. Addiction robbed me of my health, but now I was stronger than ever before. Addiction jerked me around like a puppet, but now I was the one pulling the strings. Addiction blinded me from my feelings, but now I embraced them as if my life depended on it.

I realised that addiction had thrown the kitchen sink at me but I'd flipped everything on its head. 'No matter what comes my way, especially in sobriety, I can turn it into a positive,' I thought, exhilarated by my realisation.

I then began reflecting on my greatest adversary. Before that fateful day with the fire extinguisher, anxiety was my master, but now I just watched it float by. Even when anxiety, or any troubling feeling for that matter, took me by surprise, I could catch it in its tracks before it took hold.

The elation didn't last, however, and I soon found myself pondering the loneliness of my former life. Addiction is a solitary endeavour, and I had isolated myself from anyone who was ever close. I hadn't thought about this before. I had lived a terribly lonely existence. Buying drugs alone. Doing drugs alone. Lying in my bed alone. Nearly everything I did, I did alone. Even when I was around people, I felt alone, trapped in my mind, ensnared in my world of addiction.

But here I was, revelling in the spoils of a huge social victory. I'd sought out connections with strangers, and because they wanted to connect too, amazing opportunities were coming my way. I was only home a few hours and queries about further talks were already landing in my inbox.

More important than connecting with successful professionals, however, I was beginning to reconnect with family and friends. There was still work to do, and bridges to build, but bonus time is a great teacher, and it was finally becoming clear: life is about people.

20

MAGIC AND MIRACLES

'Sobriety is not the opposite of addiction, connection is.'
JOHANN HARI

NOVEMBER 2019

The orange streetlights flicker through the rain-speckled window, illuminating the bedroom walls. There's a young child in the room, peering into the night. He seems lost. The floorboards creak beneath me as I walk towards him, but he doesn't look around. When I get to the window, I can see he is upset, so I decide to join him, and we gaze into the night together.

The child becomes increasingly agitated as cars pass by, so he climbs down from the window and jumps into his bed. He twists and turns under the covers, but before long, he leaps back up to the window and begins to cry.

He doesn't acknowledge me at first, but when I put my hand on his, he looks up. The child is me, seven-year-old me, the one who stared out the window waiting for his parents to come home from the pub, worrying they would never make it home. I reach out and hug him tightly. He squeezes back, and we both feel a sense of release.

I relive this event often – not to punish myself, but to heal my inner-child, the one who was overwhelmed by the trauma in his life. By showing strength now, and telling my younger self, *'Everything is okay, I'll look after you,'* incredible healing takes place. We carry much of our pain in our bodies, and this practice helps me to soften my childhood anguish.

I do this with many painful events from my life, especially the ones that fed my anxiety. My infant self, operated on without an anaesthetic, is the one who needs it most. I used to be blind to this. I used to think of him as an organism, which was part of the detachment I created to distance myself from the pain.

Thanks to psychologist Allison Keating, one of my interviewees, I was able to make sense of my earliest trauma, the one that set the tone for a life of anxiety. My infant self never stopped looking for that anaesthetic, and when I was seventeen years old, I found it in the form of heroin. Heroin provided the numbness I craved since that operation, and it cut me off from my pain. But it did more than that. It cut me off from my feelings, and from the people around me, as I disconnected myself from life.

Just like the child at the window, I sometimes sit with my infant self, cradling him in my arms. I'm strong now, and comfortable in my own skin. I no longer need heroin to escape my pain. And when I sit with this defenceless baby, I let him know everything is going to be okay.

* * *

Reconnecting with my inner-child has not only helped me to heal, it has helped me to see things from other people's perspectives. In doing so, I've been able to forge deeper connections with people. This was a long road, but people being people, I had a lot of help along the way.

On New Year's Eve 2018, Adam Robinson, a person I greatly admire and an amazing thought leader, suggested I journal on this question: 'What parts of your life are converging towards something amazing, and what are they converging towards?'

How times have changed. I wouldn't have been caught dead journalling back in my youth. I didn't even know it was a thing. Instead, eighteen years ago to the day, I was collecting two bags of heroin in a laneway as the New Year rang in. I was planting my flag in the world of heroin, unaware of the path that lay ahead.

I journalled on Adam's question for over an hour that night, dumping my brain onto the pages. Several things jumped out: boldly reaching out to people. Building new relationships. My programme for helping others. My family and friends helping me. Writing and speaking to share my message. Spending time with high-energy people. Happiness, opportunities and growth.

As I dug deeper, and continued to make links between the themes on the page, everything seemed to connect, pointing towards one common thread: 'Life isn't about me, it's about other people.'

It struck me how self-obsessed I'd been. Even in recovery, because of my inability to look at the world through the eyes of others, I hadn't truly connected with anyone, including my family.

Around the same time, Adam sent me a draft of his new book. He had no idea about my struggles with seeing things from others' perspectives. Nor, I imagine, did he know how addiction can turn its victims into self-obsessed 'me' machines. So when he sent me the draft, I couldn't believe how much it related to my current challenges.

His book, called *An Invitation to the Great Game*, is a fictional story about love, magic and everyday miracles. Within this parable are three powerful rules for winning the game of life.

The first rule: whenever possible, connect with others. This lesson highlights how we need to look into people's eyes, create that universal spark and listen attentively.

The second rule: with enthusiasm, create joy and delight for others. In other words, bring happiness, energy and present-moment awareness into your encounters with other people.

The third rule: lean into every moment expecting magic and miracles. This is the one that blew me away. What a way to live.

Following these three rules has had a huge impact on my life. I love creating universal sparks with people. I'm always looking to 'life it up'. And now, every time I meet someone, or an opportunity arises, I lean in expecting magic, and more times than not, the rabbit jumps out of the hat.

***

My aunt Tess passed away on 9 November 2019. She was incredibly brave in her fight against cancer, but what I could not believe, even facing death, was her concern for the wellbeing of others.

In her final days in hospital, at the height of her pain, she had a caring message, and a song, for the entire family. She even had thoughtful words for the nurses and doctors. 'No need to worry about me. I'm ready to go,' she said. 'Just make sure you look after yourselves, you all work too hard.'

When it was time to say goodbye, I wasn't sure what to say, so I just told her how I felt. 'Tess, I'm in awe of you, of how brave you are, and I'm just so thankful that your blood runs in my veins.' She smiled, I kissed her on the cheek, and we said goodbye for the last time.

Before Tess passed, the day she gave me back the letter I had written her in detox, we had an amazing chat about life. On reflection, this conversation was really about connection. Tess was the hub of the family, the one who kept us all united, so she wanted to make sure it stayed that way after she was gone.

She also had such a colourful way with words. 'I love the bones of ye,' she'd often say, but what I remember most from our conversation that day was this: 'You can't cuddle a sofa.' What did she mean? She was reminding me about the importance of people, all people, but especially the people you love. You might be able to wrap your arms around your sofa, or any material item for that matter, but it's not going to hug you back – only people can do that.

Before I left, she told me how proud she was of how I turned my life around. She also asked me to keep a promise: 'After I'm gone, I want you to stay strong for everyone, to stay connected and to be there for the family.' It's a promise I plan to keep.

* * *

They say addiction is a family sport, and eventually everyone gets to play. In my experience, this is true, but thankfully, it's the same for recovery.

Because of its severity, my addiction took centre stage. Like many families in Ireland, however, alcohol was a big issue in ours – but not any more. Recovery shone a light on all of our problems, and although it was tough, we have all come out the other side for the better.

My addiction had a particularly big impact on my mam, and although the memories are still painful for her, she often tells me how proud she is and how happy she is to see how close me, my brothers and sister have become.

I have an amazing relationship with my mam today. When I reflect on how much it's changed, it fills me with joy. Instead of dragging her to drug deals, we go for walks in the park with our pet dog, Frankie. Instead of listening to my lies, we have deep conversations about life. And instead of making her cry, I like to think I make her laugh.

My dad is old-school, but at the same time, he's a big cuddly teddy bear. He was devastated by my addiction, but he was also in denial. Deep down, he knew I was killing myself, but he never gave up on me. My dad would do anything for anybody – it's just his way. I like to think we help each other now. He's even contemplated meditation, and we've had some great chats about catching his road rage in full flight. As a former taxi man, that's some feat.

Kelvin, James and Anne witnessed me at my lowest in addiction, but despite the pain I put them through, they did everything in their power to help me and never gave up. Our relationships today are very different. Instead of watching me annihilate myself with drugs, Kelvin, James and I watch Liverpool matches together every single week – an amazing tradition that I plan to keep.

My sister Anne felt the brunt of my addiction, and it's taken a long time to rebuild that bond, but our relationship has never been stronger. Christmas reminds me of this the most. No more drug-fuelled madness, just conversations about positive mental health, and I now help her husband Wayne cook dinner – one of my favourite Christmas traditions.

Addiction would have killed me if I didn't get clean, but worse than that, I would have never met my two gorgeous nephews Ollie and Aaron, Anne's two boys. I often heard people talk about *'a softening of the heart'*, or the one that really threw me, *'it warmed my heart'*. I had no idea what they were talking about until these two little guys came into my life.

Ollie, who's five, is an old soul and has the most beautiful little spirit. I love our excursions together, especially our hikes up the Dublin mountains. Aaron is two, but unlike Ollie, he's a little terrier. He's also the funniest kid I've ever met, with a smile that would melt your heart.

In the summer of 2019, Anne, myself and the two boys climbed the Sugarloaf Mountain in Wicklow. It was a wonderful summer's day. I had climbed it with Ollie before, but we never reached the summit. Now that he was five, I was determined to reach it with him. Aaron was a lot younger, however, so it was going to be a struggle. I said I'd carry Aaron for the steeper part, but he's as stubborn as he is funny, and he wanted to walk himself.

It's quite a steep trek and his little legs couldn't take it. He still refused to be carried, so Anne waited with Aaron while Ollie and I made our climb to the top. It was amazing to see how far he'd come in a year, as he scampered up the mountain ahead of me. He was bursting with excitement as we neared the peak, and when we finally made it, he shouted something that will stay with me forever, *'Brian, Brian, I can see the whole world.'* So could I.

When I think about how I felt in addiction – isolated, lonely, detached and disconnected – I've never been more grateful for the life I have today. I was also afraid of my emotions and used drugs to numb the pain – but not any more. Today, I feel more connected and alive than ever before, and instead of running away from my emotions, I embrace them, especially when I'm afraid. In my experience, the best things in life are often on the other side of fear. This is where true connection lies: in our challenges, our vulnerabilities, our suffering and our fears.

I feel a strong sense of connection today– to my friends, to nature, to life, but most of all to my family. There is a powerful bond between us, something I hadn't felt before, and the best part is that it's getting stronger every day.

* * *

'What's next?' I often wonder. When I was in detox, I scrawled, 'Follow your passion and live it' in huge letters in my diary. As wild as I was back then, on many levels, I was also seeing the world very clearly. When I got out of treatment, I could have played it safe and got a normal job, but thankfully, I followed my instincts and went to college.

I've since found my passion, which has transformed into my life purpose: with a relentless belief that we are what we think, my mission is to show people that change is possible, demonstrating actionable steps through a lived experience.

Teaching kids about the tools in my 'programme for life' is a huge part of this purpose, and with the gift of bonus time, I'm willing to push the boundaries that will help me achieve it. I will continue to take big risks, embrace failure and laugh at rejection. I will keep leaning into every moment expecting magic and miracles. And, most important, I will continue to dream big and act boldly. Our younger generation have it tougher than ever, so if pushing these boundaries can help, I'm willing to throw myself right into it.

Bonus time, the gift that just keeps giving, has taught me many lessons over the last six years, none of which are more important than living in the present moment. By grounding myself in the now, I don't torment myself over lost time or missed opportunities. I can never reclaim the years I lost to addiction, so why dwell on it? Instead, I'm launching myself into the unknown so I can follow my life purpose.

Part of this journey involves reaching out to people further along the path, those who can help me to spread my message. This includes leading psychologists, self-development gurus, corporate heavy hitters, as well as sports stars and celebrities – anyone who can help me to get through to the younger generation. You'd expect these actions to bring a certain amount of anxiety, but they don't. Am I afraid they might say no? Thankfully, I'm not. People are busy, so it happens often, but if you don't ask, the answer is always no. That's the way I see it, and with the hindsight of a second chance at life, now it just feels like common sense.

So how do I feel when I receive my latest no? It hurts a little, sure, but I no longer weave a story in my head about what I should or shouldn't have done. Nor do I worry about what others think or say. We all like to be liked – it's human nature – but with the help of bonus time, I rarely worry about situations that are out of my control, and that includes what others think of me.

Concerns like these can make it difficult to put yourself out there, but that's only when your mind gets involved. It never ceases to amaze me when I witness my mind talking to itself. Telling me to be afraid when there's nothing to fear. Telling me to doubt myself for no reason. But I don't negotiate with my mind any more, which has brought an incredible freedom into my life. Rather than talking myself out of good opportunities because I'm worried about failure, I dive right in and figure it out when I get there.

That brings me to my greatest adversary. Do I still struggle with anxiety? It delights me to say that I do not. I still get anxious, of course – the natural kind – especially when I'm jumping into the unknown. But by focusing on the present moment, and practising my self-observation techniques, anxiety no longer consumes me. I changed the story that ruled my life; this is by far my greatest achievement.

We are but the stories we tell ourselves and believe. My old story, the one I told myself in addiction, was: 'I cannot cope with anxiety and I need heroin to survive.' This was my identity, and it was how I lived my life until I landed in hospital in August

2013. On that fateful night, however, I surrendered. I stopped fighting with my own mind. I dropped my story. In doing so, everything changed.

The sirens fell silent and the darkness lifted. It was time to write another story, and my new story is very different: 'I'm the happiest person I know. I can cope with anything life throws my way, and by turning negatives into positives, adversity doesn't stop me – it fuels my ability to thrive.'

I like this story – it helped me to climb out of my drug-riddled chicken coop and allowed me to soar.

It's important to realise that it's never too late. Everyone's situation is different, but second chances are all around us – you just have to look. Life is about connecting with people, having fun and pushing yourself forward. If you're not doing that, maybe it's time to write a new story.

That's how I plan to live the rest of my life. I will keep taking chances, I will keep writing new stories, and I will continue living each day as if life is a bonus.

APPENDIX: MY PROGRAMME

I have written extensively about my programme for life. You can find this work, including the tools, tactics and habits that have transformed my life, at the links below:

Website: www.brianpennie.com
Blog: www.brianpennie.com/blog/ and https://medium.com/@brianpennie

You can sign up to my email list through my website, where you'll receive a programme of nine core strategies that transformed my life. You'll also receive a weekly newsletter where I share my latest articles and videos, as well as other great content that has crossed my path.

You can find my social media handles via my website, where I share content to help people make positive changes in their lives. I'm active on Instagram, Twitter, Facebook, LinkedIn and Quora.

ACKNOWLEDGEMENTS

Writing this book has been an emotional rollercoaster, but also a million times more rewarding than I could have imagined. It helped me to truly feel the pain I caused my family and, in doing so, strengthened our relationships along the way. None of this would have been possible without my mam and dad, my sister Anne, and my brothers Kelvin and James. They stood by me throughout my addiction, quite literally saving my life, and they were willing to relive our darkest moments as I interviewed them for this book. Thankfully, my nephews Ollie and Aaron, and their father Wayne, weren't there for the madness, but they have become a huge part of my life since I found sobriety. Thanks to you all. I will be forever grateful for your unwavering love and support.

Huge thanks to three amazing people: my literary agent Faith O'Grady from Lisa Richards, and my incredible editors Sarah Liddy and Catherine Gough from Gill Books. Writing a book is a relentless process, but thanks to these people, it was one of the most gratifying journeys of my life.

I also want to thank the fabulous Fiona McCluskey and Eavan Kenny from the Lisa Richards agency, who have been guiding lights for me in the past year, and Teresa Daly and Avril Cannon from Gill Books, who were hugely supportive in the design, publicity and marketing of this book.

A massive thank you to Niall Breslin. I hadn't even thought about writing a book until we bumped into each other at my first ever lecture at UCD in 2018. Niall opened up many doors for me, including introducing me to Faith and Sarah, which led to this book. He also introduced me to Lynn Ruane, now a good friend, who gave me amazing advice during the writing process: speak your truth. Lynn didn't just advise me to do that, she showed me how.

A very special thank you to those who received my uninvited emails throughout 2019 asking for an interview. This endeavour, part of my quest to develop my programme for life, led me to contact many of Ireland's leading performers across business, sport and the arts. I am truly grateful for the time these people took from their busy lives, which I hope will enable me to help others on their respective journeys. In order of interview, a huge thank you to: Dr Dave Alred MBE, Fergal Naughton, Professor Ian Robertson, Alan Foy, Anne Heraty, Alison Cowzer, Carolan Lennon, Dr Rick Hanson, Catherine Duffy, Julie Sinnamon, Dr Claire Gillan, David Harney, Professor Philip Nolan, Nick Palmer, Paul Gilligan, Louise Phelan, Dr Lydia Lynch, Stephen Flynn (aka The Happy Pear), Amy Huberman, Dara Ó Briain, Allison Keating, Conor O'Kelly, Phillip Matthews, Brian McGeough, Keith Barry and, lastly, another person Niall Breslin introduced me to, my dear friend Fiona Brennan.

The world is a better place thanks to people who want to develop and lead others. What makes it even better are people who share the gift of their time to mentor those who need their guidance. Several such people, who should be on the list above, went above and beyond to help me on my journey. Bernard Byrne, who was instrumental in launching my speaking career, provides me with regular guidance as I navigate this new world. Brian McKiernan has also given me tremendous guidance, including a deeply thoughtful email that helped me to stay on course with my PhD. John Boyle, who provided me with the title of this book, has been a continued source of support. Hugh O'Byrne, who I fortuitously met at my local gym, mentors me on a regular basis, throwing cluster bombs of wisdom every time we meet. Finally, Mick Slein, a master in the art of mentorship, has given me an incredible amount of time and advice, and connected me with so many people that I've lost count.

One such connection was Dublin footballer Philly McMahon. Philly, whose brother John died from heroin addiction, was an interview I'll never forget. What I thought was going to be a great chat about the lessons he learned as a footballer, entrepreneur and writer, turned into one of the most therapeutic conversations of my life. Philly is all about seeing the world from the perspective of others, something I seriously lacked. It's only after writing this book that I've realised it wasn't an interview, it was one of the biggest lessons of my life.

So many others have helped me on my journey, going above and beyond, but a special thank you to: Mark Doyle, who gave me incredible opportunities after my first talk in AIB; Ciaran Boyle, who pushed me forward after that talk; Cian Corbett, who continues to teach me the art of digital marketing; Judith McAdam, who has guided me spiritually over the past few years; Saoirse Duffy, who gave me amazing feedback on several of the early chapters; my friends in Kenilworth Products, especially Wayne and Mick, who were there for me through it all; the staff of the Rutland Centre, particularly Barry Costello, who gave me an incredible opportunity with my PhD research; Dr Rob Whelan, who has been amazingly supportive as my PhD supervisor; Dr Hugh Gallagher and the staff at the methadone clinics in Coolmine and Buzzardstown House, who had to put up with me at my worst for twelve years; the staff and clients of the Lantern detox facility, who saw me at my darkest and brightest in the space of a few weeks; the staff of Aiséirí and Tabor House addiction centres; and, last but not least, Dr Jo-Hanna Ivers, who sparked a hope for the future when I was deep in withdrawal.

I also want to thank several others who had a direct impact in the creation of this book. My aunt Tess, who even in her final hours showed me the importance of connection. Sue Booth-Forbes, host of Anam Cara, and Michelle Orabona, a resident at this amazing writers' retreat, both played a role in shaping the direction of this book. To my incredible friends in our writing group, Creative Ink. I was invited into this international group of creatives back in 2018, and their feedback and support has been crucial in developing my skills as a writer. I would like to thank the whole group, but a special thank you to Michael Thompson, Niklas Goeke and Liz Huber.

Finally, I want to thank my dearest friends, some who were part of and witnessed the madness, and some whom I met after it. To Rory and Deco – thank you for the memories before we fell over the edge, and for helping me to conjure up the moments that I had forgotten.

To my gym buddies at the National Sports Centre. Thanks to all of you for taking me under your wings six years ago, for the constant advice and support, and for showing up at 6 a.m. every morning. I want to thank some of you for the great workout sessions, and the rest of you for the laughs in the Jacuzzi.

To Niamh Duffy, thank you for the amazing chats in Maynooth, your feedback on the book and the most unlikely of friendships – one I cherish every day. To Michelle Kelly, thank you for reminding me about the importance of having fun, for all the heart-stopping laughs (medicine for my soul), your feedback on the book and for just being you. To my best friend Gar, who was there from the very start and who, despite us heading down different paths, stayed with me until the very end. And now that I'm clean, thanks for rekindling the great laughs and for asking me to be Penny's godfather.

Finally, because I wouldn't be here without them, I want to thank my amazing family again. I love you all.